-*BLEEP!*-

A Guide to Popular American Obscenities

BLEEP!

is now...

available on cassette!

-*BLEEP!*-

A Guide to Popular American Obscenities

David Burke

Optima Books

Los Angeles   San Francisco

Publisher: Optima Books
Editor: Robert Graul
Managing Editor: Debbie Wright
Editing, Design, and Production: Optima PrePress
Front Cover Illustration: Jim Graul
Inside Illustrations: Dave Gallup
Photography: Marc Berenson

This publication is designed to provide accurate and authoritative information in regard to the subject matter covered. It is sold with the understanding that the publisher is not engaged in rendering legal, accounting, or other professional services. If legal advice or other expert assistance is required, the services of a competent professional person should be sought. FROM A DECLARATION OF PRINCIPLES JOINTLY ADOPTED BY A COMMITTEE OF THE AMERICAN BAR ASSOCIATION AND A COMMITTEE OF PUBLISHERS.

Library of Congress Preassigned Catalog Card Number: 92-60861
ISBN 1-879440-07-5
Printed in the United States of America
93 10 9 8 7 6 5 4 3 2 1

This book is dedicated to my family in New York...
Irv, Sharon, Michael, Jilly, & Steve

PREFACE

What purpose could a book about obscenities possibly serve other than simply to create shock value by listing gratuitous vulgar words and expressions? There are three simple answers: 1) to avoid embarrassment; 2) to fully understand American entertainment; and 3) survival.

Although some would prefer not to acknowledge this fact, obscenities are a living part of the American-English language. They are heard in movies, television and radio shows, news broadcasts, seen in books, newspapers, magazines and generally used in everyday life.

Those who are not completely familiar with the American-English language often find themselves in awkward or embarrassing situations by using a word in such a way as to create a *double-entendre* or a sexual innuendo. When I was in high school, our vice-principal, a non-native speaker of English, made a speech to an auditorium full of students. At one point in her lecture, she mentioned that her son, Dick, went to our high school some years ago. She then casually asked us:

"How many Dicks do we have here in the auditorium?"

Not having a firm grasp on popular American obscenities as did every student in attendance, she was quite unaware that she had just made a serious yet entertaining faux pas since *"dick"* is a very common slang term for "penis" leading to more than just one interpretation of her comment.

Even on popular American television shows, obscenities are commonly used yet cleverly couched in innuendos. One of the most obvious and funniest I've heard was on the very popular American television broadcast of *"The Tonight Show"* with Johnny Carson who interviews various celebrities. During one of the shows, movie star Zsa Zsa Gabor sat down next to Johnny holding a cat on her lap. Then in an effort to unnerve Johnny, Ms. Gabor purposely used a suggestive innuendo by asking:

"Johnny, do you want to pet my pussy?"

Naturally, the audience burst out in laughter as they waited in anticipation to see his reaction since the term *"pussy,"* not only means "cat" but is also a vulgar slang synonym for "vagina." However, to the surprise of Ms. Gabor and the rest of the audience, he countered with:

"I'd be glad to if you'd just move that damn cat!"

In addition, a knowledge of obscenities, and especially drug slang, can also be vital as a means of survival. Many foreign visitors to America are concerned that they may get involved with the "wrong element" due to unfamiliarity with certain slang terms.

BLEEP! is the first step-by-step approach to exploring the most common expletives and obscenities used in America. This knowledge is an essential tool in self-defense for non-native speakers as well as native-born Americans!

BLEEP! presents chapters such as Vulgar & Non-vulgar Insults for Behind the Wheel, Body Parts, Bodily Functions and Sounds, Handy-Hand Gestures at a Safe Distance, and the special "Buffets" where a word from each column may be chosen to create a personalized "colorful" expression. Word games, fill-ins, *"cussword"* puzzles, entertaining drills as well as a thesaurus and detailed glossary are presented for easy reference. In addition, a thermometer ranging from mild to hot begins each section.

This book will also provide an important demonstration on how our most common slang terms, idioms, and gestures can be misconstrued as insulting, offensive and even obscene in other English-speaking countries where completely different meanings are applied!

BLEEP! is a self-teaching guide divided into four parts:

- **DIALOGUE**

    Twenty to thirty popular American expressions and terms (indicated in boldface) are presented as they may be heard in an actual conversation. A translation of the dialogue in standard English is always given on the opposite page followed by an important phonetic version of the dialogue as it would actually be spoken by an American. This page will prove vital to any non-native since Americans tend to rely heavily on contractions and shortcuts in pronunciation.

- **VOCABULARY**

  This section spotlights all of the slang words and expressions that were used in the dialogue and offers more examples of usage, synonyms, antonyms, and special notes.

- **PRACTICE THE VOCABULARY**

  These word games include all of the new terms and idioms previously learned and will help you to test yourself on your comprehension. (The pages providing the answers to all the drills are indicated at the beginning of this section.)

- **A CLOSER LOOK**

  This section offers the reader an inside look at common slang words and expressions pertaining to a specific category.

Whether you're a native-born American who spends a great deal of time traveling to foreign countries or a non-native speaker visiting America, **BLEEP!** will prove to be an essential yet hilarious guide to the darker and more *"colorful"* side of the language as well as a valuable manual for avoiding the unintentional use of obscenities from country to country.

David Burke
Author

NOTE

For a close look at the most popular slang used in America, refer to the "Street Talk" series by the same author:

STREET TALK -1:
How to Speak and Understand American Slang

STREET TALK -2:
Slang Used by Teens, Rappers, Surfers, & Popular American Television Shows

STREET TALK -3:
Popular American Business Slang & Jargon

SEE COUPON ON BACK PAGE FOR DETAILS

ACKNOWLEDGMENTS

A special thanks goes to Janet Graul, Vivian Margolin, and Debbie Wright for making the copyediting phase of this book so enjoyable. Their patience, expertise, and attitude are, as always, so appreciated.

I am especially grateful to Bob Graul for his contribution in the technical end of this book's production. His commitment to quality, accuracy, and detail are absolutely unsurpassed.

I am particularly thankful to Jim Graul, who designed and created such an ideal cover for **BLEEP!** and to Dave Gallup who created the most wonderful, light-hearted illustrations in each chapter. Their creativity, professionalism, and ability to produce exceptional images were astounding.

I was also extremely fortunate to work with Mark Barensen who photographed the gesture section of this book. To find someone as patient, creative, professional, and talented as Mark was an unexpected stroke of luck.

I owe a special debt of gratitude to all of the people throughout the U.S. who I badgered for information regarding obscenities and gestures. I was always met with kindness and an eagerness to offer a total stranger some, oftentimes, "unusual" information.

legend

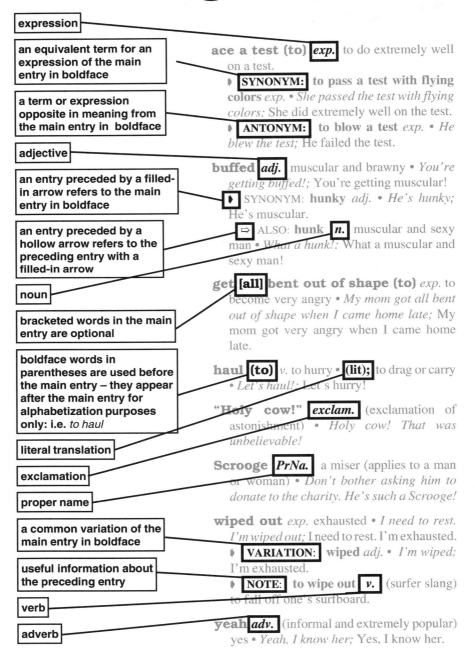

expression

an equivalent term for an expression of the main entry in boldface

a term or expression opposite in meaning from the main entry in boldface

adjective

an entry preceded by a filled-in arrow refers to the main entry in boldface

an entry preceded by a hollow arrow refers to the preceding entry with a filled-in arrow

noun

bracketed words in the main entry are optional

boldface words in parentheses are used before the main entry – they appear after the main entry for alphabetization purposes only: i.e. *to haul*

literal translation

exclamation

proper name

a common variation of the main entry in boldface

useful information about the preceding entry

verb

adverb

ace a test (to) *exp.* to do extremely well on a test.
▸ SYNONYM: to pass a test with flying colors *exp.* • *She passed the test with flying colors;* She did extremely well on the test.
▸ ANTONYM: to blow a test *exp.* • *He blew the test;* He failed the test.

buffed *adj.* muscular and brawny • *You're getting buffed!;* You're getting muscular!
▸ SYNONYM: hunky *adj.* • *He's hunky;* He's muscular.
➡ ALSO: hunk *n.* muscular and sexy man • *What a hunk!;* What a muscular and sexy man!

get [all] bent out of shape (to) *exp.* to become very angry • *My mom got all bent out of shape when I came home late;* My mom got very angry when I came home late.

haul (to) *v.* to hurry • *(lit);* to drag or carry • *Let's haul!;* Let's hurry!

"Holy cow!" *exclam.* (exclamation of astonishment) • *Holy cow! That was unbelievable!*

Scrooge *PrNa.* a miser (applies to a man or woman) • *Don't bother asking him to donate to the charity. He's such a Scrooge!*

wiped out *exp.* exhausted • *I need to rest. I'm wiped out;* I need to rest. I'm exhausted.
▸ VARIATION: wiped *adj.* • *I'm wiped;* I'm exhausted.
▸ NOTE: to wipe out *v.* (surfer slang) to fall off one's surfboard.

yeah *adv.* (informal and extremely popular) yes • *Yeah, I know her;* Yes, I know her.

CONTENTS

-*BLEEP!*-

A Guide to Popular American Obscenities

UNIT ONE

This unit is rated...

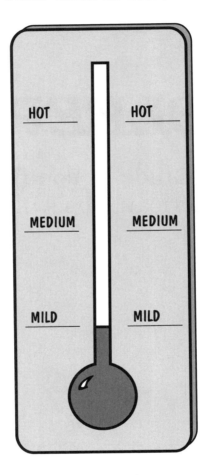

MILD

The terms and expressions in this unit are made up of euphemisms which are mild substitutes for words or groups of words that may offend.

EUPHEMISMS
– The Camp Out –

LESSON ONE

The Camp Out...

DIALOGUE

Scout leaders Tim and Bob are demonstrating the necessary techniques for surviving in the wild.

Tim: **Geez**! How the **heck** do you get this **friggin'** thing to open! With all the **crud** we brought, you'd think we could bring a decent tent! **Drat**!

Bob: **Gosh**! Those **darn** things are always a **mother** to open.

Tim: **Guy**! What an **F-ing** nightmare. There aren't even any instructions anywhere. This is starting to get me really **P.O.**'d!

Bob: Now, don't have a **you-know-what** fit in front of the kids.

Tim: You're right. **Gad**! It's just that every time you rent one of these things they turn out to be a **bleeping** pain in the **arse**. **Pardon my French**, but you remember what a **B.I.T.C.H.** the last one was.

Bob: **Shoot**, yeah! **Gee**, last time you were mumbling the **F-word** all over the place. **Golly**! I didn't know you knew so many **four-letter words**!

LESSON ONE

Translation of dialogue in standard American-English

The Camp Out...

DIALOGUE

Scout leaders Tim and Bob are demonstrating the necessary techniques for surviving in the wild.

Tim: **How frustrating**! How **do you possibly** get this **annoying** thing to open! With all the **materials** we brought, you'd think we could bring a decent tent! **I'm so upset**!

Bob: **That's a shame**! Those **bothersome** things are always **extremely difficult** to open.

Tim: **I can't believe this**! What an **absolute** nightmare. There aren't even any instructions anywhere. This is starting to get me really **angry**!

Bob: Now, don't have a **huge** fit in front of the kids.

Tim: You're right. **This is so irritating**! It's just that every time you rent one of these things they turn out to be a **big annoyance**. **Forgive my use of obscenities**, but you remember what a **difficulty** the last one was.

Bob: **Absolutely! Surprisingly enough**, last time you were mumbling the **obscenity that begins with the letter "F"** all over the place. **What a surprise**! I didn't know you knew so many **obscene words**!

LESSON ONE

Dialogue in slang as it would be heard

The Camp Out...

DIALOGUE

Scout leaders Tim 'n Bob 'r demonstrating the necessary techniques for surviving in the wild.

Tim: **Geez**! How the **heck** d'ya get this **friggin'** thing ta open! With all the **crud** we brought, y'd think we could bring a decent tent! **Drat!**

Bob: **Gosh**! Those **darn** things 'r always a **mother** ta open.

Tim: **Guy**! Whad 'n **F-in'** nightmare. There arn' even any instructions anywhere. This's startin' ta get me really **P.O.**'d!

Bob: Now, don't have a **you-know-what** fit 'n fronna the kids.

Tim: Ye'r right. **Gad**! It's jus' thad ev'ry time ya rent one 'a these things they turn out ta be a **bleepin'** pain 'n the **arse**. **Pardon my French**, but a remember whad a **B.I.T.C.H.** the last one was.

Bob: **Shoot**, yeah! **Gee**, las' time you were mumbling the **F-word** all over the place. **Golly**! I didn' know ya knew so many **four-ledder words**!

4

Vocabulary

arse *n.* • **1.** idiot, fool, jerk • *Don't act like such an arse!;* Don't act like such a jerk! • **2.** buttocks • *When I went skiing yesterday, I kept falling on my arse;* When I went skiing yesterday, I kept falling on my butt.

♦ ORIGIN: This is commonly used as a euphemism for *"ass"* n. (lit); buttocks. The term *"ass"* is actually a shortened version of *"asshole"* meaning a "contemptible person" or literally "anus." For some reason, the shortened version, *"ass,"* is considered somewhat vulgar but not obscene. However, its complete form, *"asshole"* is indeed regarded as obscene and offensive. Both terms are extremely popular.

B.I.T.C.H. *n.* • (lit); female dog • **1.** unpleasant woman • *She's a real B.I.T.C.H.;* She's a really unpleasant woman. • **2.** extremely difficult • *This work is such a B.I.T.C.H!;* This work is extremely difficult!

♦ NOTE: To create a euphemism out of an obscene or coarse word, many people simply just spell it out. This tends to relieve the severity of the word since we don't actually hear the term in its entirety. The term *"bitch"* is considered only somewhat coarse to most people and is therefore commonly heard in most situations. There are some, however, who feel that it is still unpleasant language and will only spell it out.

♦ NOTE: The use of *B.I.T.C.H.* in the examples above, are extremely popular in the "un-spelled" form of the term and are heard frequently: *She's a real bitch!* • *This work is such a bitch!*

bleeping *adj.* This is commonly used as a euphemistic replacement for the adjective *"fucking"* which means "intense." (The term *"fuck"* will be discuss in depth in lesson five). Its origin comes from television and radio where a "bleep" sound is commonly used to replace obscene words.

♦ VARIATION: **bleepity bleep** *n.* • *That bleepity-bleep cop gave me a ticket!;* That fucking police officer gave me a ticket!

crud • **1.** *n.* any unidentifiable or unusual substance • (lit); excrement • *What's that crud you're drinking?;* What's that bizarre substance you're drinking? • **2.** *exclam.* an exclamation used in surprise or anger • *Crud! I left my wallet at work!;* I'm so angry! I left my wallet at work! • **3.** *n.* excrement (when used in the following expression, this term takes on a more vulgar meaning) • *I have to go take a crud;* I have to go defecate.

♦ ORIGIN: This is commonly used as a euphemism for *"crap"* which is considered vulgar yet extremely popular.

darn • **1.** *n.* unpleasant • *Do you have to play that darn music all day?;* Do you have to play that unpleasant music all day? • **2.** *exclam.* an exclamation used in astonishment and anger • *Darn! Look at that new car!;* I'm really astonished! Look at that new car! • *Darn! I locked myself out of the house again!;* I'm so angry! I locked myself out of the house again! (NOTE: When used in anger, the exclamation *"Darn it!"* is used as a common substitution) • **3.** *v.* to damn • *Darn you!;* May you be damned to hell!

♦ ORIGIN: This is a commonly used euphemism for the term *"damn"* which is not really considered vulgar as much as it is deemed harsh. As with many words coming from the church, many feel that the use of these terms is in bad taste and prefer to use euphemisms.

"Drat!" *exclam.* an exclamation used in annoyance • *Drat! I can't find my glasses!*

♦ NOTE: This is a commonly used euphemism for the exclamation *"Damn!"*

F-ing • **1.** *adj.* absolute, complete • *Our picnic was an F-ing disaster yesterday because of the rain;* Our picnic was a complete disaster yesterday because of the rain. • **2.** *adv.* absolutely, completely • *What an F-ing great stereo!;* What an absolutely great stereo! • **3.** used before a verb to indicate great annoyance • *Why do you always F-ing come over here and bother me every two minutes?!* • **4.** used before a noun to indicate great annoyance • *I don't want to drive her to the airport but what F-ing choice do I have?!*

♦ ORIGIN: This is commonly used as a euphemism for the adjective/adverb *"fucking"* which is considered extremely vulgar yet very popular.

➤ SYNONYM: SEE: **Friggin'.**

F-word (the) *n.* a euphemism for the vulgar term *"fuck"* • *Mom! I just heard Barry use the F-word!;* Mom! I just heard Barry say "fuck!"

‣ ALSO: **the S-word** *n.* a euphemism for the vulgar term *"shit."*

four-letter word *n.* Since most of the worst obscene terms in the American-English language contain four letters, they have been nicknamed "four-letter words" • *My mother never uses four-letter words;* My mother never uses swear words.

‣ NOTE: It's interesting to note that the French equivalent of the American *"four-letter word"* is *"un mot à cinq lettres"* which means "a five-letter word." This is due to the fact that the most commonly used obscenity in France is *"merde,"* meaning "shit," containing five letters.

friggin' • **1.** *adj.* absolute, complete • **2.** *adv.* absolutely, completely • **3.** used before a verb to indicate great annoyance • **4.** used before a noun to indicate great annoyance.

‣ ORIGIN: This is commonly used as a euphemism for the adjective/adverb *"fucking"* which is considered extremely vulgar yet very popular.

‣ NOTE: It's very common in colloquial speech to reduce the "-ing" ending to "-in'." The term *"frigging"* is almost always used in its reduced form, *"friggin'."*

‣ SYNONYM: SEE: **F-ing.**

"Gad!" *exclam.* a commonly used euphemism for "God," used to denote excitement, surprise or annoyance • **1.** (excitement) *Gad! What a beautiful house!* • **2.** (surprise) *Gad! Did you see that shooting star?* • **3.** (annoyance) *Gad! Why doesn't he just leave me alone?!*

‣ VARIATION (1): **"Gadzooks!"** *exclam.* used primarily by the older generation or in jest.

⇨ ORIGIN: Originally pronounced, "God's hooks!" which referred to the nails on the cross.

‣ VARIATION (2): **"Egads!"** *exclam.* used primarily by the older generation or in jest.

⇨ ORIGIN: "Oh, God!"

"Gee!" *exclam.* a commonly used euphemism for *"Jesus,"* used to denote excitement, surprise, or annoyance. *"Gee!"* may be used in place of *"Gad!"* in all three instances.

‣ VARIATION (1): **"Gee whillikers!"** used primarily by the older generation or in jest.
‣ VARIATION (2): **"Gee whiz!"** *exclam.*
‣ VARIATION (3): **"Geez Louise!"** *exclam.*

"Geez!" *exclam.* a commonly used euphemism for *"Jesus,"* used to denote excitement, surprise, or annoyance. *"Geez!"* may be used in place of *"Gad!"* in all three instances.
‣ VARIATION: **"Geez Louise!"** *exclam.*

"Golly!" *exclam.* a very mild and commonly used euphemism for *"God,"* used to denote excitement, surprise, or annoyance. *"Golly!"* may be used in place of *"Gad!"* in all three instances.
‣ VARIATION (1): **"Golly gee!"** *exclam.* used primarily in jest.
‣ VARIATION (2): **"Golly gee whillikers!"** *exclam.* used primarily in jest.

"Gosh!" *exclam.* a very mild and commonly used euphemism for *"God,"* used to denote excitement, surprise, or annoyance. *"Gosh!"* may be used in place of *"Gad!"* in all three instances.

"Guy!" *exclam.* a mild and commonly used euphemism for *"God,"* used to denote excitement, surprise, or annoyance. *"Guy!"* may be used in place of *"Gad!"* in all three instances.

heck • **1.** *n.* used as *"the heck,"* this is a common euphemism for *"the hell"* denoting surprise, annoyance, or nonsense • (surprise) *It's great to see you! What the heck are you doing here?* • (annoyance) *What the heck do you want now?* • (nonsense) *He told you he was rich? The heck he is!;* He told you he was rich! That's nonsense! • **2.** *exclam.* used to denote excitement or annoyance • (excitement) *Heck! That's great news!* • (annoyance) *Heck! Why doesn't he just go away?!* • **3.** to add emphasis to "yes" and "no" • *Heck yes! I'd love to go with you to the carnival!* • **4. like heck** *exp.* a lot • *My broken arm hurts like heck!;* My broken arm hurts a lot!
‣ NOTE (1): The term *"heck"* is also commonly used in the following expressions:
• **to have a heck of a lot of money**; to have a lot of money.
• **the heck with it**; to hell with it (said about something very irritating.
• **all heck broke loose**; great chaos developed.
• **to be funny as heck**; to be extremely funny.

• **a heck of a good show, speech, time, etc.**; an extremely good show, speech, time, etc.
‣ NOTE (2): In all of the previous examples of *"heck," "hell"* is very commonly used. As with many words coming from the church, many feel that the use of these terms is in bad taste and prefer to use euphemisms.

mother • 1. *adj.* extremely difficult • *This bicycle is a real mother to ride!;* This bicycle is extremely difficult to ride! • **2.** *n.* a despicable person • *He's a real mother!;* He's a real despicable person!
‣ ALSO: **a mother of a** *exp.* an extremely difficult • *This is a mother of a homework assignment!;* This is an extremely difficult homework assignment.
‣ ORIGIN: This is a commonly used euphemism for the adjective and noun *"fuck"* which is considered to be one of the crudest, yet most popular, obscenities in the American-English language. The term *"fuck"* is also a popular, yet vulgar, verb meaning "to have sexual intercourse." This term will be discussed in depth in lesson five.

P.O.'d (to be) *adj.* to be extremely angry • *I'm really P.O.'d because my brother borrowed my shirt without asking!;* I'm really angry because my brother borrowed my shirt without asking!
‣ NOTE: This is a commonly used euphemism for the expression *"to be pissed off."* This expression is considered somewhat crude since it contains the verb *"to piss"* which is vulgar for "to urinate."

"Pardon my French" *exp.* "Forgive my use of obscenities."
‣ NOTE: This is a common apology used by the speaker for having just used an obscenity. The word *"French"* is used facetiously and ironically since Americans regard the language as being beautiful and romantic; quite the opposite of a vulgarism or obscenity.

"Shoot!" a commonly used euphemism for *"Shit!"* used to denote excitement, surprise, or annoyance. *"Shoot!"* may be used in place of *gad, darn, etc.*

"Shucks!" a commonly used euphemism for *"Shit!"* used to denote disappointment • *Shucks! I lost the contest!*

♦ NOTE: The uses of *"shit"* will be discussed in depth in lesson four.

you-know-what *exp.* a convenient expression used to replace an obscenity • *He's a real son of a you-know-what;* He's a real son of a bitch (or any other obscenity).
♦ NOTE: **son of a bitch** *exp.* an extremely despicable person.

PRACTICE THE VOCABULARY

[Answers to Lesson 1, p. 165]

A. Underline the appropriate word that best completes the phrase.

1. (**Guy**, **Woman**)! What a surprise!

2. I'm so tired of doing this (**beeping**, **bleeping**) homework!

3. How did I get this (**crust**, **crud**) all over my shirt?

4. How the (**heck**, **hawk**) did he get in here?

5. (**Cheese**, **Geez**)! Why do you keep asking me the same question?

6. If you don't stop bothering me, I'm gonna get really (**P.O.'d**, **F-ing**)!

7. (**Shot**, **Shoot!**) I missed the bus!

8. My party turned into a (**friggin'**, **frightening**) disaster!

9. (**Dawn**, **Darn**)! I can't find my keys!

10. This is a real (**mother**, **father**) of an assignment the teacher gave us!

B. Match the colums.

☐ 1. How did you possibly find me?

☐ 2. Do you believe all this annoying homework we have to do?

☐ 3. I'm getting really angry.

☐ 4. Pardon my use of obscenities.

☐ 5. Absolutely!

☐ 6. That bothersome material is extremely difficult to remove.

☐ 7. I'm so surprised!

☐ 8. Last time I saw her angry, she kept yelling the obscenity that begins with the letter "F."

☐ 9. What an offensive person!

☐ 10. Absolutely not!

☐ 11. What is that substance you got on yourself?

A. **Pardon my French.**

B. **Gad, yes!**

C. **Last time I saw her angry, she kept yelling the F-word.**

D. **What's that crud you got on yourself?**

E. **How the heck did you find me?**

F. **I'm getting really P.O.'d.**

G. **Do you believe all this friggin' homework we have to do?**

H. **That darn stuff's a mother to remove.**

I. **Shoot, no!**

J. **What a B.I.T.C.H.!**

K. **Golly!**

C. FILL IN THE BLANK & WORD SEARCH:

Step 1: Using the word list below, fill in the blank with the correct word that corresponds to the definition.

Step 2: Then find and circle the same word in the grid on the opposite page. Words may be spelled left to right and diagonally. The first one has been done for you.

GEEZ	YOU-KNOW-WHAT	HECK
BLEEPING	ARSE	BITCH
DRAT	DARN	FRENCH
CRUD	SHOOT	MOTHER

1. "_____ !" *exclam.* a euphemism for *"Jesus,"* used to denote excitement, surprise, or annoyance.

2. _____ *exp.* a convenient expression used to replace an obscenity.

3. _____ *n.* • **1.** idiot, fool, jerk • **2.** buttocks.

4. _____ • **1.** *n.* a common euphemism for *"the hell"* denoting surprise, annoyance, or "nonsense" • **2.** *exclam.* used to denote excitement or annoyance • **3.** to add emphasis to "yes" and "no."

5. "_____ !" a euphemism for *"Shit!,"* used to denote excitement, surprise, or annoyance.

6. "_____ !" *exclam.* an exclamation used in annoyance and a common euphemism for *"Damn!"*

7. _____ • **1.** *n.* unpleasant • **2.** *exclam.* an exclamation used in astonishment and anger • **3.** *v.* to damn.

8. "Pardon my _____" *exp.* "Forgive my use of obscenities."

9. _____ • **1.** *n.* any unidentifiable or unusual substance.

10. _____ • **1.** *adj.* extremely difficult • **2.** *n.* a despicable person.

11. _____ *adj.* This is a euphemistic replacement for the adjective *"fucking"* meaning "intense."

12. _____ *n.* **1.** unpleasant woman • **2.** extremely difficult.

– WORD SEARCH –

Y	O	U	K	N	O	W	W	H	A	T	A
D	M	I	C	O	H	S	T	E	S	A	B
L	A	R	S	E	I	O	D	C	J	T	L
E	C	O	M	B	N	W	A	K	T	E	E
G	L	O	O	E	I	W	J	K	K	S	E
G	E	S	H	O	O	T	B	H	I	T	P
A	D	E	S	K	H	D	C	E	R	H	I
I	R	Y	Z	X	M	O	T	H	E	R	N
E	A	W	H	I	P	S	O	P	E	R	G
O	T	X	R	K	F	R	E	N	C	H	L
T	W	D	A	R	N	D	J	E	E	E	Y
L	I	C	C	R	U	D	B	X	D	N	A

A CLOSER LOOK
Euphemisms

A euphemism is a mild substitute for a word or a group of words that may offend, such as an obscenity or a blasphemous exclamation. Euphemisms play an important part in any language since they allow the speaker to convey thoughts delivered with great emotion without offending others. This practice is considered to be in good taste and shows sensitivity on the part of the speaker.

Not all people choose to use euphemisms. Some prefer to communicate in terms which are quite strong, highly offensive, shocking, and inappropriate in many social situations as will be explored in later chapters.

The following are common American euphemisms which are considered to be very mild and may be used without any fear of offending, unless otherwise stated.

baloney *n.* nonsense (may be used as a euphemistic replacement for *"bullshit"* which is considered vulgar) • *You actually believed that baloney?;* You actually believed that nonsense?

blazes *n.* used in surprise to add emphasis to a question (may be used as a euphemistic replacement for *"hell"* which is considered harsh) • (lit); fire • *What the blazes is he doing here?!*
♦ VARIATION: **blue blazes** *exp.* • (lit); extremely hot fire • *What in blue blazes did you do to my car?!*

caca • **1.** *n.* nonsense (may be used as a euphemistic

replacement for *"shit"* which is considered vulgar) • (lit); excrement *That story she told you is nothing but caca;* That story she told you is nothing but nonsense. • **2.** *exclam.* used to convey moderate frustration and anger • *Caca! I lost again!*

crap • **1.** *n.* nonsense (may be used as euphemistic, yet rather crude, replacement for *"shit"*) • *Why do you keep listening to his crap?;* Why do you keep listening to his nonsense? • **2.** *n.* uncivil behavior • *I'm tired of putting up with his crap!;* I'm tired of tolerating his uncivil behavior! • **3.** *exclam.* used to convey great frustration and anger • *Crap! I can't find my wallet!*

"Dagnabbit!" *exclam.* may be used as a euphemistic replacement for *"God damn it!"* which is used to convey frustration and anger • *Dagnabbit! I lost my car keys again!*

"Dash it all!" *exclam.* used to indicate anger and frustration (may be used as a euphemism for *"Damn it!"* which is considered harsh) • *Dash it all! I missed the last bus!* How frustrating! I missed the last bus!
♦ NOTE: *"Dash it all!"* is an exclamation which is used only by the English. It has been listed here due to its popular usage by English performers in American television and movies.

derrière *n.* may be used as a euphemistic replacement for *"buttocks"* (See NOTE) • *Put your derrière right here;* Sit down right here.
♦ NOTE: Some people feel that to use the actual terms for any body part having to do with sex is in bad taste. Although the word *"buttocks"* is perfectly acceptable, there are those who prefer to use a less direct term such as *"derrière."* Since Americans

feel that French is such a beautiful and romantic language, to use a French synonym in its place seems more refined.

doggone *adj.* irritating (may be used as a euphemistic replacement for *"God damn"* which is considered irreverent) • *These doggone shoes are too tight!;* These irritating shoes are too tight!
♦ ALSO: **"Doggone it!"** *exclam.* used to indicate anger or frustration (may be used as a euphemistic replacement for *"God damn it!"* which is considered irreverent) • *Doggone it! He's late again!;* How frustrating! He's late again!

"Fooey!" *exclam.* (also spelled "phooey") used to indicate anger or frustration (may be used as a euphemistic replacement for *"Fuck"* which is considered extremely vulgar) • *Fooey! I lost the contest for the third time!;* How frustrating! I lost the contest for the third time!
♦ VARIATION: **"Fooey on him/that!"** *exp.* used to indicate contempt for someone or something (may be used as a euphemistic replacement for *"Fuck him/that!"* which is considered extremely vulgar) • *She forgot to pick you up at the airport? Fooey on her!;*

She forgot to pick you up at the airport? How contemptible!

"Fudge!" *exclam.* used to indicate disappointment, anger, or frustration (may be used as a euphemistic replacement for *"Fuck!"* which is considered extremely vulgar) • *Fudge! I was so sure I was going to win;* What a disappointment! I was so sure I was going to win.

"Goldarnit!" *exclam.* (pronounced "galdarnit") used to indicate anger or frustration (may be used as a euphemistic replacement for *"God damn it!"* which is considered irreverent) • *Goldarnit! That guy just cheated me!;* I'm angry! That guy just cheated me!
▸ NOTE: This term is mainly used in old westerns and in jest.

"Good grief!" *exclam.* used to indicate surprise and disbelief (may be used as a euphemistic replacement for *"Good God!"* which is considered, by some, to be irreverent) • *Good grief! How did you get the kitchen so dirty?;* I can't believe it! How did you get the kitchen so dirty?
▸ VARIATION: **"Good gravy!"**

exclam. used primarily in jest.

"Holy Cow!" *exclam.* used to indicate surprise and disbelief (may be used as a euphemistic replacement for *"Holy Christ!"* which is considered to be irreverent) • *Holy Cow! How did your little sister get way up there?;* What a surprise! How did your little sister get way up there?
▸ CAUTION: The expression *"Holy Cow!"* would be considered quite irreverent to natives from India where the cow is considered holy.

"Holy Cripes!" *exclam.* used to indicate surprise and disbelief (may be used as a euphemistic replacement for *"Holy Christ!"* which is considered to be irreverent) • *Holy Cripes! Did you hear what just happened?;* What a surprise! Did you hear what just happened?

"Holy Moley!" *exclam.* used to indicate surprise and disbelief (may be used as a euphemistic replacement for *"Holy Moses!"* which is considered to be irreverent) • *Holey Moley! How did you do that?;* What a surprise! How did you do that?

"Jiminy Cricket!" *exclam.* used to indicate surprise

and disbelief (may be used as a euphemistic replacement for *"Jesus Christ"* which is considered to be irreverent) • *Jiminy Cricket! Where did you find all that money?;* What a surprise! Where did you find all that money?
▶ NOTE (1): This exclamation is based on a famous cartoon character whose initials are the same as Jesus Christ and consequently may be used as a euphemistic replacement.
▶ NOTE (2): This exclamation is used primarily in jest.
▶ SYNONYM: **"Jiminy Christmas!"** *exclam.* used primarily in jest.

little boys'/girls' room *exp.* may be used as a euphemistic replacement for "bathroom" • *Excuse me, can you tell me where the little girls' room is?;* Excuse me, can you tell me where the bathroom is?
▶ NOTE: Some people feel that to use the word *"bathroom,"* (which is certainly an acceptable term) is rather crude and unrefined.

mother • **1.** *n.* despicable person (may be used as a euphemistic replacement for *"mother fucker"* which is considered extremely vulgar

• *That guy's a real mother!;* That guy's a real despicable person! • **2.** *adj.* extremely difficult • *What a mother of a homework assignment!;* What a difficult homework assignment!

number one *exp.* may be used as a euphemistic replacement for "urination" • *I have to go number one;* I have to urinate.

number two *exp.* may be used as a euphemistic replacement for "defecation" • *The little baby went number two in his diapers;* The little baby defecated in his diapers.

pecker *n.* may be used as a euphemistic replacement for "penis" • *See the baby's little pecker? It's a boy!;* See the baby's little penis? It's a boy!

peter *n.* may be used as a euphemistic replacement for "penis" • *That guy's bathing suit is so tight, you can see his peter!;* That guy's bathing suit is so tight, you can see his penis!

poop *n.* may be used as a euphemistic replacement for "defecation" • *I have to go poop;* I have to go defecate.
▶ ALSO: **poop** *n.* • **1.** specifics • *So, give me the poop on the new neighbors! What are they like?;* So, give me the

specifics on the new neighbors! What are they like? • **2.** gossip • *Did you hear the poop about our new teacher?*; Did you hear the gossip about our new teacher?

S.E.X. *n.* may be used as a euphemistic replacement for the word "sex" which is considered, by some, to be improper to say unless spelled • *I think they're finally going to have S.E.X.*

the dirty deed *exp.* may be used as a euphemistic replacement for "sex" • *Do you think they did the dirty deed last night?*; Do you think they had sex last night?

undies *n.* may be used as a euphemistic replacement for "underwear" • *I just bought some new undies;* I just bought some new underwear.

♦ NOTE: The word *"undies"* is considered infant language and is, therefore, occasionally borrowed by adults in order to desexualize the original term.

you-know-what *exp.* a euphemistic expression which is used to replace any vulgar word • *She's always so nasty! I think she's a real you-know-what!*

♦ NOTE: In this expression, it's up to the listener to guess which obscenity the speaker is replacing. Although the listener may not deduce the exact word, the sentiment is still the same.

UNIT TWO

This unit is rated...

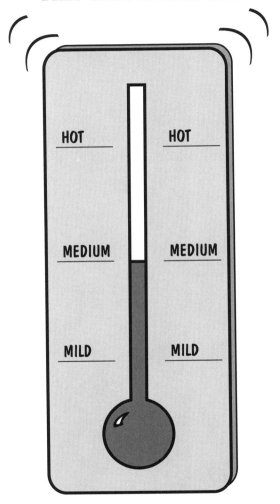

MEDIUM

This unit is composed of insults which are primarily humorous and not offensive. However, terms and expressions which are somewhat crude, will be noted.

NON-VULGAR INSULTS

– At the Market –

At the Market...

DIALOGUE

Debbie and Nancy are out shopping.

Nancy: Debbie, isn't that your old boss? What a little **runt!**

Debbie: Oh, yeah. That **creep** was the biggest **tightwad** I ever met and he's a real **crazo**, too. Oh, look! There's his wife! What a **loser!** Everyone says she's a real **tramp** but does she ever have a **bad case of the uglies!** They make a real pair, don't they? He's a **fat slob** who's **bald as a billiard ball** and she's a total **birdbrain** and **no spring chicken**.

Nancy: Wow, what a **motormouth!** She just keeps talking and talking. She seems like a real **cold fish**, too.

Debbie: You're not kidding. She's a real **bitch on wheels** and **stuck up** in a big way!

Translation of dialogue in standard American-English

At the Market...

DIALOGUE

Debbie and Nancy are out shopping.

Nancy: Debbie, isn't that your old boss? What a little **insignificant person**!

Debbie: Oh, yeah. That **despicable man** was the most **miserly person** I ever met and he's a real **crazy individual**, too. Oh, look! There's his wife! What an **inferior human being**! Everyone says she's a real **nymphomaniac** but is she ever **ugly**! They make a real pair, don't they? He's an **extremely fat** man who's **very bald** and she's totally **mindless** and **old-looking**.

Nancy: Wow, **her mouth never stops moving**! She just keeps talking and talking. She seems like a real **unfeeling person**, too.

Debbie: You're not kidding. She's a real **shrew** and **conceited** in a big way!

Dialogue in slang as it would be heard

At the Market...

DIALOGUE

Debbie 'n Nancy 'r out shopping.

Nancy: Debbie, isn' tha' cher ol' boss? Whad a liddle **runt**!

Debbie: Oh, yeah. That **creep** was the bigges' **tightwad** I ever met 'n 'e's a real **crazo**, too. Oh, look! There'z 'iz wife! Whad a **loser**! Ev'ryone says she's a real **tramp** but da' she ever have a **bad case 'a the uglies**! They make a real pair, don't they? He's a **fat slob** oo'z **bald 'ez a billiard ball** 'n she'z a todal **birdbrain** 'n **no spring chicken**.

Nancy: Wow, whad a **modormouth**! She jus' keeps talking and talking. She seems like a real **cold fish**, too.

Debbie: Yer not kidding. She's a real **bitch on wheels** 'n **stuck up** 'n a big way!

Vocabulary

bad case of the uglies (to have a) *exp.* (humorous) to be extremely ugly • *He's got a bad case of the uglies!*; He's really ugly!

‣ SYNONYM: **face that could stop a clock (to have a)** *exp.* (humorous).

bald as a billiard ball (to be as) *exp.* (humorous) to be extremely bald • *That guy's as bald as a billiard ball!*; That guy's totally bald!

‣ SYNONYM: **to be as bald as an eagle** *exp.* (humorous).

birdbrain (to be a) *n.* (humorous) to be excessively dumb • *Can you believe she forgot where she parked yesterday? What a birdbrain!*; Can you believe she forgot where she parked yesterday? She's so dumb!

‣ NOTE: This is said of someone whose brain appears to be the size of that of a bird.

bitch on wheels (to be a) *exp.* (humorous yet somewhat crude) to be exceptionally shrewish • *Why is she being so nasty? What a bitch on wheels!*; Why is she being so nasty? What a shrew!

cold fish (to be a) *exp.* (mild) to be an unemotional and unfriendly individual • *I introduced myself to her, but she was such a cold fish*; I introduced myself to her, but she was extremely unemotional and unfriendly.

crazo (to be a) *n.* (mild) to be an excessively eccentric individual • *That guy's a real crazo!*; That man is a really eccentric individual!

creep (to be a) *n.* (mild) to be a despicable person • *My little brother lied to me so that I'd give him money. What a creep!*; My little brother lied to me so that I'd give him money. What a despicable person!

fat slob (to be a) *exp.* (mild) to be an inordinately piggish and heavy individual • *I'll never invite him to my party again. He was such an embarrassment. What a fat slob!;* I'll never invite him to my party again. He was such an embarrassment. What a pig!

loser (to be a) *n.* (mild) to be an unlucky, clumsy, and miserable person • *You're dating that loser?;* You're dating that miserable person?

motormouth (to be a) *n.* (humorous) said of a person who talks incessantly as if his/her mouth were motorized • *I didn't say one word when I was with her today. She's such a motormouth!;* I didn't say one word when I was with her today. She talks incessantly!

no spring chicken (to be) *exp.* (mild) said of a person who is well past his/her prime.
  ‣ NOTE: This expression comes from farms where the *"spring chicken"* was considered to be the most desirable, young, tender, and flavorful.

runt (to be a) *n.* (mild) an individual, usually male, who is very small and frail • *He may look like a runt, but he's very strong;* He may look very small and frail, but he's very strong.

stuck up (to be) *adj.* (mild) to be conceited and arrogant • *I can't stand her. She's so stuck up!;* I don't like her at all. She's so arrogant.

tightwad (to be a) *n.* (mild) to be extremely miserly • *He refused to buy me a cup of coffee because he said it was too expensive. What a tightwad!;* He refused to buy me a cup of coffee because he said it was too expensive. He's so miserly.

tramp (to be a) *n.* (mild) to be a promiscuous person • (lit); to be like a vagabond who rarely sleeps in the same place twice • *Look, there's Donna. She's the school tramp;* Look, there's Donna. She's the school nymphomaniac.

PRACTICE THE VOCABULARY

[Answers to Lesson 2, p. 166]

A. Choose the phrase that doesn't belong.

1. **She's so stuck up!:**
   - ☐ She's so tall!
   - ☐ She's so arrogant!

2. **He has a bad case of the uglies:**
   - ☐ He's rather ugly.
   - ☐ He's extremely ugly.

3. **He's as bald as a billiard ball:**
   - ☐ He's completely bald.
   - ☐ He's a little bald.

4. **She's a real tightwad:**
   - ☐ She's an extremely generous person.
   - ☐ She's an extremely miserly person.

5. **Have you ever met such a cold fish?:**
   - ☐ Have you ever met such a nice person?
   - ☐ Have you ever met such an unfriendly person?

6. **My brother's new girlfriend is a real creep:**
   - ☐ My brother's new girlfriend is really wonderful.
   - ☐ My brother's new girlfriend is really despicable.

7. **She's a real tramp!:**
   - ☐ She's a real promiscuous person!
   - ☐ She's a real beauty!

8. **The new librarian is a bitch on wheels!:**
   - ☐ The new librarian is a good driver!
   - ☐ The new librarian is a real shrew!

9. **What a fat slob!:**
   - ☐ What a gourmet!
   - ☐ What a pig!

10. **That birdbrain forgot to pick me up at the airport:**
    - ☐ That pretty girl forgot to pick me up at the airport.
    - ☐ That neglectful person forgot to pick me up at the airport.

B. FIND-THE-WORD-CUBE

Step 1: Fill in the blanks with the correct word using the list below.

Step 2: Find and circle the word in the grid on the opposite page. The first one has been done for you.

uglies	crazo	slob
wheels	billiard	fish
motormouth	chicken	stuck
tramp	runt	creep

1. My father is bald as a _____ ball.

2. She sure does have a bad case of the _____ !

3. She's not very friendly. She's a real cold _____ .

4. Look at her screaming at herself. She's a _____ .

5. He never stops talking. He's such a _____ .

6. She's such a _____ . She sleeps with a different guy every night!

7. I can't believe he did that to you. What a _____ !

8. His apartment is always a mess. He's a real _____ .

9. Her grandmother is no spring _____ .

10. That guy's such a little _____ ! He's so small!

11. She never talks to me. She's so _____ up!

12. She's so nasty! What a bitch on _____ !

FIND-THE-WORD-CUBE

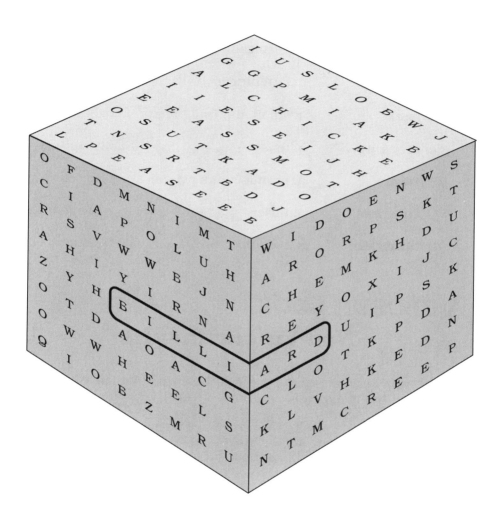

C. Choose the correct definition of the word(s) in boldface.

1. **crazo**:   a. nymphomaniac   b. eccentric

2. **creep**:   a. despicable person   b. slow person

3. **fat slob**:   a. fattening food   b. piggish person

4. **runt**:   a. small and frail person   b. buttocks

5. **stuck up**:   a. tense   b. arrogant

6. **tramp**:   a. promiscuous person b. eccentric

7. **tightwad**:   a. miser   b. piggish person

8. **birdbrain**:   a. small person   b. dumb person

A CLOSER LOOK
Non-Vulgar Insults

Whenever a large group of people gather, you'll be fairly certain to encounter many types of insults and criticisms aimed at some unsuspecting victim.

In the following list, we'll explore some of the most popular non-vulgar insults which can be used for just about any occasion:

Arrogant (to be)

cold fish (to be a) *exp.* (mild) to be unfriendly due to arrogance, shyness, unhappiness, etc.

full of hot air (to be) *exp.* (mild) said of an arrogant person who thinks he/she knows the answer to every question • *You actually believed what he said? He's so full of hot air!;* You actually believed what he said? He's such an arrogant person who thinks he knows the answer to every question!

have one's nose in the air (to) *exp.* (mild) said of someone who walks around with the chin (or nose) held high as if to look down on others.

high and mighty (to be) *exp.* (mild) to think highly of oneself.
➤ NOTE: This is said of someone who acts like a powerful king or queen who sits on an elevated throne.

hoity-toity (to be) *exp.* (mild) to be pretentious.

know-it-all (to be a) *exp.* (mild) one who boasts distastefully about the knowledge one has whether it is justified or not.

on an ego trip (to be) *exp.* (mild) to be completely self-impressed and self-absorbed.

on one's high horse (to be) *exp.* (mild) to be self-impressed.

put on airs (to be) *exp.* (mild) to be pretentious.

smart ass (to be a) *exp.* (crude yet very popular).

snooty (to be) *adj.* (mild) to be pretentious.

stuck on oneself (to be) *exp.* (mild) said of a person who is self-impressed and whose thoughts are, therefore, *"stuck on himself/herself."*

stuffed shirt (to be a) *exp.* (mild) said of someone who walks arrogantly as if wearing a stuffed shirt.

uppity (to be) *adj.* (mild) said of someone who feels that he/she is superior or above, everyone else.

Bald (to be)

bald as a billiard ball (to be) *exp.* (mild) said of someone who is completely hairless on his/her head.

bald as an eagle (to be) *exp.* (mild) to be completely hairless on one's head.

baldy *n.* (mild) name given to a bald person • *Hey, Baldy!;* Hey, you bald person!

curly *n.* (mild) name given to a bald person • *How 'ya doin', curly?;* How are you, bald person?

skin head (to be a) *n.* (mild) to be a bald person.
  ♦ NOTE: This is also the name given to a member of one of the Neo-Nazi organizations.

Coward (to be a)

baby (to be a) *n.* (mild) name given to a fearful person since babies are known for being easily frightened • *He's such a baby!;* He's such a fearful person!
  ♦ VARIATION: **big baby** *n.* an adult who acts like a baby.

chicken-shit (to be) • (vulgar) • **1.** *adj.* scared • *I'm too chicken shit to go parachuting!;* I'm too afraid to go parachuting! • **2.** *n.* coward • *What a chicken- shit!;* What a coward!
  ♦ VARIATION: **chicken** *adj.* & *n.* (mild).

fraidy cat (to be a) *n.* (mild) a fearful person.

gutless (to be) *adj.* (mild).
  ♦ NOTE: In American slang, *"guts"* is used to mean "courage."
  ♦ ALSO: **gutless wonder** *n.*

(mild) an extremely fearful person.
  ♦ ANTONYM: **gutsy (to be)** *adj.* (mild).

jellyfish (to be a) *n.* (mild) a meek and fearful person.

milktoast (to be a) *n.* (mild) to be a spineless person.
  ♦ NOTE: Also seen as "milquetoast."

scaredy-cat (to be a) *n.* (mild) coward.
  ♦ NOTE: This term is commonly used among children.

sissy (to be a) *n.* • **1.** (mild) to be a fearful person • **2.** (derogatory) a homosexual male.

yellow (to be) *adj.* coward
  ♦ VARIATION: **to be yellow-bellied** *adj.*

Crazy, to be
(NOTE: None of the synonyms for "crazy" are vulgar).

bananas (to be) *adj.*
  ♦ VARIATION: **to go bananas** *exp.* to go crazy • *He went bananas;* He went crazy.

bats in the belfry (to have) *exp.* (humorous).
  ♦ NOTE: This is a humorous expression signifying that

the subject has something wrong in his/her head.
‣ VARIATION: **to be batty** *adj.*

bonkers (to be) *adj.*
‣ VARIATION: **to go bonkers** *exp.* to become crazy • *When she lost the contest, she went bonkers;* When she lost the contest, she became crazy.

both oars in the water (not to have) *exp.* (humorous) said of a slightly crazy person • *She doesn't have both oars in the water;* She's rather crazy.

cook on all four burners (not to) *exp.* said of a person who is slightly crazy.

cracked (to be) *exp.*
‣ ALSO: **to crack [up]** *v.* to become crazy.

crackpot (to be a) *n.* one who is crazy and unpredictable, an eccentric.

crazo (to be a) *n.* to be a deranged person or an eccentric.
‣ NOTE: This is a variation of the term "crazy."

cuckoo (to be) *adj.* to be eccentric and unpredictable.

daffy (to be) *adj.*

ding-a-ling (to be a) *adj.* to be a deranged person or an eccentric.

dingy (to be) *adj.* to be crazy or foolish.

dippy (to be) *adj.* to be slightly crazy.

dorky (to be) *adj.* to be idiotic and clumsy.
‣ NOTE: This adjective is primarily used by the younger generation.

flaky (to be) *adj.* to be rather peculiar and unreliable.

flip one's lid (to) *exp.* to become crazy.

flip one's wig (to) *exp.* to become crazy.

flip out (to) *exp.* • **1.** to become crazy • *He used to be a genius but he suddenly flipped out for no reason!;* He used to be a genius but he suddenly became crazy! • **2.** to became extremely excited • *She flipped out over her new car!;* She became extremely excited over her new car!

flipped (to be) *adj.*
‣ VARIATION: **to be flipped out** *exp.*

freak out (to) *exp.* to become completely crazy.

fried (to be) *adj.* said of someone who seems to have brain damage (usually due to drugs).

fruitcake (to be a) *n.* to be a crazy person.

gone (to be) *adj.* • (lit); to have left one's senses.

in the ozone (to be) *exp.* to have left one's senses and be as far away from them as the ozone layer.

know enough to come in from the rain (not to) *exp.* said of a person who does not have the common sense to come inside to escape the rain.

kook (to be a) *n.* to be a peculiar and unpredictable person.
  ♦ VARIATION: **kooky (to be)** *adj.* to be peculiar and unpredictable.

loony (to be) *adj.* to be peculiar and unpredictable.
  ➤ NOTE: This comes from the noun "lunatic" meaning a "crazy person."

loony tune (to be a) *n.*
  ♦ NOTE: This is a common series of cartoons created by Warner Bros. studios and is used here as a play-on-words since it contains the word *"loony."*

mad as a hatter (to be) *exp.* • (lit); to be as crazy as one who sells hats.
  ♦ NOTE: Many decades ago, hat sellers were known for being crazy since the hats they wore contained lead-based dyes which would be absorbed by the skin and cause insanity.

meshuga (to be) *adj.* to be crazy.
  ♦ NOTE: This comes from Yiddish.
  ♦ VARIATION: **meshungina** *adj.*

missing a few marbles (to be) *exp.* to be slightly crazy.
  ♦ VARIATION (1): **not to have all one's marbles** *exp.*
  ♦ VARIATION (2): **to lose one's marbles** *exp.* to become crazy.

not all there (to be) *exp.* to be slightly crazy.

not playing with a full deck (to be) *exp.* (humorous) said of someone who is slightly crazy.
  ♦ NOTE: This expression comes from card playing where an incomplete deck of cards results in an inconsistent and unusual game. Here, the lack of a full deck refers to the lack of a complete set of brains.
  ♦ VARIATION: **to be a few cards short of a desk** *exp.*

nothing upstairs (to have) *exp.*
  ♦ NOTE: In this expression, *"upstairs"* refers to one's head.

nut case (to be a) *n.*

nuts (to be) *adj.* (very popular).
‣ VARIATION: **to be just plain nuts** *exp.*

nutty (to be) *adj.* to be nonsensical.
‣ VARIATION: **A common play-on-words of this expression is** *"to be nuttier than a fruitcake"* which is known for being full of nuts.

off one's nut (to be) *exp.* (humorous).

off one's rocker (to be) *exp.* (humorous).

off one's trolley (to be) *exp.* (humorous).

off the deep end (to go) *exp.* to became completely crazy.

out of it (to be) *exp.* to be incoherent, inaccurate, and slow.

out of one's gourd (to be) *exp.* to have left one's senses.
‣ NOTE: **gourd** *n.* (humorous) head.

out of one's head (to be) *exp.* to have left one's senses.

out of one's mind (to be) *exp.* to have left one's senses.

out of one's skull (to be). *exp.* to have left one's senses.

out of one's tree (to be) *exp.* to have left one's senses.

out there (to be) *exp.* to be very bizarre.

out to lunch (to be) *exp.* (humorous) to have left one's senses.
‣ VARIATION: **to be O.T.L.** *exp.* a common abbreviation of *"to be out to lunch."*

over the edge (to be) *exp.* to have fallen into a state of madness.

psycho (to be) *adj.* to be extremely crazy.
‣ NOTE: This is a common abbreviation of "psychotic."

schizo (to be) *adj.* to have two personalities.
‣ NOTE: This is a common abbreviation of "schizophrenic."
‣ VARIATION (1): **to be schizoid** *adj.*
‣ VARIATION (2): **to be schized out** *exp.*

screw loose (to have a) *exp.* to be slightly crazy.
‣ NOTE: It would be less common to hear *"to have a loose screw."*
‣ VARIATION: **to have a few screws loose** *exp.*

screwball (to be a) *n.* to be a crazy person.

screwy (to be) *adj.* to be peculiar.

sickie (to be a) *n.* to be an extremely crazy or perverted person.

sicko (to be a) *n.* to be an extremely crazy or perverted person.

slaphappy (to be) *n.* to be in a euphoric state where everything seems hilarious; giddy.

slow on the draw (to be) *exp.* (humorous) to be dull-witted.
♦ NOTE: This is a humorous expression coming from westerns where cowboys would duel with guns. The cowboy with the slowest reflexes, or slowest at drawing his gun, would inevitably lose. This expression is now commonly used to indicate someone who is slow at reasoning.

slow on the uptake (to be) *exp.* to be slow at common reasoning.

snap one's twig (to) *exp.* to become suddenly crazy.
♦ VARIATION: **to snap** *v.*

spacey (to be) *adj.* to be oblivious and irresponsible.

space cadet (to be a) *n.* to be an oblivious and irresponsible person.

♦ VARIATION: **to be a space case** *exp.*

the elevator doesn't go all the way to the top *exp.* (humorous).
♦ NOTE: This is a humorous expression inferring that the subject doesn't use his/her entire brain.

the lights are on but nobody's home *exp.* (humorous).
♦ NOTE: This is a humorous expression describing a person who is awake but completely unaware.

thick (to be) *adj.* to be dull-witted.
♦ NOTE: This adjective describes a person who's head is so thick that information can not penetrate.

touched in the head (to be) *exp.* to be eccentric and unpredictable.

wacky (to be) *adj.* to be eccentric and unpredictable.

whacko (to be) *adj.* to be extremely eccentric and unpredictable.
♦ NOTE: The adjective *"whacko"* is considered slightly more extreme than *"wacky."*

Despicable Person (to be a)

bitch (to be a) *n.* (somewhat coarse) • **1.** unpleasant woman • *You like her? She can be such a bitch!;* You like her? She can be so unpleasant! • **2.** unpleasant man (especially used among gays) • *What a bitch!;* What an unpleasant man! • **3. difficult** • *This job is a real bitch!;* This job is really difficult!
➤ NOTE (1): **bitchy** *adj.* (somewhat coarse) unpleasant (may be used for a man or woman) • *I asked her a simple question and she got all bitchy with me!;* I asked her a simple question and she became extremely unpleasant with me!
➤ NOTE (2): **to bitch** *v.* (somewhat coarse) to complain • *Stop bitching and just try to enjoy yourself;* Stop complaining and just try to enjoy yourself.

creep (to be a) *n.* (mild).

dirtbag (to be a) *n.* (mild).

douche bag (to be a) *exp.* (crude) despicable person • *I can't believe he did that to you. What a douche bag!;* I can't believe he did that to you. What a despicable person!

dweeb (to be a) *n.* fool (mild and very popular among the younger generation).

fink (to be a) *n.* (mild).
♦ NOTE: This is an older term used mainly in jest.

low-down no-good (to be) *adj.* (mild) vile, contemptible.
♦ NOTE: This is a very popular adjective used in conjunction with any one of the nouns in this section.

low-life (to be a) *n.* (mild) a very low individual.

maggot (to be a) *n.* (mild) • (lit); fly larva.

M.F. (to be an) *n.* a euphemistic abbreviation for *"mother fucker,"* an extremely vulgar synonym for a "despicable person."
♦ VARIATION: **mo-fo** *n.*

rat (to be a) *n.* (mild).

rat fink (to be a) *n.* (mild).
♦ NOTE: This is an older term used mainly in jest.

sleaze ball (to be a) *n.* (mild) an extremely low and contemptible person.
♦ VARIATION: **sleazy** *adj.* low and contemptible.

slime (to be) *n.* (mild) a low and despicable person • (lit); thick slippery liquid.

slime ball (to be a) *n.* (mild) a low and despicable person • (lit); a ball of thick slippery liquid.
  ♦ VARIATION: **slimebucket** *n.* • (lit); a bucket of thick slippery liquid.

snake (to be a) *n.* (mild) said of a person who is as low as a snake.

  ♦ VARIATION: **snake in the grass** *exp.*

S.O.B. (to be an) *n.* a euphemistic abbreviation of *"son of a bitch".*

stinker (to be a) *n.* (mild) • (lit); one who smells repulsively.

twerp (to be a) *n.* (mild).

Fat (to be)
(NOTE: All synonyms for "fat" are mild)

blimp (to be a) *exp.* • (lit); to be (as fat as) a dirigible.
  ♦ VARIATION: **to be a blimpo** *adj.*

broad in the beam (to be) *exp.* (humorous) to be fat across the rear.

chunky (to be) *adj.* to be somewhat fat.

cow (to be a) *n.* to be as fat as a cow.
  ♦ ALSO: **to be a fat cow** *exp.*

pig (to be a) *adj.* to be as fat as a pig.
  ♦ ALSO: **to be a fat pig** *exp.*

fat slob (to be a) *exp.* to be fat and disgusting.

fat stuff *n.* a fat person.

fatso (to be a) *n.* a slang transformation of the adjective "fat."
  ♦ ALSO: **to be a fatty** *exp.*

hippo (to be a) *adj.* to be as fat as a hippopotamus.
  ♦ NOTE: The term *"hippo"* is a common abbreviation for "hippopotamus."

hog (to be a) *exp.* to be fat as a hog.

lard-ass (to be a) *exp.* to have fat buttocks.
  ♦ NOTE: **ass** *n.* (vulgar) buttocks.

lardo (to be a) *n.* to be a fat person.
  ♦ NOTE: The term *"lardo"* is a slang transformation of the noun "lard" meaning "fat."

love handles (to have) *exp.* an affectionate expression referring to the ring of fat around one's midsection.

porker (to be a) *n.* to be extremely fat as well as an overzealous eater.
➧ VARIATION: **pig** *adj.* to be fat as a pig.

spare tire (to have a) *exp.* to have a ring of fat all around one's midsection, resembling the shape of a tire.

tub of lard (to be a) *exp.* to be an extremely fat individual • (lit); to be a container of fat.
➧ VARIATION: **to be a tub** *adj.*

walrus (to be a) *n.* to be as fat as a walrus.

whale (to be a) *n.* to be as fat as a whale.
➧ VARIATION: **to be a beached whale** *exp.* to be extremely fat and motionless such as after eating a huge meal.

Fool

airhead (to be an) *n.* (mild) an irresponsible and unthinking person • (lit); one who has nothing but air in the head.

birdbrain (to be a) *n.* (mild) an irresponsible and unthinking person • (lit); one who has a brain the size of that of a bird.

blockhead (to be a) *n.* (mild) a ridiculous and unthinking person • (lit); one who has a block of wood (which has no brains) for a head.

blubberhead (to be a) *n.* (mild) an unthinking person • (lit); one who has nothing but blubber for a brain.

bonehead (to be a) *n.* (mild) a nonsensical and unthinking person • (lit); one who has nothing but a bone for a head.

boob (to be a) *n.* (mild) an ridiculous and unthinking person, a fool.

butthead (to be a) *n.* (somewhat crude) • **1.** an unthinking person • **2.** a despicable person.

chump (to be a) *n.* (mild) an unthinking and gullible person.

dimwit (to be a) *n.* (mild) a foolish and unthinking person, an idiot • (lit); one whose cleverness is dim or faint.

dip stick (to be a) *n.* (mild) an unthinking person.
➧ VARIATION: **dip** *n.* • *What a dip!;* What a fool!
➧ NOTE: A *"dip stick"* is literally a stick which is

used to verify the oil level in a car. Due to its similarity in sound, it is commonly used as a euphemism for the term *"dip shit"* meaning "fool."

dode (to be a) *n.* (mild) fool.
 ‣ NOTE: This is one of the newest slang terms for "fool" and is used mainly by the younger generation.

dodo (to be a) *n.* (mild) fool.

dolt (to be a) *n.* (mild) a foolish person.

dork (to be a) *n.* (very popular among the younger generation) an extremely foolish person, a stupid and awkward person.

dumb bunny (to be a) *n.* an affectionate term for a foolish person.

dumb Dora (to be a) *n.* (mild) a foolish woman or girl.

dumb ox (to be a) *n.* (mild) an extremely foolish person.
 ‣ NOTE: This compares a person to an ox which is considered extremely slow and stupid.

dumbass (to be a) *n.* (crude) • an extremely foolish person.

dumbbell (to be a) *n.* (mild) a foolish person.

dumbo (to be a) *n.* (mild) a foolish person.

dumdum (to be a) *n.* (mild) an affectionate term for a foolish person.

dummy (to be a) *n.* (mild) an affectionate term for a foolish person.

dunce (to be a) *n.* (mild) a foolish person.

dunderhead (to be a) *n.* (mild) a foolish and unthinking person.

fathead (to be a) *n.* (mild) an extremely foolish person.
 ‣ NOTE: This describes someone who has nothing but fat in place of a brain.

geek (to be a) *n.* (extremely popular and mild) a dull and stupid person.
 ‣ NOTE: This was made popular by the younger generation but is becoming more and more used by the older generation. This term is commonly heard on television.

goob (to be a) *n.* (mild) an extremely foolish person.
 ‣ NOTE: This term is used primarily by the younger generation. It comes from a fictional character used in an old popular television show called "The Andy Griffith Show" where a character named Goober was known for being extremely foolish. Teens

have simply shortened the name to *"goob"* and changed the first letter to lowercase.
‣ VARIATION: **goober** *n.*

goof ball (to be a) *n.* (mild) a silly and amusing person.

goofus (to be a) *n.* (mild) a fool.

goon (to be a) *n.* (mild) a fool.

jackass (to be a) *n.* (somewhat crude) • **1.** an imbecile • **2.** a despicable person.

jerk (to be a) *n.* (mild) an extremely foolish, unthinking, and despicable person.

jughead (to be a) *n.* (mild) a foolish and unthinking person • (lit); a person who has an empty jug in place of a head.

knucklehead (to be a) *n.* (mild) an affectionate term for a silly person.

lamebrain (to be a) *n.* (mild) a foolish and unthinking person • (lit); a person with an impaired brain.

lunkhead (to be a) *n.* (mild) a foolish and unthinking person.

meathead (to be a) *n.* (mild) a foolish and unthinking person • (lit); a person with nothing but a big piece of meat in place of a head.

nerd (to be a) *n.* (mild) to be a foolish-looking person.
‣ VARIATION (1): **to be nerdy** *adj.*
‣ VARIATION (2): **to be nerded out** *exp.*

nincompoop (to be a) *n.* (humorous) a fool.
‣ NOTE: This term is primarily used in cartoons or in jest.

ninny (to be a) *n.* (humorous) a fool.
‣ NOTE: This term is primarily used in cartoons or in jest.

nitwit (to be a) *n.* (mild) a foolish and unthinking person.

numbskull (to be a) *n.* (somewhat humorous) an affectionate term for a foolish and unthinking person.

pinhead (to be a) *n.* (somewhat humorous) a foolish and unthinking person • (lit); one who has a head the size of that of a pinhead with a brain to match.

scatterbrain (to be a) *n.* (mild) one who is forgetful and unreliable.

schmo (to be a) *n.* (mild) a fool.
‣ NOTE: This comes from Yiddish.

spaz (to be a) *n.* (mild) a very foolish and dull person.
➤ NOTE: This is an abbreviation of the term "spastic" meaning "one who has muscle spasms due to injury or illness."

stupe (to be a) *n.* (mild) a foolish and unthinking person.
♦ NOTE: This is a shortened version of "stupid."

turkey (to be a) *n.* (mild) an extremely foolish and unthinking person.

twit (to be a) *n.* (mild) a foolish and worthless person.

Miserly (to be)

cheap (to be) *adj.* (mild) said of one who only buys goods which are inexpensive regardless of the quality.
♦ VARIATION: **to be a cheapskate** *n.* (mild) a disdainful term for one who only buys goods which are inexpensive regardless of the quality.

close to one's wallet (to be) *exp.* (mild) a figurative expression said of one who guards his/her wallet closely.

close-fisted (to be) *exp.* (mild) a figurative expression said of one who keeps the fist tightly closed around his/her money to keep from spending.

last of the big spenders (to be the) *exp.* (mild) a facetious expression said of a miser.
♦ VARIATION: **to be the last of the big-time spenders** *exp.* (mild).

penny-pinching (to be) *adj.* (mild) a figurative expression signifying one who has difficulty spending as little money as a penny to which he/she holds on tightly.
♦ ALSO: **to be a penny-pincher** *n.*

piker (to be a) *n.*

skinflint (to be a) *n.*

tight (to be) *adj.* (mild) to be rigid with one's money.
♦ VARIATION: **to be as tight as a drum** *exp.* to be very rigid with one's money.
♦ VARIATION: **to be a tightwad** *n.* (mild).

tight-fisted (to be) *adj.* (mild) a figurative expression signifying one who has difficulty spending money which he/she holds onto tightly.

Old (to be)

a few miles on him/her (to have) *exp.* (humorous).
♦ NOTE: This is a common expression traditionally applied to an old car.

been around (to have) *exp.* (mild) • **1.** to be old • **2.** to have had sex with a variety of people.

codger (to be a) *n.* (mild) to be an old eccentric and irritable man.
♦ VARIATION: **to be an old codger** *n.*

fogy (to be a) *n.* (mild) someone with outdated ideas.
♦ VARIATION: **to be an old fogy** *n.*
♦ NOTE: Also spelled *"fogey."*

fossil (to be a) *n.* (humorous) refers to someone (or something) old and out-of-date.
♦ NOTE: This term is traditionally applied to old remnants or bones from a past geological era.
♦ VARIATION: **to be an old fossil** *n.*

gramps *n.* (mild) a disrespect-ful name given to an old man • *Hey, gramps!; Hello, old man!*

granny *n.* (mild) a disrespect-ful name given to an old woman • *Hurry up, granny!; Hurry up, old woman!*

long in the tooth (to be) *exp.* (mild) said of someone who is getting old.

old coot (to be an) *exp.* (mild) a foolish and cantankerous person.

old fart (to be an) *n.* (somewhat crude yet humorous) • **1.** said of someone with outdated ideas • **2.** said of someone with no enthusiasm for physical activity • (lit); to be an old flatulence.

old poop (to be an) *n.* (humorous) • **1.** said of someone with outdated ideas • **2.** said of someone with no enthusiasm for physical activity • (lit); to be an old bowel movement.

old-timer (to be an) *n.* • (lit); (mild) one who has been living for a long time.

older than dirt (to be) *exp.* (humorous) to be extremely old.
♦ VARIATION (1): **to be older than Methusela** *exp.* (mild).
♦ VARIATION (2): **to be older than Moses** *exp.* (mild).
♦ VARIATION (3): **to be older than the hills (to be)** *exp.* (mild).

oldster (to be an) *n.* (mild).

on one's last legs (to be) *exp.* (mild) to be so old and decrepit as to be close to death.
  ♦ NOTE: This term is also commonly applied to an old appliance which is about to cease functioning.

one foot in the grave (to have) *exp.* (mild) to be close to death.

over the hill (to be) *exp.* (mild).
  ♦ NOTE: In this expression, "*the hill*" represents youth.

pops *n.* a name given to an old man (which can be disrespectful depending on the context).
  ➤ NOTE: This is also an affectionate term for one's father.

pruneface (to be a) *n.* (humorous) a name given to an old person whose face is wrinkled like a prune.
  ♦ VARIATION: **to be an old prune** *exp.*

relic (to be a) *n.* (humorous) • (lit); to be an artifact from a past era.
  ♦ VARIATION: **to be an old relic** *n.*

Promiscuous (to be a)

easy (to be) *adj.* (mild) to be quick to have sex with a variety of partners.

easy lay (to be an) *n.* (very popular and somewhat crude) • *I heard the new girl in school is an easy lay!*; I heard the new girl in school is real promiscuous!

floozy (to be a) *exp.* (mild).

loose (to be) *adj.* (mild).

round heels (to have) *exp.* (mild) said of a girl who is always on her back with her heels dragging on the ground, being passed from one sex partner to the other.

skank *n.* (mild) an extremely promiscuous person.
  ♦ NOTE: This term is popular mainly among the younger generation.

slutty (to be) *n.* (somewhat crude) to act like a prostitute and have frequent sex.
  ♦ VARIATION: **to be a slut** *n.* • (lit); to be a prostitute.

swinger (to be a) *n.* (mild) to be ready for all types of recreational sex at any moment.

trampy (to be) *adj.* (mild) to act like a prostitute and have frequent sex.
 ♦ VARIATION: **to be a tramp** *exp.* to be like a vagabond who rarely sleeps in the same place twice.

Short (to be)

dinky (to be) *adj.* (mild) to be exceptionally small.

half-pint (to be a) *n.* (humorous) to be very short.
 ♦ VARIATION: **to be pint-sized** *adj.*

peewee (to be a) *n.* (mild) an abusive name given to a short person.

puny (to be) *adj.* (mild) to be very short.

runt (to be a) *n.* (mild) an abusive name given to a short person.

shorty (to be a) *n.* (mild) an abusive name given to a short person.

shrimp (to be a) *n.* (mild) an abusive name given to a short person.
 ♦ NOTE: The term *"shrimp"* is literally a very small crustacean which is used to mean "a very short person" due to its small size.

small fry (to be a) *exp.* (mild) • **1.** an abusive name given to a very short person • **2.** an affectionate term used to describe a child.

squirt (to be a) *n.* (mild) a abusive name given to a very short person.

Talkative (to be)

bag of wind (to be a) *exp.* (humorous).
 ♦ NOTE: This expression is said of someone who talks so much that all they appear to be doing is exhaling.
 ♦ VARIATION: **to be a windbag** *n.*

big mouth (to have a) *n.* (mild).

blabbermouth (to be a) *n.* (mild).
 ♦ NOTE: **to blabber** *v.* to talk excessively.

blowhard (to be a) *n.* (mild) one who talks excessively about unrealistic ideas.

diarrhea of the mouth (to have) *exp.* (humorous yet crude).
‣ VARIATION: **to have verbal diarrhea** *exp.*

flap one's gums (to) *exp.* (humorous) • (lit); to move one's mouth open and closed continuously due to excessive talking.

gasbag (to be a) *n.* (humorous).

go on (to) *exp.* (mild) to talk continuously.
‣ VARIATION: **to go on and on** *exp.*

long-winded (to be) *exp.* (mild) said of someone whose excessive chatter produces large amounts of wind.

loudmouth (to be a) *n.* (mild) to be a talkative and loud person.

motormouth (to be a) *n.* (humorous) to be an extremely talkative person.

rattle on (to) *exp.* (mild) to talk nonstop.

talker (to be a) *n.* (mild) to be a talkative person.

windbag (to be a) *n.* (mild) said of someone whose excessive chatter produces large amounts of wind.

yacker (to be a) *n.* (mild) to be a talkative person.
‣ NOTE: **to yack** *v.* to talk excessively.

Thin (to be)

bag of bones (to be a) *exp.* (mild) to be extremely thin.

bean pole (to be a) *exp.* (humorous).

bird legs (to have) *exp.* (mild) said of a person with extremely thin legs.

skin and bones (to be) *exp.* (mild) to be extremely thin.
‣ VARIATION: **to be nothing but skin and bones** *exp.*

stick (to be a) *n.* (mild) to be very thin.

thin as a rail (to be) *exp.* (mild) to be extremely thin.

Ugly (to be)

beaten with the ugly stick (to be) *exp.* (humorous) said of someone who is extremely ugly.
‣ VARIATION: **to be hit with the ugly stick** *exp.* (humorous).

butt ugly (to be) *exp.* (crude yet humorous) to be extremely ugly • (lit); to be as ugly as one's buttocks.

dog (to be a) *n.* (mild) to be an ugly person.
‣ VARIATION: **to be a bow-wow** (which is the sound made by a barking dog) *exp.* (humorous).

face only a mother could love (to have a) *exp.* (humorous) to be extremely ugly.

face that could stop a clock (to have a) *exp.* (humorous) to be extremely ugly.

face that would crack a mirror (to have a) *exp.* (humorous) to be extremely ugly.

gross (to be) *adj.* (mild) to be hideously ugly or disgusting.

hard on the eyes (to be) *exp.* (mild) to be extremely ugly.

look like death warmed over (to) *exp.* (mild) to look ugly or sick.

pig (to be a) *n.* (mild) • **1.** to be an ugly and dirty person. • **2.** to be very fat.

troll (to be a) *n.* (mild) to be an ugly person.

ugly as sin (to be) *exp.* (mild) to be extremely ugly.

ugo (to be) *adj.* (humorous) a slang transformation of the adjective "ugly."

UNIT THREE

This unit is rated...

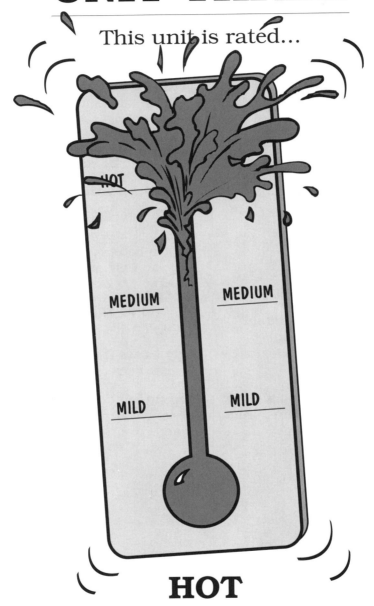

HOT

MEDIUM

MEDIUM

MILD

MILD

HOT

This unit is composed of terms and expressions which are extremely vulgar and offensive and should, therefore be used with caution.

VULGAR INSULTS
– At School –

LESSON THREE

Dialogue in slang

At School...

DIALOGUE

Robert and Alicia are having lunch.

Robert: What a **pisser**! I really **fucked up** the test. I should have been more of a **kiss-ass** to that **shit-head** of a teacher. What **bull shit**!

Alicia: This really **bites**. I think he **gets his rocks off** flunking us, the **son of a bitch.**

Robert: I couldn't believe what a **fucker** he was to that new girl today.

Alicia: Donna? The one who's got **shit for brains**? She deserved it. She's a real **asshole**, too. I don't know what her problem is. Maybe she's **on the rag**.

50

LESSON THREE

At School...

DIALOGUE

Robert and Alicia are having lunch.

Robert: What an **aggravating situation**! I really **failed** the test. I should have been a **nicer person** to that **idiot** of a teacher. This is **ridiculous**!

Alicia: This **is really annoying**. I think he **enjoys** flunking us, the **despicable person**.

Robert: I couldn't believe what a **vile person** he was to that new girl today.

Alicia: Donna? The one who's **totally stupid**? She deserved it. She's a real **hateful person**, too. I don't know what her problem is. Maybe she's **menstruating**.

Dialogue in slang as it would be heard

At School...

DIALOGUE

Robert 'n Alicia 'r having lunch.

Robert: Whad a **pisser**! I really **fucked up** the test. I should've been more of a **kiss-ass** ta that **shit-head** of a teacher. What **bull shit**!

Alicia: This really **bites**. I think 'e **gets 'is rocks off** flunking us, the **son of a bitch**.

Robert: I couldn' believe whad a **fucker** 'e was ta that new girl t'day.

Alicia: Donna? The one oo'z got **shit fer brains**? She deserved it. She's a real **asshole**, too. I dunno what 'er problem is. Maybe she's **on the rag**.

Vocabulary

asshole (to be an) *n.* (vulgar) to be a despicable person • (lit); to be an anal sphincter • *He lied and got me into trouble. Can you believe what an asshole he is?*; He lied and got me into trouble. Can you believe what a despicable person he is?

bite (to) *v.* (vulgar) to be terrible • *It bites that she did that to you;* It's terrible that she did that to you.
▸ CAUTION: It is important to note that *"to bite"* is a variation on the popular expression *"to bite the big one,"* *"the big one"* being a euphemism for "penis." Therefore, *"to bite"* should be used with caution due to its reference.
▸ SYNONYM: **to suck** *v.* (vulgar).
⇨ CAUTION: It is important to note that *"to suck"* is a shortened version of the popular expression *"to suck dick,"* *"dick"* being a slang synonynm for "penis." Therefore, *"to suck"* should be used with caution due to its reference.

bullshit (to be) *exp.* (vulgar) to be nonsense • (lit); to be bull excrement • *That's a bunch of bullshit!;* That's complete nonsense!
▸ NOTE: Any expression containing the term *"shit"* is vulgar.

fuck up (to) *exp.* (vulgar) to ruin; to bungle • *I fucked up my car;* I ruined my car.
▸ NOTE: This comes from the verb *"to fuck,"* meaning "to fornicate." This is one of the most vulgar yet popular obscenities in the American-English language.

fucker (to be a) *n.* (vulgar) to be an extremely despicable person • (lit); to be a fornicator • *That guy stole my wallet! What a fucker!;* That guy stole my wallet! What an extremely despicable person!
▸ VARIATION: **to be a mother-fucker** *exp.*

gets one's rocks off (to) *exp.* (vulgar) to enjoy greatly • (lit); said of a man who relieves his testicles (*"rocks"*) of semen by having sex • *He gets his rocks off by singing;* He really enjoys singing.

kiss-ass (to be a) *exp.* (vulgar) said of someone who does anything to get in the good graces of someone • *He keeps buying the boss lunch all the time. What a kiss-ass;* He keeps buying the boss lunch all the time. He'll do anything to get in the boss's good graces.
  ‣ SYNONYM: **to brown-nose** *v.* (vulgar) said of someone who "kisses someone's ass" to such a degree as to get his/her nose brown.

on the rag (to be) *exp.* (vulgar) to be in a bad mood • (lit); to be menstruating • *You're sure on the rag today!;* You're sure in a bad mood today!
  ‣ NOTE: In this expression, *"rag"* refers to a woman's sanitary napkin used during menstruation. Oddly enough, this expression is now also heard in reference to a man who is in a bad mood.
  ‣ VARIATION: **to be O.T.R.** *adj.* a common abbreviation and euphemism of the expression *"to be on the rag."*

pisser (to be a) *n.* (vulgar) to be aggravating • *I got yelled at again by the teacher. What a pisser!;* I got yelled at again by the teacher. How aggravating!
  ‣ NOTE: **to be pissed [off]** *exp.* (crude) to be angry.

shit for brains (to have) *exp.* (vulgar) to be extremely stupid • (lit); to have excrement for brains • *Can you believe what he did? He must have shit for brains!;* Can you believe what he did? He must be a complete idiot!
  ‣ VARIATION: **shit-for-brains** *exp.* an incredibly stupid person • *Hey, shit-for-brains!;* Hey, stupid!

shit-head (to be a) *n.* (vulgar) a despicable person • *What a mean thing he did to you! What a shit-head!;* What a mean thing he did to you! What a despicable person!

son of a bitch (to be a) *exp.* (vulgar) an extremely despicable person • (lit); to be a son of a female dog • *I'm gonna kill that son of a bitch!;* I'm going to kill that despicable person!
  ‣ VARIATION: **to be an S.O.B.** *exp.* a common euphemistic abbreviation of *"son of a bitch."*

PRACTICE THE VOCABULARY

[Answers to Lesson 3, p. 167]

A. Underline the word that best completes the phrase.

1. That (**fucker**, **trucker**) just stole my car!

2. I failed the test again. What a (**kisser**, **pisser**)!

3. How could he do that to you? I can't believe what a shit-(**foot**, **head**) he is!

4. Why do you always bother me? Is this how you get your (**stones**, **rocks**) off?

5. Why are you reacting with such hostility? What are you, on the (**rag**, **cloth**)?

6. I hate that (**son**, **daughter**) of a bitch!

7. I don't believe what you're telling me. It's a bunch of (**rabbit**, **bull**) shit!

8. I totally fucked (**up**, **down**) my homework assignment!

9. He keeps offering to do favors for the teacher. What a kiss-(**boob**, **ass**)!

10. You actually trust him to get the job done? He's got shit for (**hooters**, **brains**)!

11. That (**asshole**, **pothole**) lied to me!

12. My teacher gave us homework to do over vacation! This really (**eats**, **bites**, **drinks**).

B. "CUSSWORD" PUZZLE
Fill in the puzzle by using the words from the list.

shit	ass	fucker
son	rocks off	pisser
brains	rag	kiss

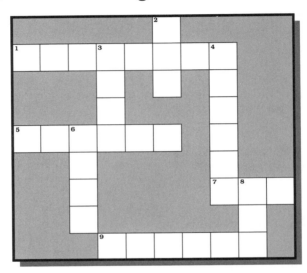

ACROSS

1. **to get one's** _____ *exp.* to enjoy greatly • (lit); said of a man who relieves his testicles of semen by having sex.

5. **to be a** _____ *n.* to be aggravating.

7. **to be on the** _____ *exp.* to be in a bad mood • (lit); to be menstruating.

9. **to have shit for** _____ *exp.* to be extremely stupid.

DOWN

2. **to be a** _____ **of a bitch** *exp.* an extremely despicable person • (lit); to be a son of a female dog.

3. **to be a** _____**-ass** *exp.* said of someone who does anything to get in the good graces of someone.

4. **to be a** _____ *n.* to be an extremely despicable person • (lit); to be a fornicator.

6. **to be bull** _____ *exp.* to be nonsense.

8. **to be an** _____**hole** *n.* to be a despicable person • (lit); to be an anal sphincter.

A CLOSER LOOK (1):
Vulgar Insults
(Common Obscenities from Behind the Wheel)

To paraphrase an American comedian: "The intensity of the delivery of an insult is proportionate to the distance between the two people." In other words, the greater the distance between the speaker and the target, the stronger the insult! Then what better place to deliver a rip-roaring obscenity than from behind the armor of one's car?!

Here are some of the more colorful vulgar insults you're liable to encounter while driving on just about any highway in America. All terms are synonyms for "despicable person" unless otherwise noted:

ass hole *n.* (vulgar) • (lit); anal sphincter.

ass wipe *n.* (vulgar) • (lit); toilet paper.

bastard *n.* (vulgar) • (lit); an illegitimate son.
  ♦ NOTE: This applies to males only.

butt-head *n.* (humorous yet somewhat crude).

butt-hole n. (vulgar) • (lit); anal sphincter.

cock-sucker *n.* (extremely vulgar) • (lit); one who is active in oral sex.
  ♦ NOTE: **cock** *n.* (extremely vulgar) penis.

cunt *n.* (extremely vulgar, applies to women only) • (lit); vagina.

dick *n.* (very popular yet crude).
  ♦ NOTE: This applies to males only.
  ♦ VARIATION: **dick head** *n.*

dumb-fuck *n.* (vulgar) idiot.

fuck-face *n.* (vulgar yet very popular) an extremely despicable person.

fucker *n.* (vulgar yet extremely popular) an extremely despicable person.

fuck-head *n.* (vulgar) a despicable person.

mother-fucker *n.* (extremely vulgar yet popular) an exceedingly despicable person.

prick *n.* (vulgar) • (lit); penis.

putz *n.* (vulgar) • (lit); penis.
  ♦ ORIGIN: Yiddish.

shit ass *n.* (extremely vulgar).

shit for brains • **1.** *exp.* to *have shit for brains;* to be an idiot • **2.** *n.* jerk, fool.

shit head *n.* (vulgar yet very popular) • (lit); one with a head full of excrement.

shit hole *n.* (extremely vulgar) • (lit); anal sphincter.

shmuck *n.* (vulgar) • (lit); penis.
  ⟩ ORIGIN: Yiddish.

son of a bitch *n.* (vulgar) • (lit); son of a female dog.

A CLOSER LOOK (2):
The Obscenity "Buffet"

Now, you can create you own personalized obscene phrase by choosing one entry from each column:

TAKE-OFF	+ADJECTIVE[1]+	ADJECTIVE[2] +	INSULT
What a(n)	big	cock-sucking	*ass hole!*
Why, you	big, fat	fucking	*ass wipe!*
You,	dirty	mother-fucking	*bastard!*
	disgusting	scum-sucking	*cock-sucker!*
	fat		*cunt!*
	filthy		*dick!*
	goddamn		*dumb-fuck!*
	gross		*fuck-face!*
	lousy		*fuck-head!*
	stinking		*fucker!*
	stupid		*mother-fucker!*
	slimey		*prick!*
	ugly		*putz!*
			shit-ass!
			shit-head!
			shmuck
			son of a bitch!

A CLOSER LOOK (3):
"Vulgar" Initials

Initials are popular in everyday speech as a way to euphemistically represent an obscene phrase. This is a very common practice which enables the speaker to use obscenities by couching them behind inoffensive initials.

The following list represents some of the most commonly used initials of this kind:

B.F. *n.* despicable person • *He's such a B.F.!*; He's such a despicable person.
♦ NOTE: This is a euphemistic abbreviation of *"butt fucker"* which is considered extremely vulgar.

B.F.D. *exp.* used to indicate great indifference • *I know you lost the contest but B.F.D. You'll try again next time*; I know you lost the contest but don't be concerned. You'll try again next time.
♦ NOTE: This is a euphemistic abbreviation of *"big fucking deal"* which is considered vulgar.

B.J. *exp.* oral sex • *I heard she gave him a B.J. last night*; I heard she gave him oral sex last night.
♦ NOTE: This is a euphemistic abbreviation of *"blow job"* which is considered vulgar.

B.S. *exp.* nonsense • *That's a bunch of B.S.!*; That's a bunch of nonsense!
♦ NOTE: This is a euphemistic abbreviation of *"bullshit,"* (literally "bull excrement") which is considered vulgar.

C.Y.A. *exp.* a euphemistic replacement for *"Cover your ass!"* meaning "Protect yourself from possible blame!" • *Make sure to tell the boss in writing that the client was the one who changed the design, not you. Remember, C.Y.A.!*; Make sure to tell the boss in writing that the client was the one who changed the design, not you. Remember, protect yourself from possible blame!

"F.U!" *interj.* "Fuck you!"
♦ NOTE: This is a common reproach to a despicable person • *I can't believe you'd do such a rotten thing. F.U.!*; I can't believe you'd do such

a rotten thing. Fuck you! • In this interjection, the letter "U" is used to represent "you" since the sounds are identical.

J.O. (to) *v.* masturbation • *I'm gonna go J.O.*; I'm going to go masturbate.
♦ NOTE: This is a euphemistic abbreviation of the verb to *"jack off"* which is con- sidered vulgar.

M.F. *exp.* despicable person • *He's such an M.F.!*; He's such a despicable person!
♦ NOTE: This is a euphemistic abbreviation of *"mother- fucker"* which is considered vulgar.

O.P.P. *exp.* one's sexual organs • *He got into O.P.P. last night*; He had sex last night.
♦ NOTE: These are some of the newest slang initials in the American repertory and are known only by the younger generation. Unbeknownst to most parents, *"O.P.P."* comes from rap music and stands for "other people's pussy" (*"pussy"* is a vulgar slang synonym for vagina) or "other people's penis."

O.T.R. *exp.* in a terrible mood • *Don't talk to her now. She's O.T.R.*; Don't talk to her now. She's in a terrible mood.
♦ NOTE: This is a euphemistic

abbreviation of *"on the rag"* which is a vulgar expression applied to women who are menstruating. Although the term *"rag"* is used in slang to mean "sanitary napkin," this expression is occasionally applied to a male who is in a bad mood as well.

P.W.'d (to be) *exp.* to be subservient to one's wife • *His wife does nothing but yell at him all the time and he does everything she tells him to do! He sure is P.W.'d!*; His wife does nothing but yell at him all the time and he does everything she tells him to do! He sure is subservient to his wife!
♦ NOTE: This is a euphemistic abbreviation of the extremely vulgar expression *"to be pussy-whipped;" "pussy"* being a vulgar slang synonym for "vagina."

S.B.D. *exp.* (humorous) silent, yet potent flatulence • *Who cut the S.B.D.?*; Who has the silent flatulence?
♦ NOTE: This is a euphemistic abbreviation of "silent-but- deadly" which is considered humorous.

S.O.B. *exp.* a despicable person • *I'm gonna kill that S.O.B.!*; I'm going to kill that despicable person!
♦ NOTE: This is a euphemistic

abbreviation of *"son of a bitch"* which is considered vulgar.

S.O.L. *exp.* extremely unfortunate • *I'm sorry but you missed dinner because you're so late. I guess you're just S.O.L.;* I'm sorry but you missed dinner because you're so late. I guess you're just extremely unfortunate. ◗ NOTE: This is a euphemistic abbreviation of *"shit out of luck"* which is considered vulgar.

S.O.S. exp. an army term for "chipped beef on toast" which was referred to as *"shit on a shingle"* or "S.O.S."

T. & A. *exp.* nudism, or more literally, breasts and buttocks • *My parents don't let me go to movies that have a lot of T. & A.;* My parents don't let me go to movies that contain a lot of nudism. ◗ NOTE: This is a euphemistic abbreviation of *"tits and ass"* which is considered crude.

T.S. *exp.* a shame • *I know you don't want to do your homework, but T.S.! You have no choice!;* I know you don't want to do your homework, but that's a shame! You have no choice! ◗ NOTE: This is a euphemistic abbreviation of *"tough shit"* which is considered vulgar.

THE MANY USES OF

$\mathfrak{Shit}$

"Something tells me Steve got **shit-faced** during lunch..."

Dialogue in slang

The Hollywood Studio Tour...

DIALOGUE

Julie and Mike are talking about one of their co-workers.

Julie: Malcolm got **shit-faced** again on the job.

Mike: You **shitting** me? How **the shit** can he drink all that **shit** without **catching shit** from the boss? His work's even **for shit**.

Julie: **Beats the shit** out of me! He's been **pulling shit** like this for a long time.

Mike: **Shit, yeah**! Last week he did the **shittiest** job on this **shitload** of work he had to do which he **doesn't know shit about** anyway. He thinks he's **hot shit** but I think he's **shit** lazy. He'd better **shit or get off the pot**.

Julie: One of these days he's gonna be **shit out of luck** and **up shit creek** when he gets on the boss's **shitlist**.

Mike: **No shit**!

Translation of dialogue in standard American-English

The Hollywood Studio Tour...

DIALOGUE

Julie and Mike are talking about one of their co-workers.

Julie: Malcolm got **intoxicated** again on the job.

Mike: Are you **kidding** me? How **is it possible that** he can drink all that **substance** without **getting reprimanded** by the boss? His work is even **mediocre**.

Julie: **I have no idea**! He's been **successful at devious acts** like this for a long time.

Mike: **Absolutely**! Last week he did the **worst** job on this **large quantity** of work he had to do which he **doesn't know anything about** anyway. He thinks he's **exceptional** but I think he's **extremely** lazy. He'd better **start to take some action**.

Julie: One of these days he's going to be **completely out of luck** and **in big trouble** when he gets in the boss's **bad graces**.

Mike: **You're not kidding**!

Dialogue in slang as it would be heard

The Hollywood Studio Tour...

DIALOGUE

Julie 'n Mike 'r talking about one 'a their co-workers.

Julie: Malcolm got **shit-faced** again on the job.

Mike: You **shiddin'** me? How **the shit** can 'e drink all that **shit** without **catching shit** from the boss? His work's even **fer shit**.

Julie: **Beats the shit** oudda me! He's been **pulling shit** like this fer a long time.

Mike: **Shit, yeah**! Last week 'e did the **shiddiest** job on this **shitload** 'a work 'e had ta do which 'e **doesn' know shid aboud** anyway. He thinks 'ees **hot shit** bud I think ee'z **shit** lazy. He'd bedder **shid 'r ged off the pot**.

Julie: One 'a these days ee'z gonna be **shid oudda luck** 'n **up shit creek** when 'e gets on the boss's **shitlist**.

Mike: **No shit!**

Vocabulary

"Beats the shit out of me" *exp.* "I don't know"

catch shit from (to) *exp.* to get reprimanded by • *I'm gonna catch shit from my parents when they see what I did to the car;* I'm going to get reprimanded by my parents when they see what I did to the car.

for shit (to be) *exp.* to be useless • *This car's for shit!;* This car's useless!

hot shit (to be) *exp.* to be impressive • *He thinks he's such hot shit;* He thinks he so impressive.
♦ VARIATION: **"He thinks he's hot shit but he's just runny diarrhea"** *exp.*

know shit about something (not to) *exp.* not to know the slightest thing about something • *She doesn't know shit about cooking;* She doesn't know the slightest thing about cooking.
♦ VARIATION: **not to know jack shit about something** *exp.*

"No shit!" *exp.* • *"You're not kidding!"*.
♦ VARIATION: **"Shit no!"** *exp.* "Absolutely not!" • *–Did you like the dinner he made last night? –Shit no!;* –Did you like the dinner he made last night? –Absolutely not!
♦ ANTONYM: **"Shit yes!"**

pull some shit on someone (to) *exp.* to do something nasty to someone • *I'm not talking to him anymore because he pulled some shit on me yesterday;* I'm not talking to him anymore because he did something nasty to me yesterday.

shit • **1.** *n.* unidentifiable substance • *What's that shit you're drinking?;* What's that substance you're drinking? • **2.** *adv.* extremely • *He's shit stupid!;* He's really stupid!

shit or get off the pot (to) *exp.* to take action or abandon the project • (lit); to defecate or get out of the bathroom • *Why are you taking so long to do something about resolving this situation? Shit or get off the pot!;* Why are you taking so long to do something about resolving this situation? Take action or abandon the project!

shit out of luck (to be) *exp.* to be extremely unfortunate • *I tried to get tickets for the concert, but they were sold out. I guess I'm just shit out of luck;* I tried to get tickets for the concert, but they were sold out. I guess I'm just unfortunate.

shit someone (to) *exp.* to tease someone • *Are you shitting me?;* Are you teasing me?

"Shit, yeah!" *exp.* "Absolutely!"

shit-faced (to be) *adj.* to be intoxicated • *I got shit-faced last night;* I got intoxicated last night.

shitlist *n.* a mental or physical roster of people one dislikes • *If you get on the boss's shitlist, you'll be sorry;* If you become one of the people the boss doesn't like, you'll be sorry.

shitload (a) *adv.* a lot • *I have a shitload of work to do today;* I have a lot of work to do today.

shittiest *adj.* worst • *He did the shittiest job painting his house;* He did the worst job painting his house.

the shit *exp.* used to modify interrogative pronouns *who, what, where, when, why, how* • *Who the shit is that?;* Who could that possibly be? • *What the shit did I spill on myself?;* What could I have possibly spilled on myself?

up shit creek (to be) *exp.* to be in a big predicament • *If I don't get this work done in five minutes, I'm gonna be up shit creek;* If I don't get this work done in five minutes, I'm going to be in a big predicament.
  ‣ NOTE: Although it's incorrect, many people transform this expression to *"to be up shit's creek."*

PRACTICE THE VOCABULARY

[Answers to Lesson 4, p. 168]

A. Complete the phrases by choosing the appropriate words from the list below.

shittiest	catch shit	shit
for shit	pulled some shit	shit-faced
shit creek	shitlist	shitload
shit out of luck	hot shit	the shit

1. Who _____ does he think he is that he can just come here and tell me what to do?!

2. I'm so glad to be home. I had the _____ day today!

3. I can't stand her. She thinks she's such _____ .

4. I think I got on the boss's _____ because I accidentally insulted her.

5. I really got _____ last night! That's the last time I drink vodka!

6. This stereo's _____ ! I want a refund!

7. I'm gonna _____ when I get home. I promised my parents I'd come home at 11:00 and it's already midnight!

8. I'm really angry with her. She really _____ on me yesterday.

9. Beats the _____ outta me where he is!

10. I'm gonna be up _____ if he ever finds out what I've done!

11. We're _____ . They just sold the last ticket to the movie!

12. I wish I could go with you but I've got a _____ of work to do.

B. Match the two colums.

☐ 1. She's thinks she's so impressive.

☐ 2. I don't know.

☐ 3. He did something nasty to me.

☐ 4. Take action or abandon the project.

☐ 5. I think I'm getting intoxicated.

☐ 6. We're going to be in a big predicament if we don't get this work done.

☐ 7. This is the worst haircut I've ever had!

☐ 8. Absolutely!

☐ 9. I don't know the slightest thing about cooking.

☐ 10. This bicycle is defective.

☐ 11. I have a lot of work to do today.

☐ 12. Are you teasing me?

A. **We're gonna be up shit creek if we don't get this work done.**

B. **Beats the shit out of me.**

C. **This bicycle's for shit.**

D. **Shit or get off the pot.**

E. **This is the shittiest haircut I've ever had!**

F. **I don't know shit about cooking.**

G. **I have a shitload of work to do today.**

H. **Shit, yeah!**

I. **Are you shitting me?**

J. **He pulled some shit on me.**

K. **I think I'm getting shit-faced.**

L. **She thinks she's such hot shit.**

C. "CUSSWORD" PUZZLE
Fill in the puzzle by using the words from the list.

beats	pull	off the pot	load
luck	hot	shit	on
list	yeah	faced	

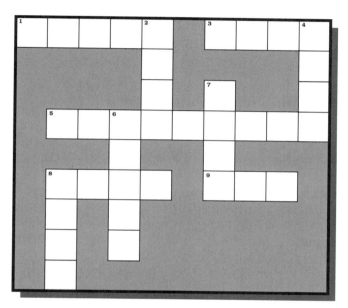

ACROSS

1. " _____ **the shit out of me**" *exp.* "I don't know."

3. _____ **some shit on someone (to)** *exp.* to do something nasty to someone.

5. **shit or get _____ (to)** *exp.* to take action or resign.

8. **shit out of _____ (to be)** *exp.* to be unfortunate.

9. _____ **shit (to be)** exp. to be impressive.

DOWN

2. **up_____ creek (to be)** *exp.* to be in a big predicament.

4. **shit-_____** *n.* a mental or physical roster of people that one dislikes.

6. **shit-_____ (to be)** *adj.* to be intoxicated.

7. "**Shit, _____ !**" exp. "Absolutely!"

8. **shit-_____ (a)** *adv.* a lot.

A CLOSER LOOK (1):
Additional Uses of "Shit"

The term *"shit,"* meaning "excrement," is one of the most popular obscenities used in America as well as countries whose languages are Latin-based. It's interesting to note that in France, the French equivalent *"merde,"* is commonly used by itself to mean simply "good luck."

The following list demonstrates how *"shit"* easily lends itself to a variety of colorful and popular expressions.

NOTE: All expressions containing the term *"shit"* are considered vulgar.

beat the shit out of someone (to) *exp.* to beat someone severely • *When I find him, I'm gonna beat the shit out of him!*; When I find him, I'm going to beat him severely!

"Big shit!" exp. "It's not a big problem!" • *Why are you so upset about losing? Big shit!*; Why are you so upset about losing? It's not a big problem!

built like a brick shithouse (to be) *exp.* to be extremely solid and muscular (may be said of a man or woman) • *Your boyfriend is built like a brick shithouse!*; Your boyfriend is really solid and muscular!

chickenshit (to be) • **1.** *adj.* to be afraid • *Just go up and talk to her. Don't be so chickenshit*; Just go up and talk to her. Don't be so afraid. • **2.** *n.* to be a coward • *He's such a chickenshit*; He's such a fearful person!

crock of shit (to be a) *exp.* to be nonsense • *You believed that crock of shit?*; You believed that nonsense? ♦ VARIATION: **a crock** *n.* • *That's a crock!*; That's nonsense!

deep shit (to be in) *exp.* to be in serious trouble • *I'm gonna be in deep shit when my mother sees what I've done to the rug*; I'm going to be in serious trouble when my mother sees what I've done to the rug.

dip shit (to be a) *exp.* to be a fool • *Did you see the stupid thing he did? What a dip* *shit!;* Did you see the stupid thing he did? What a fool!

"Does a bear shit in the woods?" *exp.* said in response to something obvious • *Do I think she's pretty? Does a bear shit in the woods?;* Do I think she's pretty? Obviously!

"Eat shit!" *exp.* a strong reproach to a despicable comment • *How dare you say that to me! Eat shit!;* How dare you say that to me! You disgust me!

full of shit (to be) *exp.* to talk absolute nonsense • *He told you he owned three cars? He's full of shit!;* He told you he owned three cars? He's talking absolute nonsense!

give a shit (not to) *exp.* not to care at all • *I don't give a shit what you do;* I don't care at all what you do.

give someone shit (to) *exp.* • **1.** to lie to someone • *Don't give me that shit! That's not true and you know it!;* Don't give me those lies! That's not true and you know it! • **2.** to give someone opposition • *Don't give me shit. Just do what I tell you;* Don't hassle me. Just do what I tell you.

"Holy shit!" *exp.* "This is terrible!" • *Holy shit! I forgot to pick my father up from the airport!;* This is terrible! I

forgot to pick my father up from the airport!

horse shit *exp.* nonsense • (lit); horse excrement • *That's a bunch of horse shit!;* That's utter nonsense!

mean shit (not to) *exp.* nothing • *This contract doesn't mean shit!;* This contract doesn't mean anything!

"No shit!" *exp.* "You're not serious!" • *She married Jeff yesterday? No shit!;* She married Jeff yesterday? You're not serious!
  ♦ VARIATION: **"Shit no!"** *exp.* "Absolutely not!"

piece of shit (to be a) *exp.* to be a despicable person • *I can't believe you deceived me like that, you piece of shit!;* I can't believe you deceived me like that, you despicable person!

run like shit (to) *exp.* to run quickly • *Run like shit! They're after us!;* Run quickly! They're after us!

scare the shit out of someone (to) *exp.* to scare someone terribly • *You scared the shit out of me when you jumped out of the closet!;* You scared me terribly when you jumped out of the closet!
  ♦ ALSO: **to be scared shitless** *exp.* to be scared

terribly • (lit); to be so scared that one defecates.

shit • **1.** *v.* to defecate • *I gotta go shit;* I have to go defecate. • **2.** *n.* one's personal belongings • *Go get your shit and let's leave;* Go get your belongings and let's leave. • **3.** *adv.* nothing • *He gave me shit for my birthday;* He didn't give me anything for my birthday. • **4.** *n.* grief, trouble • *Why are you giving me so much shit?;* Why are you giving me so much trouble? • **5.** *n.* a despicable person • *She's such a shit!;* She such a despicable person!

shit a brick (to) *exp.* to be extremely frightened or shocked • *When I saw my girlfriend walk in the door, I thought I was gonna shit a brick!;* When I saw my girlfriend walk in the door, I became shocked!

shit-eating grin (to have a) *exp.* to have an expression of gloating • *Look at him with his shit-eating grin!;* Look at him gloating!

shit from shinola (not to know) *exp.* not to know anything • *He doesn't know shit from Shinola about football;* He doesn't know a thing about football.
♦ NOTE: Shinola is a brand name for shoe polish.

shit-kicker *n.* • **1.** farmer • *I'm tired of the city. Maybe I should just spend the rest of my life being a shit-kicker;* I'm tired of the city. Maybe I should just spend the rest of my life being a farmer. • **2.** boot • *I'm gonna go put on my shit kickers;* I'm gonna go put on my boots.
♦ NOTE: This expression originated from farmers who spend a great deal of time with animals and consequently, pass many hours cleaning manure from their boots.

shit on someone (to) *exp.* to betray someone • *I couldn't believe that my best friend could shit on me like that;* I couldn't believe that my best friend could betray me like that.

shitfit (to have a) *exp.* to have a tantrum • *When my father sees what I did to his new tie, he's gonna have a shitfit!;* When my father sees what I did to his new tie, he's going to have a tantrum!

shithead (to be a) *exp.* to be a despicable person • *Your brother won't let you borrow his tennis racket? What a shithead!;* Your brother won't let you borrow his tennis racket? What a despicable person!

shithouse *n.* bathroom • *I gotta go to the shithouse;* I have to go to the bathroom.

shitter *n.* toilet • *I have to go to the shitter;* I have to go to the toilet.

shitty (to be) *adj.* to be disgraceful • *He did a shitty job decorating the house for the party;* He did a disgraceful job decorating the house for the party.

shoot the shit (to) *exp.* to chat • *I'm going over to Barry's to shoot the shit;* I'm going over to Barry's house to have a chat.

take shit (to) *exp.* to accept abuse • *Why do you keep taking shit from him?;* Why do you keep accepting abuse from him?

take a shit (to) *exp.* to defecate • *The dog took a shit right on the rug;* The dog defecated right on the rug.

than shit *adv.* to the extreme • *He's funnier than shit;* He's extremely funny • *She's meaner than shit!;* She's extremely mean!

"The shit's gonna hit the fan!" *exp.* "A great disturbance is about to occur!" • *When my father comes home and sees what I did to his car, the shit's gonna hit the fan!;* When my father comes home and sees what I did to his car, a great disturbance is going to occur.

"The shit rolls downhill" *exp.* "The blame is passed down to the person with the least amount of influence."

the shits (to have) *exp.* to have diarrhea • *I must have eaten something spoiled because I've been having the shits all day;* I must have eaten something spoiled because I've been having diarrhea all day. ♦ VARIATION: **to have the runny shits** *exp.*

think one's shit doesn't stink (to) *exp.* to think unrealistically highly of oneself • *She's so arrogant! She thinks her shit doesn't stink!;* She's so arrogant! She thinks unrealistically highly of herself!

tough shit (to be) *exp.* • **1.** used to signify "that's a shame" with a feeling of indifference and hostility from the speaker • *If you don't like the way I drive, tough shit!;* If you don't like the way I drive, too bad! • **2.** to be menacing; "cool" • *That guy's tough shit!;* That guy is menacing!

treat someone like shit (to) *exp.* to treat someone with great disrespect • *Why did you treat her like shit last night?;* Why did you treat her with such disrespect last night?

Shit-at-a-Glance Buffet

The following charts will give you an easy overview of some of the many ways in which *"shit"* is commonly used as just seen in the previous pages.

SHIT (noun) BEGINS THE PHRASE				
shit +	*ass!*		=	despicable person
	bag			despicable person
	creek			big trouble
	faced			intoxicated
	fit			tantrum
	happens			bad things happen
	head			despicable person
	hole			anal sphincter
	house			bathroom
	list			mental or physical list of disliked people
	load			great quantity
	no!			absolutely not!
	on a shingle			chipped beef on toast
	on a stick			exclamation of anger
	out of luck			completely unfortunate
	scared			extremely frightened
	wad			despicable person
	yes!			absolutely!

SHIT (verb) BEGINS THE PHRASE			
to shit +	a brick	=	to be very frightened
	on someone		to act despicably to someone
	or get off the pot		to take action
	someone		to tease someone

SHIT (noun) IS AT THE END OF THE PHRASE		
big		what's the big concern
(to) catch		to get reprimanded
(to) chew the		to chat
chicken		fearful person
(a) crock of		nonsense
dip		fool
for		useless
horse	+ **shit** =	nonsense
hot		impressive
no		you're not serious
not to know		not to know the slightest thing (about something)
piece of		despicable person
(to) pull		to do something nasty to someone
(to) take a		to defecate
(to) take		to accept abuse

A CLOSER LOOK (2):
Bodily Functions & Sounds

Although everyone has the same bodily functions, it would appear that to admit such a truth causes a certain amount of shame since they reduce us to an unbecoming primal animalistic state. This is perhaps the reason for the many slang expressions and euphemisms representing bodily functions & sounds which seem to alleviate some embarrassment when announced. Here are some of the most common:

Defecate (to) / Excrement

B.M. *n.* a common abbreviation of "bowel movement" • *The baby had a B.M. in her diapers;* The baby had a bowel movement in her diapers.
‣ ALSO: **to B.M.** *v.* • *Your little sister just B.M.'d on the floor;* Your little sister just defecated on the floor.

buffalo chips *n.pl.* (mild) dried excrement left on prairies by buffalos.
‣ ALSO: **cow chips** *n.pl.* dried excrement left by cows.

business (to do one's) *exp.* a euphemism for "to defecate" • *Steve's in the bathroom doing his business;* Steve's in the bathroom defecating.
‣ NOTE: This expression is more commonly used with children than it is with adults.

cow patty *n.* (mild) dried excrement left by cows.
‣ VARIATION: **cow pie** *n.* (mild).

crap (to) • (vulgar) **1.** *v.* to defecate • *I gotta go crap;* I have to go defecate. •
2. *interj.* used to indicate anger • *Crap! I locked myself out of my house!;* I'm so angry! I locked myself out of my house!
‣ VARIATION: **to take a crap** *exp.* (extremely popular yet vulgar) • *I have to take a crap;* I have to defecate.
‣ ALSO (1): **the crap** *exp.* to the extreme • *With our current budget, we could publicize the crap out of this book!;* With our current budget, we could publicize this book to the extreme!
‣ ALSO (2): **to scare the crap out of someone** *exp.* (extremely popular yet

vulgar) to scare someone greatly • *They scared the crap out of me when they all yelled "surprise!;" They scared really scared me when they all yelled "surprise!"*

dump (to) *v.* (crude) • (lit); to unload • *The dog dumped on the rug;* The dog defecated on the rug.
▸ VARIATION (1): **to dump a load** *exp.* (crude) • *I have to go dump a load;* I have to go defecate.
▸ VARIATION (2): **to take a dump** *exp.* (extremely popular yet crude) • *He's been in there taking a dump for the past 15 minutes!;* He's been in there defecating for the past 15 minutes!

go to the can (to) *exp.* (somewhat crude) • *I'll be right back. I have to go to the can;* I'll be right back. I have to go to the bathroom.
▸ VARIATION: **to go to the can man** *exp.* (rhyming slang and somewhat crude) • *I gotta go to the can man;* I have to go to the bathroom.

go to the john (to) *exp.* (extremely popular and mild) • *Why don't you go to the john before we leave on our trip?;* Why don't you go to the bathroom before we leave on our trip?

golden apples *n.* (mild) dried excrement left on prairies.

grunt (to) *v.* (humorous yet crude) • (lit); to make unintelligible animal noises • *I gotta go grunt;* I have to go defecate.
▸ NOTE: This verb is used to signify the grunting sounds made by someone who is defecating.

have Montezuma's revenge (to) *exp.* (humorous and mild) to have diarrhea • *I think I caught Montezuma's revenge!* I think I caught a case of diarrhea.
▸ NOTE (1): Many people visiting the United States travel to Mexico during their stay. Unfortunately, these people often return with a severe case of diarrhea after having drunk the water which contains parasites. It is said that this is Montezuma's revenge, the former emperor of Mexico (1480-1520), toward those who once invaded his country. This condition is also referred to as *"las touristas"* meaning "that which is acquired by tourists."

lay a log (to) *exp.* (a crude and very descriptive expression).
▸ NOTE: **log** *n.* a bowel movement (due to its long cylindrical shape).

make (to) v. (mild) • *The baby looks like he's about to make in his pants;* The baby looks like he's about to defecate in his pants.

nature's call exp. (mild) time to go to the bathroom • *I'll be right back. It's nature's call;* I'll be right back. I have to go to the bathroom.
♦ VARIATION: **"Nature's calling"** exp. "I have to go to the bathroom."

number two (to go) exp. (mild) to defecate • *I have to go number two!;* I have to go defecate!
♦ ALSO: **to go number one** exp. to urinate.

pinch a loaf (to) exp. (crude).
♦ NOTE: **loaf** n. a bowel movement • (lit); a mass of meat.
♦ NOTE: This expression signifies the pinching action of the anal sphincter when a bowel movement is released.

poo-poo (to go) v. (mild).
♦ NOTE: This is a common euphemism used with children • *Do you have to go poo-poo?;* Do you have to defecate?

poop (to go) v. (mild, used primarily with children) • *Do you need to poop before we leave?;* Do you need to defecate before we leave?
♦ ALSO: **poop** n. term of

affection • (lit); excrement • *I love you, you old poop!*

regular (to be) adj. (mild) to have regular bowel movements (without the displeasure of constipation).

road apple n. (mild) humorous term for "excrement" found in the road.

shit (to) v. (very popular yet extremely vulgar) • *I'm gonna go shit;* I'm going to go defecate.
♦ NOTE (1): The past participle of the verb *"to shit"* is *"shit"* although many use *"shat"* in jest: *The dog shat on the new carpet!;* The dog defecated on the new carpet!
♦ NOTE (2): SEE: **to shit**, *p. 72.*
♦ ALSO (1): **to take a shit** exp. (extremely popular yet vulgar) • *I'm gonna go take a shit before we leave;* I'm going to go defecate before we leave.
♦ ALSO (2): **to have the shits** exp. (vulgar) to have diarrhea.

squat (to) v. (crude) • (lit); to crouch.
♦ NOTE: When used to signify "to defecate," the verb *"to squat"* is considered somewhat crude.

the runs (to have) exp. (mild) to have diarrhea.

trots (to have the) *exp.* (mild) to have diarrhea.

turd *n.* (mild) • **1.** excrement • *Your dog just laid a turd on the couch;* Your dog just defecated on the couch. • **2.** despicable person • *That guy's such a turd!;* That guy's such a despicable person!
➤ ALSO: **bird turd** *n.* (humorous rhyming slang) bird excrement • *There are bird turds all over my car!;* There's bird excrement all over my car!

Flatulence *(to have)*

break wind (to) *exp.* (mild).

cut one (to) *exp.* (mild).

cut the cheese (to) *exp.* (mild)
➤ NOTE: This expression originated due to the strong offensive smell produced when certain cheeses are cut.

fart (to) *v.* (extremely popular yet somewhat crude) to have flatulence or be flatulent • *Who farted?;* Who has flatulence?
➤ VARIATION: **fart** *n.* flatulence • This noun is commonly used with *"to cut"* meaning "to release."

float an air biscuit (to) *exp.* (humorous and mild).

let one fly (to) *exp.* (mild).

let one go (to) *exp.* (mild) • *Who let one go?;* Who has flatulence?

pass gas (to) exp. (mild).

S.B.D. *exp.* (humorous) silent, yet potent, flatulence • *Who cut the S.B.D.?;* Who has the silent flatulence?
➤ NOTE: This is a euphemistic abbreviation of "silent but deadly" which is considered humorous.

toot (to) *v.* (mild and humorous).

Menstruate *(to)*

"Aunt Flo's here" *exp.* (somewhat crude yet humorous).
➤ NOTE: This is a play-on-words since the proper name *"Flo"* is a homonym of the verb *"flow"* referring to the flowing of one's blood during menstruation.

"Big Red dropped in" *exp.* (somewhat crude yet humorous).

get the curse (to) *exp.* (mild) • (lit); to get the affliction.

have a visitor (to) *exp.* (mild and humorous).

have one's period (to) *exp.* (mild and extremely popular) • (lit); to have one's term (of menstruation).

on the rag (to be) *exp.* (vulgar yet very popular).
  ‣ NOTE: This expression is also commonly used to mean "to be in a mad mood."
  ‣ VARIATION: **to be O.T.R.** *adj.* a common abbreviation and euphemism of the expression *"to be on the rag."*

that time of the month (to be) *exp.* (mild and very popular) • *You don't look well. Is it that time of the month?;* You don't look well. Are you menstruating?

"The red flag's up" *exp.* (somewhat crude yet humorous).
  ‣ NOTE: In this expression the *"red flag"* refers to "blood."

"The Red Sea's in" *exp.* (crude yet humorous).
  ‣ NOTE: In this expression, the *"red sea"* refers to "blood."

Urinate (to)

back teeth floating (to have one's) *exp.* a humorous, yet crude, description of someone who has to urinate so badly it's as if the urine were rising to the level of one's back teeth • *My back teeth are floating!;* I have to urinate badly!

can (to go to the) *n.* (somewhat crude) to go to the bathroom (and defecate or urinate, depending on the context).
  ‣ VARIATION: **to go to the can, man** *exp.*

go (to) *v.* (mild).

john (to go to the) *n.* (mild) to go to the bathroom (and defecate or urinate, depending on the context).

leak (to) *v.* (mild) • (lit); to dribble liquid.
  ‣ VARIATION: **to take a leak** *exp.* (extremely popular yet somewhat crude).

make a pit stop (to) *exp.* (mild) to stop one's routine temporarily and go to the bathroom.
  ‣ NOTE: This expression comes from the sport of auto

racing where drivers will temporarily exit the race in order to make car repairs which are performed in the *"pit."* This is commonly called *"making a pit stop."*

"Nature's calling" *exp.* (mild) "I have to go to the bathroom."
‣ NOTE: This expression refers to either urination or defecation, depending on the context.

number one (to go) *exp.*
‣ ANTONYM: **to go number two** *exp.* to defecate.

pee (to) *v.* (extremely popular yet somewhat crude).

pee-pee (to go) *v.* (mild).
‣ NOTE: This verb is commonly used with children as a diminutive form of the verb *"to pee."*

piddle (to) *v.* (humorous).
‣ NOTE: This verb is primarily used with children.

piss (to) *v.* (vulgar).
‣ VARIATION: **to take a piss** *exp.* (very popular yet vulgar).

powder one's nose (to) *exp.* (mild).
‣ NOTE: This is an excuse a woman may give for having to go the bathroom to either defecate or urinate, since to be completely truthful would be considered crude.

tinkle (to) *v.* (mild).
‣ NOTE: This verb, primarily used with children, signifies the tinkling sound that is produced when one urinates in the toilet.

wee (to go) *v.* (mild).
‣ NOTE: This verb is primarily used with children.
‣ ALSO: **to go wee-wee** *exp.* (a very popular expression used with children).

whiz (to) *v.* (vulgar).
‣ VARIATION: **take a whiz (to)** *exp.* (very popular yet vulgar).

Vomit (to)

barf (to) *v.* (extremely popular and mild).

blow chow (to) *exp.* (crude, due to its descriptive nature)
• (lit); to explode with food.
‣ NOTE (1): **to blow** *n.* to explode.
‣ NOTE (2): **chow** *n.* food.

blow chunks (to) *exp.* (very crude, due to its extreme

descriptive nature) • (lit); to explode with chunks of food.
♦ NOTE: **to blow** *n.* to explode.

buick (to) *v.* (humorous).
♦ NOTE: This verb, also the name of an American car, signifies the sound one makes when vomiting.

drive the porcelain bus (to) *exp.* (humorous).
♦ NOTE: This is a humorous description of someone who is kneeling and holding the porcelain bowl of the toilet while vomiting.

hurl (to) *v.* (humorous).
♦ NOTE: This is one of the newest slang verbs for "to vomit" which was popularized in an American movie called "Wayne's World." This verb is now extremely popular among teenagers.

laugh at the lawn (to) *exp.* (humorous).
♦ NOTE: This is a humorous expression, used in reference to an individual describing a cat vomiting after eating grass.

pray to the porcelain god (to) *exp.* (humorous).
♦ NOTE: This is a humorous description of someone kneeling in front of the toilet vomiting.

puke (to) *v.* (extremely popular yet crude).

Ralph (to) *v.* (humorous).
♦ NOTE: This humorous verb signifies the sound one makes while vomiting.

retch (to) *v.* (humorous).
♦ NOTE: This humorous verb signifies the sound one makes while vomiting.

shout at one's shoes (to) *exp.* (humorous).
♦ NOTE: This humorous expression describes someone who is bending over vomiting toward one's shoes.

sick (to be) *adj.* (extremely popular and mild) • *I'm gonna be sick;* I'm going to throw up.
♦ NOTE: Although the adjective *"sick"* simply means "ill," when preceded by *"going to be,"* the connotation changes to "sick and vomiting."

talk to Huey on the big white phone (to) *exp.* (humorous).
♦ NOTE: This humorous expression describes someone who is vomiting, and making a "Huey" sound into the toilet which looks like a large white telephone receiver.

technicolor yawn (to have a) *n.* (humorous).
♦ NOTE: This describes one's mouth opening to reveal a

variety of multicolored foods being vomited.

throw up (to) *n.* (extremely common and mild).
▸ NOTE: This is perhaps one of the most common synonyms for "to vomit" and is used by everyone.

upchuck (to) *v.* (very common and mild).
▸ NOTE: It would be incorrect to say *"to chuck up."*

york (to) *v.* (humorous).
▸ NOTE: This verb describes the sound one makes when vomiting.

A CLOSER LOOK (3):
The Many Synonyms for "Toilet"

Andy Gump *n.* (mild) a portable toilet devised by an inventor named Andy Gump.

can *n.* (crude yet very popular).
▸ NOTE: This term is often used in the expression, *"I have to go to the can, man."*

cat box *n.* (mild) • (lit; a cardboard box that indoor cats use for urination and defecation • *I'll be right back. I have to go use the cat box;* I'll be right back. I have to go use the toilet.
▸ NOTE: This term is used among women only.
▸ VARIATION: **sandbox** *n.* (mild).

crapper *n.* (vulgar).
▸ NOTE (1): This comes from the verb *"to crap,"* meaning "to defecate."
▸ NOTE (2): This term comes from the inventor of the first flush toilet, Sir John Crapper.

facilities *n.pl.* (mild) a euphemistic term for toilet.

head *n.* (crude).
▸ NOTE: This is a standard nautical term for "toilet." Oddly enough, when used outside of a ship, it is considered crude.

john *n.* (somewhat crude yet extremely popular) • *I have to go to the john;* I have to go to the bathroom.
▸ NOTE: This term comes from the inventor of the first flush toilet, Sir John Crapper.

little boys' room *exp.* (mild).
 ‣ NOTE: This is a common term given to a public bathroom for little boys. This term is used euphemistically in reference to an adult in an attempt to soften the indelicacy of announcing a trip to the toilet.

little girls' room *exp.* (mild).
 ‣ NOTE: This is a common term given to a public bathroom for little girls. This term is used euphemistically in reference to an adult in an attempt to soften the indelicacy of announcing a trip to the toilet.

pot *n.* (somewhat crude).
 ‣ NOTE: This term comes from the obsolete "chamber pot" which was simply a portable bowl used for urination and defecation.
 ‣ VARIATION: **potty** *n.* Used only with children, this is a mild diminutive of *"pot"*.

shithouse *n.* (vulgar yet extremely popular).
 ‣ NOTE: This comes from the verb *"to shit"* which is vulgar for "to defecate."
 ‣ VARIATION: **shitter** *n.* (vulgar).

throne *n.* (humorous).
 ‣ NOTE: This term is a humorous comparison of a toilet to a royal throne.

THE MANY USES OF Fuck

Dialogue in slang

The New Car...

DIALOGUE

Steve and George are driving when all of a sudden the car fails.

Steve: What the **fuck**? That **mother-fucking dumbfuck** mechanic **fucking fucked up** my **fucking** car after **fucking** with it for two days!

George: **Fuck** a duck! That's **fucked**!

Steve: I'm so **fucking** tired of getting **fucked** over. **Fuck** that shit!

George: What the **fuck**. Don't **fucking** pay him!

Steve: **Fucking** A!

Translation of dialogue in standard American-English

The New Car...

DIALOGUE

Steve and George are driving when all of a sudden the car fails.

Steve: What's **happening**? That **damn stupid** mechanic **absolutely ruined** my **darn** car after **fiddling** with it for two days!

George: **How unbelievable**! That's **awful**!

Steve: I'm so **darn** tired of getting **cheated out of my money**. **I don't accept that**!

George: **That's not a problem**. **Just** don't pay him!

Steve: **You're not kidding**!

Dialogue in slang as it would be heard

The New Car...

DIALOGUE

Steve 'n George 'r driving when all of a sudden the car fails.

Steve   What the **fuck**? That **mother-fuckin' dumbfuck** mechanic **fuckin' fucked up** my **fuckin'** car after **fuckin'** with it fer two days!

George: **Fuck** a duck! That's **fucked**!

Steve: I'm so **fuckin'** tired 'a gettin' **fucked** over. **Fuck** that shit!

George: What the **fuck**. Don't **fuckin'** pay 'im!

Steve: **Fuckin'** A!

Vocabulary

dumbfuck (to be a) *n.* to be an idiot • *Can you believe what a dumbfuck he is?;* Can you believe what an idiot he is?

"Fuck a duck!" *exclam.* exclamation denoting surprise or disdain • *Fuck a duck! That's ridiculous!*

fuck something up (to) *exp.* • **1.** to ruin something • *I totally fucked up my car* [or] *I totally fucked my car up;* I totally ruined my car. • **2.** to blunder • *I forgot to mail the letter which needed to arrive today! I guess I really fucked up;* I forgot to mail the letter which needed to arrive today! I guess I really blundered. • **3.** to injure something • *I fucked up my back this morning* [or] *I fucked my back up this morning;* I injured my back this morning.
♦ ALSO: **fuck-up** *n.* one who always blunders.

"Fuck that noise!" *exp.* "That's ridiculous!" • *He wants me to take him to the airport at 1:00 in the morning?! Fuck that noise!;* He wants me to take him to the airport at 1:00 in the morning?! That's ridiculous!
♦ NOTE: In this expression, it is important to stress *"that"* by raising the pitch of the voice slightly.

fucked (to be) *adj.* to be intolerable • *That's fucked that she could do such a mean thing to you!;* That's intolerable that she could do such a mean thing to you!

fuck someone over (to) *exp.* • **1.** to cheat someone • *Every time I trust someone, I get fucked over;* Every time I trust someone, I get cheated. • **2.** to betray someone • *I got fucked over by my best friend;* I was betrayed by my best friend.
♦ VARIATION: **to fuck someone over royally** *exp.* to betray someone completely • *She royally fucked me over!* [or] *She fucked me over royally!;* She completely betrayed me!

fuck with something (to) *exp.* to toy with something • *I fucked with the car for an hour trying to repair it, but it's still not working;* I toyed with the car for an hour trying to repair it, but it's still not working.

fucking *adv.* • **1.** completely • *She fucking embarrassed me in front of all my friends!;* She completely embarrassed me in front of all my friends! • **2.** used to add emphasis to the verb that follows • *Don't fucking bother me!;* Just don't bother me! • *Don't even ask me if you can borrow my car. I'm not fucking lending it to you!;* Don't even ask me if you can borrow my car. I'm simply not lending it to you! • **3.** infuriating • *I spent $500 on this fucking washing machine and it doesn't even work!;* I spent $500 on this infuriating washing machine and it doesn't even work!

"Fuckin' A!" *exp.* "Absolutely!" • *"Do you think he's a jerk?" "Fuckin' A!;"* • "Do you think he's a fool?" "Absolutely!"
♦ NOTE: The *"-ing"* ending in this expression is commonly reduced to *"-in'."*
♦ VARIATION: **fuckin' A right** *exp.* absolutely correct.

mother-fucking *exp.* extremely infuriating • *I'm so tired of my mother-fucking car breaking down every week!;* I'm so tired of my infuriating car breaking down every week!
♦ NOTE: Adding *"mother"* before *"fucking"* makes this a stronger expression: *fucking* = contemptible • *mother-fucking* = extremely contemptible.

"What the fuck" • **1.** *exclam.* (as a question) "How is this possible?" • *What the fuck? I can't remember where I put my keys!;* How is this possible? I can't remember where I put my keys! • **2.** *exp.* (as a statement) "It's not a big issue" • *What the fuck. If you don't want to go to her party, just don't!;* It's not a big issue. If you don't want to go to her party, just don't!

PRACTICE THE VOCABULARY

[Answers to Lesson 5, p. 169]

A. Choose the correct definition.

1. **to fuck with something**:
   a. to hit something   b. to toy with something

2. **dumbfuck**:
   a. idiot   b. accident

3. **"Fuckin' A!"**:
   a. "That's ridiculous!"   b. "Absolutely!"

4. **"That's fucked!"**:
   a. "That's beautiful!"   b. "That's intolerable!"

5. **"Fuck that noise!"**:
   a. "It's too loud!"   b. "That's ridiculous!"

6. **to fuck someone over**:
   a. to cheat someone   b. to have sex with someone

7. **fucking**:
   a. wonderful   b. infuriating

8. **to fuck something up**:
   a. to ruin something   b. to enjoy something

9. **"Fuck a duck!"**:
   a. "That's amazing!"   b. "I'm hungry!"

10. **"What the fuck"**:
    a. "It's not a big issue"   b. "Please speak louder"

B. Choose the word(s) from the list below that best complete(s) the phrase.

dumbfuck	**fuck that noise**	**fucked up**
fuckin' A	**mother-fucking**	**what the fuck**
fucked	**fucked with**	**fucked over**

1. Can you believe how much my _____
    mechanic charged me for the repairs on my car?

2. You've _____ that for three hours. Why
    don't you just go to bed and work on it again in the
    morning?

3. What she did to you is really _____ .

4. The last time I trusted a used car salesperson, I got
    completely _____ .

5. What a _____ ! He's just so stupid!

6. Do I think he's an idiot? _____ !

7. He asked to borrow your car after ruining your last one?
    _____ !

8. I thought I could fix my bicycle myself. Now it's really
    _____ !

9. We can't go to that restaurant. It's too expensive! Oh,
    _____ . We don't do it very often. Let's go.

A CLOSER LOOK (1):
Additional Uses of "Fuck"

The verb *"to fuck"* is one of the most commonly heard, yet most vulgar, obscenities in the American-English vocabulary.

In fact, don't be surprised if you encounter this very word in France. I remember how surprised I was living in Paris when I heard a little French boy shout it out repeatedly at the zoo. I couldn't believe that his parents didn't even reprimand him for such an outburst. When he was yelling what I thought was *"Fuck! Fuck!"* he was actually just trying to get his parents to look at the seals, *"Phoques! Phoques!"*

It's interesting how *"fuck"* went through a metamorphosis of being a perfectly acceptable word to a severe obscenity. Some sources say that many centuries ago, the verb *"to fuck"* simply meant "to seed" a crop, for example. Later, it was used in reference to "seeding" a woman or having sex. It was also used as an acronym which was placed in large letters below a prisoner convicted of adultery who remained locked in the stockade. The letters F.U.C.K. represented "For Unlawful Carnal Knowledge."

In present day, *"Fuckin'"* (the shortened version of *"fucking"*) is probably one of America's most overused obscene adjectives, especially in crowded cities where people are hurried, impatient and aggressive such as in New York. In fact, a common lighthearted joke about New Yorkers is — QUESTION: What is the New York alphabet? ANSWER: *Fuckin' A, Fuckin' B, Fuckin' C, etc.*

All of the following expressions containing *"fuck"* are vulgar:

absofuckin'lutely *adv.* absolutely • *Do I like her? Absofuckin'lutely!;* Do I like her? Absolutely! ➤ NOTE: The "-ing" ending in this expression is commonly reduced to "-in'."

bum-fuck *adj.* distant • *She wants me to drive to all the way to bum-fuck Idaho!;* She wants me to drive her all the way to distant Idaho!

butt fuck (to) *exp.* to have sexual intercourse through the anus • *I think they're into butt fucking;* I think they enjoy sexual intercourse through the anus. ⟩ ALSO: **butt fucker** *exp.* despicable person • *What a*

butt fucker!; What a
despicable person!

**come-fuck-me boots/dress/
etc.** *exp.* said of any article
of clothing that is sexually
alluring • *Did you see that
come-fuck-me dress she's
wearing?;* Did you see that
alluring dress she's wearing?
♦ VARIATION: **fuck-mes** *exp.* •
*I'm wearing my fuck-mes
tonight!*

"Excuse the fuck outta me!"
exp. "Well, excuse me!"

"Fuck!" *exp.* • **1.** used to
signify anger or frustration •
Fuck! I just missed my flight!
• **2.** used to signify
amazement • *Fuck! She's
beautiful!*

fuck (to) *v.* • **1.** to have sex •
*All he ever thinks about is
fucking;* All he ever thinks
about is having sex. • **2.** to
cheat • *You paid way too
much for your car. I'm afraid
you got fucked!;* You paid
way too much for your car.
I'm afraid you got cheated.
♦ VARIATION (1): **to fuck
one's brains out** *exp.* to
have aggressive or prolonged
sex with someone.
♦ VARIATION (2): **to fuck like
a bunny** *exp.* to have
aggressive, speedy, and
frequent sex.

fuck around (to) *exp.* • **1.** to
spend time idly • *We're just*

*gonna go fuck around
outside today;* We're just
going to go spend time idly
outside today. • **2.** to have
sex • *He's out fucking
around tonight;* He's out
having sex tonight.
♦ NOTE: The difference
between definitions **1.** and
2. depend on the context.

fuck off (to) *exp.* to shirk
one's responsibilities and
play • *I worked for two
weeks on this project while
my partner fucked off the
whole time!;* I worked for two
weeks on this project while
my partner was out shirking
his responsibilities and
playing the whole time.
♦ ALSO: **"Fuck off!"** *interj.*
"Leave me alone!"

"Fuck no!" *exp.* "Absolutely
not!" • *"You like that food?"
"Fuck no!;"* "You like that
food?" "Absolutely not!"
♦ ANTONYM: **"Fuck yes!"** *exp.*
"Absolutely!"

fuck with someone (to) *exp.*
to harass someone • *Don't
fuck with him. He's
dangerous!;* Don't harass
him. He's dangerous!

**"Fuck you/him/her/them/it
etc.!"** *exclam.* used in
contempt • *I can't believe
you tried to cheat me! I
thought you were my friend.
Well, fuck you!*

fucker (to be a) *n.* to be a despicable person • *That fucker lied to me!*; That despicable person lied to me!

fuckface (to be a) *n.* to be a despicable person • *Did you hear the derogatory way he was talking about you? What a fuckface!*; Did you hear the derogatory way he was talking about you? What a despicable person!

fuckhead (to be a) *n.* to be a despicable person • *How can you like that fuckhead?*; How can you like that despicable person?

fuckin' *adv.* absolute(ly), extreme(ly) • *I don't fuckin' know!*; I absolutely don't know! • *He's a fuckin' idiot!*; He's an absolute idiot!
▸ NOTE: The "–ing" ending in this adverb is commonly reduced to "–in'."

give a fuck (not to) *exp.* not to care at all • *I don't give a fuck what you do!*; I don't care at all what you do!
▸ VARIATION: **not to give a flying fuck** *exp.*

good fuck (to be a) *exp.* to be a satisfying sex partner • *I hear she's a good fuck*; I hear she's a satisfying sex partner.

mindfuck (to) *v.* to mislead • *You actually believe what he's saying? I'm telling you, he's mindfucking you*; You actually believe what he's saying? I'm telling you, he's misleading you.

motherfucker (to be a) *exp.* to be a despicable person •
1. *n.* despicable person (a euphemistic replacement for "mother fucker" which is considered extremely vulgar) • *That guy's a real mother!*; That guy's a real despicable person! • **2.** *adj.* extremely difficult • *What a mother of a homework assignment!*; What a difficult homework assignment!
▸ VARIATION (1): **to be an M.F.** *exp.* a euphemistic abbreviation of *"to be a mother fucker."*
▸ VARIATION (2): **to be a mo-fo** *exp.* a euphemistic abbreviation of *"to be a mother fucker."*

the fuck *exp.* used to denote surprise, annoyance, or "nonsense" • (surprise) *It's great to see you! What the fuck are you doing here?* • (annoyance) *What the fuck do you want now?* • ("nonsense") *He told you he was rich? The fuck he is!*; He told you he was rich! That's nonsense!

Fuck-at-a-Glance Buffet

The following charts will give you an easy overview of some of the many ways in which *"fuck"* is commonly used as just seen in the previous pages.

FUCK (infinitive) BEGINS THE PHRASE			
to fuck +	*around*	=	to spend time idly
	off		to shirk one's responsibilities
	someone over		to cheat someone
	something up		to bungle something
	with someone		to provoke someone
	with something		to toy with something

FUCK (noun) IS AT THE END OF THE PHRASE		
bum-	+ **fuck** =	far away
dumb-		idiot
not to give a		not to care
the		used to denote surprise, annoyance, or nonsense
to be a good		to be a good sex partner
to mind-		to mislead

FUCK (noun/verb) BEGINS THE PHRASE			
Fuck +	*a duck!*	**=**	That's ridiculous!
	-er!		Despicable person!
	-face		Despicable person
	-head		Despicable person
	-in'		Absolute(ly), extreme(ly)
	-in' A!		Absolutely!
	no!		Absolutely not!
	that noise!		That's ridiculous!
	yes!		Absolutely!

A CLOSER LOOK (2):
Sexual Slang

This is perhaps one of the most prolific of slang groups in the American repertory most likely attributed to the universal practice of sex.

The following synonyms represent some of the first examples of slang that most young non-native speakers learn when arriving in America:

Fornicate (to)

all over each other (to be)
exp. (mild) • **1.** said of two people who are kissing each other aggressively • **2.** said of two people who are having aggressive sex • *No matter where they are, they're always all over each other;* No matter where they are, they're always kissing each other aggressively (or having aggressive sex).
♦ NOTE: The difference between definitions **1.** and **2.** depend on the context.

ball (to) *v.* (vulgar) • *Did you ball her yesterday?;* Did you have sex with her yesterday?
♦ NOTE: This verb comes

from the slang connotation of *"balls"* meaning "testicles."

bang (to) *v.* (vulgar) • *Did you see them leave the party early? I bet they went to go bang in the car!;* Did you see them leave the party early? I bet they went to go have sex in the car!
♦ ALSO: **to gang bang** *exp.* to have sex with many partners at the same time; to have an orgy.

boink (to) *v.* (humorous) • *I think she wants to boink you;* I think she wants to have sex with you.

bump (to) *v.* (humorous) • *I know he asked you to go to the movies but I think all he wants to do is bump!;* I know he asked you to go to the movies but I think all he wants to do is have sex!

bump and grind (to) *exp.* (mild) to have aggressive sex • *They did a lot of bumping and grinding all night long!;* They had aggressive sex all night long.

deed (the) *n.* (mild) sex • *Wanna go do the deed?;* Do you want to go have sex?
♦ VARIATION: **the dirty deed** *exp.* • *Let's go do the dirty deed;* Let's go have sex.

dick (to) *v.* (vulgar) • *All he ever talks about is dicking her!;* All he ever talks about is having sex with her!
♦ NOTE: This comes from the slang noun *"dick,"* meaning "penis."

do it (to) *exp.* (mild).
♦ NOTE: In this expression, *"it"* refers to "sex."

do the do (to) *exp.* (a mild term from rap music slang) • *I think Janice and Tim are out doin' the do somewhere;* I think Janice and Tim are out having sex somewhere.
♦ NOTE: It's extremely common in slang, especially rap slang, to reduce the *"-ing"* ending to *"-in'"* as seen in *"doin' the do."*

do the nasty (to) *exp.* (a mild term from rap music slang) • *Are you going out tonight to do the nasty?;* Are you going out tonight to have sex?

do the wild thing (to) *exp.* (an acceptable term from rap music slang) • *Do you think they did the wild thing last night?;* Do you think they had sex last night?

fool around (to) *exp.* (mild) • *Wanna go fool around later?;* Do you want to go have sex later?

fuck (to) *v.* (extremely vulgar) • **1.** to have sex • *All he ever thinks about is fucking;* All he ever thinks about is

having sex. • **2.** to cheat • *You paid way too much for your car. I'm afraid you got fucked!;* You paid way too much for your car. I'm afraid you got cheated.
♦ NOTE: SEE: Additional Uses of Fuck, p. 95

get it on (to) *exp.* (somewhat crude) • *She got it on with her boyfriend all weekend;* She had sex with her boyfriend all weekend.

get laid (to) *exp.* (somewhat crude) • *I got laid last night for the first time;* I had sex last night for the first time. • *Did she lay you after the party?;* Did she have sex with you after the party?

get some ass (to) *exp.* (vulgar) • *So, did you get some ass tonight?;* So, did you have sex tonight?
♦ VARIATION: **to get a piece [of ass]** *exp.*

go all the way (to) *exp.* (mild) to get past foreplay and into sex • *Wanna go all the way now?;* Do you want to get past foreplay and into sex now?

grind (to) *v.* (crude) to pound one's sex organs into those of one's partner • *They were grinding all night;* They were having sex all night.

have a nooner (to) *exp.* (mild) to have quick sex during lunch • *He always leaves the office during lunch. I think he has a nooner every day;* He always leaves the office during lunch. I think he has quick sex during lunch every day.

have a one-night stand (to) *exp.* (mild) to have a sexual affair with someone for just one night • *I don't even remember her name. She was just a one-night stand;* I don't even remember her name. She was just someone I had sex with one night.

have a quickie (to) *exp.* (mild) to have speedy sex • *We don't have time to leave for my house. How about a quickie right here?;* We don't have time to leave for my house. How about speedy sex right here?

hop in the saddle (to) *exp.* (humorous) • *He hops in the saddle with every girl he meets;* He has sex with every girl he meets.
♦ NOTE: This expression comes from westerns where a cowboy would commonly *"hop in the saddle"* with a beautiful girl and ride off into the sunset.
♦ VARIATION: **to hop in the**

sack *exp.* ("*sack*" being a slang term for "bed").

hump (to) *v.* (somewhat crude) to rub one's sex organs against another person • *As soon as I walked into his house, his dog started humping my leg!;* As soon as I walked into his house, his dog started rubbing his sex organs against my leg!

jump (to) *v.* (mild) to attack sexually • *As soon as they got home, he jumped her!;* As soon as they got home, he attacked her sexually.

jump one's bones (to) *exp.* (somewhat crude) • *He's not really interested in you. He just wants to jump your bones!;* He's not really interested in you. He just wants to have sex with you!

make whoopie (to) *exp.* (mild) • *Let's go home and make whoopie;* Let's go home and have sex.

nookie *n.* (humorous) sex • *How about a little nookie?;* How about having a little sex?

play bouncy-bouncy (to) *exp.* (humorous) • *I think they're playing bouncy-bouncy upstairs;* I think they're having sex upstairs.
♦ NOTE: This expression comes from the bouncing noise which comes from the springs of a bed during sex.

poke (to) *v.* (crude yet humorous) • *Are you gonna poke her tonight?;* Are you going to have sex with her tonight?

put out (to) *exp.* (mild) to engage someone in sex • *If you're hoping to have sex with her, forget it. She doesn't put out;* If you're hoping to have sex with her, forget it. She doesn't engage in sex.

roll in the hay (to) *exp.* (humorous) • *How about a roll in the hay?;* How about some sex?

romp (to) *v.* (mild) • (lit); to frolic • *Let's go romp in the basement;* Let's go have sex in the basement.

score (to) *v.* (mild) • *Did you finally score with Anne?;* Did you finally have sex with Anne?

screw (to) *v.* (vulgar) • *All she ever wants to do is screw;* All she ever wants to do is have sex.
♦ NOTE: This verb comes from the image of a screw penetrating an object.

shtup (to) *v.* (humorous) • *They shtupped the first day they met;* They had sex the

first day they met.
♦ NOTE: This verb, coming from Yiddish, is considered humorous due to the pronunciation.

wham bam, thank you ma'am *exp.* quick sex

(humorous and popular) • *Our date last night was nothing but wham bam, thank you ma'am!;* Our date last night was nothing but quick sex.
♦ VARIATION: **slam bam thank you ma'am** *exp.*

Indecent/Pornographic

blue (to be) *adj.* (mild) • *The language in the movie was very blue;* The language in the movie was very vulgar.
♦ NOTE: When said of a person, the connotation of *"blue"* changes to "melancholy."

dirty (to be) *adj.* (mild and very popular) • *Are you reading this dirty book?;* Are you reading this pornographic book?

filth *n.* (mild) indecency • (lit); dirt • *How can they show this kind of filth on television?;* How can they show this kind of indecency on television?

hardcore (to be) *adj.* (mild) to be very pornographic and explicit • *That movie was real hardcore;* That movie was very pornographic and explicit.
♦ ANTONYM: **to be softcore** *adj.* said of a sexy film

which does not contain penetration.

in the gutter (to be) *exp.* (mild) to be indecent • *Your mind is always in the gutter;* Your mind is always focusing on indecent acts.
♦ NOTE: This is actually a parody on the term *"dirty,"* a synonym for "pornographic," since that which is found in the gutter is extremely dirty.

off-color (to be) *adj.* (mild) to be somewhat pornographic.

porn *n.* (mild) pornography • *That film is nothing but porn!;* That film is nothing but pornography!
♦ VARIATION: **porno** *adj.* (mild)

raunchy (to be) *adj.* (mild) to be pornographic and somewhat rough • *He's into raunchy sex;* He enjoys rough sex.
♦ VARIATION: **to be into raunch** *exp.* (mild) to enjoy rough and even painful sex.

raw (to be) *adj.* (mild) to be pornographic and unrefined.

smutty (to be) *adj.* (mild) to be pornographic.

steamy (to be) *adj.* (mild) to be sexy • *That's a steamy dance she's doing;* That's a sexy dance she's doing.

T and A *exp.* (mild) a common abbreviation and euphemism for "tits and ass" used to signify "nudity" • *There's a lot of T and A in that movie;* There's a lot of nudity in that movie.

X-rated (to be) *adj.* (mild) to be pornographic.
▸ NOTE: Movies which contain graphic sexuality are rated X and are restricted to anyone under the age of 18 years old. This expression may also be used to indicate anything which is sexy • *This party is turning X- rated!;* This party is becoming indecent!

Kiss (to)

eat face (to) *exp.* • *Did they eat face last night?;* Did they kiss last night?

French kiss (to) *exp.* to kiss with the tongue • *Can you believe he actually tried to French kiss me?;* Can you believe he actually tried to kiss me with his tongue?
▸ SYNONYM: **to wet kiss** *exp.*

lay one on the lips (to) *exp.* • *She tried to lay one on my lips but I turned away;* She tried to kiss me but I turned away.

pucker up (to) *exp.* to prepare to give a kiss • *Pucker up 'cause I'm gonna give you a big kiss!;* Get prepared because I'm going to give you a big kiss!

slip someone the big wet one (to) *exp.* (crude) to kiss with one's tongue.
▸ NOTE: In this expression, *"the big wet one"* refers to "the tongue."

smooch (to) *v.* • *I saw mom and dad smooching in the living room today;* I saw mom and dad kissing in the living room today.

suck face (to) *v.* • *I'm not going out with him. All he ever wants to do is to suck face;* I'm not going out with him. All he ever wants to do is to kiss.

Masturbate (to)

(NOTE: All slang synonyms for *"to masturbate"* are considered crude since they deal with self-gratification)

beat off (to) *v.* • *He beats off to dirty magazines;* He masturbates to pornographic magazines.
▶ NOTE (1): This is probably the most common, yet vulgar, slang expression for "to masturbate."
▶ NOTE (2): This verbs comes from the beating motion associated with masturbation.

beat one's meat (to) *exp.* • *He beats his meat every night;* He masturbates every night.
▶ NOTE: The term *"meat"* is commonly used in slang to mean "penis."

bleed the weasel (to) *exp.* (humorous) • *I can hear him bleeding the weasel next door;* I can hear him masturbating next door.
▶ NOTE: This is a humorous, yet crude, expression comparing the action of masturbating with that of *"bleeding a weasel."*

choke the chicken (to) *exp.* (humorous) • *All he ever thinks about is choking the chicken;* All he ever thinks about is masturbating.
▶ NOTE: This is a humorous, yet crude, expression

comparing the action of masturbating with that of *"choking a chicken."*

circle jerk (to) *exp.* to stand in a circle and masturbate simultaneously • *Can you believe he's actually into circle jerking?;* Can you believe he actually enjoys group masturbation?

collar the cock (to) *exp.* (humorous) • *I started collaring the cock when I was 13 years old;* I started masturbating when I was 13 years old.
▶ NOTE (1): This is a humorous, yet crude, expression comparing the action of masturbating with that of *"collaring a cock."*
▶ NOTE (2): This is a sexual play-on-words since the word *"cock"* means "a male chicken" in standard English as well as "penis" in American slang.

date with Rosy Palm and her five sisters (to have a) *exp.* (humorous) • *I have a date with Rosy Palm and her five sisters tonight;* I'm going to masturbate tonight.
▶ NOTE: This expression comes from a play-on-words

since the term "Rosy" is both a proper name as well as a synonym for the color "pink." Therefore, in this expression *"Rosy Palm"* represents one's own hand or "rosy palm" along with one's fingers which will all be used in masturbation.

flog the Bishop (to) *exp.* (humorous) • *My new roommate flogs the Bishop three times a day!;* My new roommate masturbates three times a day!
♦ NOTE: This humorous, yet crude, expression was created since the head of the penis resembles the hat worn by the Bishop. The expression, therefore, compares the action of masturbating to *"flogging the Bishop"* or "flogging one's penis."

grease the bayonet (to) *exp.* (humorous) • *I think I need to go grease the bayonet;* I think I need to go masturbate.
♦ NOTE: This is a humorous, yet crude, expression comparing the action of masturbating with that of *greasing a bayonet* which is long and hard like an erect penis.

hand job (to give oneself a) *exp.* • *He's probably in his room giving himself a hand*

job; He's probably in his room masturbating.

jack off (to) *exp.* (very popular yet crude) • *Is it true she jacked you off last night?;* Is it true she masturbated you last night?

jerk the joint (to) *exp.* • *My little brother just jerked the joint yesterday for the first time;* My little brother just masturbated for the first time.
♦ NOTE: This is a somewhat humorous, yet crude, expression comparing the action of masturbating with that of *"jerking a joint"* or more literally, "tugging one's attachment."

jerkin' the gherkin *exp.* (humorous) • *He's been jerkin' the gherkin for an entire hour in there!;* He's been masturbating for an entire hour in there!
♦ NOTE (1): This is a humorous, yet crude, rhyming expression which compares the action of masturbating with that of *"jerking a gherkin pickle."*
♦ NOTE (2): **gherkin** *n.* penis (due to its similar shape to a pickle).

milk the chicken (to) *exp.* (humorous yet crude) • *If I milk the chicken before I go to work, I get too tired;* If I

masturbate before I go to work, I get too tired.
♦ NOTE: This is a humorous, yet crude, expression comparing the action of masturbating and reaching orgasm with that of *"milking a chicken."* The *"chicken"* in this expression refers to a penis which resembles the shape of a chicken's neck.

play the skin flute (to) *exp.*
(humorous) • *Is he playing the skin flute again?*; Is he masturbating again?
♦ NOTE: **skin flute** *exp.* penis.

play with oneself (to) *exp.*
(extremely popular and mild) to masturbate or toy with one's genitals • *It's very natural for children to start playing with themselves at an early age*; It's very natural for children to play with their genitals at an early age.

polish the lance (to) *exp.*
(humorous) • *I'm so turned on now! I think I need to go polish the lance*; I'm so sexually excited now! I think I need to go masturbate.
♦ NOTE: This is a humorous, yet crude, expression comparing the action of masturbating with that of *"polishing a lance"* which is long and hard like a penis.

roll the fuzzy dice (to) *exp.*
(humorous, yet crude) • *I'm gonna go roll the fuzzy dice*; I'm going to go masturbate.
♦ NOTE: This is a humorous, yet crude, expression based on gambling slang, to *"roll the dice"* which has been altered since *"fuzzy dice"* refer to the testicles.

rub the rod (to) *exp.*
(humorous) • *Is he rubbing the rod upstairs again?*; Is he masturbating upstairs again?
♦ NOTE: This is a humorous, yet crude, expression comparing the action of masturbating with that of *"rubbing a rod"* which is long and hard like a penis.

shake hands with the governor (to) *exp.*
(humorous) • *I think he's shaking hands with the governor*; I think he's masturbating.
♦ NOTE: The term *"governor"* is a humorous, yet uncommon, term for "penis" since one's sex organs tend to "govern" the actions of many people.

shift gears (to) *exp.*
(humorous) • *He's a little young to be shifting gears, isn't he?*; He's a little young to be masturbating, isn't he?
♦ NOTE: This is a humorous expression comparing the

action of masturbating with that of *"shifting gears"* in a car.

slap the snake (to) *exp.* (humorous) • *All he ever thinks about is slapping the snake!;* All he ever thinks about is masturbating.
♦ NOTE: This is a humorous, yet crude, expression comparing the action of masturbating with that of *"slapping a snake"* which is long and cylindrical like a penis.

stroke oneself (to) *exp.* • *He likes to stroke himself in front of people;* He likes to masturbate in front of people.

tickle the tiger (to) *exp.* (humorous) • *He tickles the tiger whenever he goes to bed;* He masturbates whenever he goes to bed.
♦ NOTE: The word *"tiger"* is used to mean "penis" in this expression due to the similarity between the large head of the tiger and the large head of the penis.

tune one's organ (to) *exp.* (humorous) • *I think I need to go tune my organ;* I think I need to go masturbate.
♦ NOTE: This expression is a play-on-words since the term "organ" refers to a

musical instrument as well as a "penis."

whack off (to) *exp.* (popular yet crude) • *Did you know he whacks off all the time in his car?;* Did you know he masturbates all the time in his car?
♦ NOTE: This verb may also be spelled *"wack off."*

whip the weenie (to) *exp.* • *It sounds like he's upstairs whipping the weenie;* It sounds like he's upstairs masturbating.
♦ NOTE: The term *"weenie,"* literally meaning "sausage," is used to signify "penis" in slang.

whip the worm (to) *exp.* (humorous) • *I know where you're going. You're gonna go whip the worm, aren't you?;* I know where you're going. You're going to go masturbate, aren't you?
♦ NOTE: In this expression, the term *"worm"* is used to mean "penis" due to its long cylindrical shape.

yank the yak (to) *exp.* (humorous) • *He's yanking the yak;* He's masturbating.
♦ NOTE: In this expression, the term *"yak,"* literally a long-haired ox, is used to mean "penis."

Naked (to be)

au naturel (to be) *adj.* (mild).
♦ NOTE: This comes from French meaning "to be natural."

bare-assed (to be) *adj.* (crude yet very popular) • (lit); to have one's naked buttocks exposed.

buck naked (to be) *exp.* (mild) • (lit); to be as naked as a male deer.

butt naked (to be) *exp.* (mild) to be completely nude.

in the raw (to be) *exp.* (humorous) said of one who is exposing his/her "raw meat."

in one's birthday suit (to be) *exp.* (humorous) said of one who is in the same "clothing" as at birth.

in the buff (to be) *exp.* (mild).
♦ VARIATION: **to be buffo** *adj.*

naked as a jaybird (to be) *exp.* (mild) to be completely naked.

without a stitch of clothing (to be) *exp.* (mild) to be completely naked.

Oral Sex (to have)

blow (to) *exp.* to perform oral sex • *Did you get blown last night?*; Did you have oral sex last night?

blow job (to give a) *exp.* to perform oral sex • *She gave him a blow job last night*; She performed oral sex on him last night.

deep-throat (to) *exp.* to perform oral sex by taking the entire penis down one's throat • *She deep-throated him without gagging*; She perform oral sex on him by taking his entire penis down her throat without gagging.

give head (to) *exp.* (very popular) to perform oral sex • *I could hear her giving him head last night!* I could hear her performing oral sex on him last night!

go down on someone (to) *exp.* to perform oral sex on someone • *He went down on her on their first date!*; He performed oral sex on her on their first date!

play the skin flute (to) *exp.* a humorous expression signifying oral sex with a male • *So, did you play the skin flute last night?*; So, did you perform oral sex with him last night?

sixty-nine (to) *exp.* to perform mutual oral sex at the same time by both partners inverting their positions much like the transposed digits "6" and "9" in the number *"sixty-nine."*

suck [off] (to) *v.* to perform oral sex • *Can you believe he actually offered her money to suck him [off]?;* Can you believe he actually offered her money to perform oral sex on him?

Orgasm (to have an)

blow (to) *v.* (crude) • (lit); to explode • *I'm gonna blow!;* I'm going to have an orgasm!

cream one's jeans (to) *exp.* (extremely vulgar) • *I almost creamed my jeans when I saw her;* I almost had an orgasm when I saw her.
  ♦ NOTE: **to cream** *v.* to get sexually excited • *I'm creaming over her;* I'm getting really sexually excited over her.

cum (to) *v.* (extremely popular and mild) • *I'm gonna cum!;* I'm going to reach orgasm!
  ♦ VARIATION: **to come** *v.*
  ♦ NOTE: The past participle of *"to cum"* and *"to come"* is *"came."*

get off (to) *exp.* (mild) • **1.** to reach orgasm • *Did you get off last night?;* Did you reach orgasm last night? • **2.** to enjoy greatly • *You really get off annoying people, don't*

you?; You really enjoy annoying people, don't you?

get one's rocks off (to) *exp.* (vulgar) • **1.** said of a man who relieves his testicles of semen by having sex • *I really got my rocks off last night;* I had some great sex last night. • **2.** to enjoy greatly • *He gets his rocks off by annoying people;* He really enjoys annoying people.

shoot (to) *v.* (mild) • (lit); to discharge.

shoot one's load (to) *exp.* (vulgar) • (lit); to discharge one's cargo.
  ♦ NOTE: This expression is considered to be vulgar due to the descriptive nature of *"load."*
  ♦ VARIATION: **to shoot one's wad** *exp.* (vulgar) • (lit); to discharge one's mass (of semen).

Orgy (Group Sex)

circle jerk *n.* (vulgar) a group of men who masturbate while standing in a circle.

daisy chain *n.* (mild) a group of men or women or both who are engaged in sex together

gang bang *n.* (crude yet popular).
♦ NOTE: **to bang** *v.* (humorous) to fornicate.

group grope *n.* (crude).
♦ NOTE: **to grope** *v.* to caress.

Sexual Diseases

A.I.D.S. *n.* Acquired Immune Deficiency Syndrome.

blue balls (to have) *exp.* to have gonorrhea.

chancres *n.pl.* syphilis.

clap *n.* gonorrhea.

crabs *n.pl.*

herpes *n.pl.* cold sores.

H.I.V. *n.* Human Immunodeficiency Virus.

social disease *n.* gonorrhea.

S.T.D. *n.* sexually transmitted disease.

V.D. *n.* venereal disease, syphilis.

Sexually Aroused

boner (to have a) *n.* (crude yet very popular).
♦ NOTE: This term signifies a penis which is as erect and as hard as a bone.
♦ VARIATION: **to have a bone** *n.* (crude).

cream (to) *v.* (vulgar) said of one who is sexually aroused and reaching orgasm • (lit); to orgasm.

♦ VARIATION: **to cream one's jeans** *exp.* (very vulgar) • (lit); to orgasm.

hard-on (to have a) *n.* (crude yet extremely popular) said of a man with an erect penis.

have the hots for (to) *exp.* (mild) to be so sexually excited by someone as to feel warm due to one's accelerated pulse.

horny (to be) *adj.* (crude yet extremely popular) to be extremely sexually excited.
♦ ALSO: **to be a horn dog** *n.* to be an extremely sexual person.

hot (to be) *adj.* (mild) • **1.** to be sexually aroused • **2.** to be sexy.
♦ VARIATION: **to be hot to trot** *exp.* (mild) • **1.** to be sexually aroused • **2.** to be sexy.
♦ VARIATION: **to be hot and bothered** *exp.* to be sexually aroused.

hot for some (to be) *exp.* (mild) to be sexually aroused by someone.
♦ VARIATION: **to have the**

hots for someone *exp.* (mild).

ready (to be) *adj.* (mild).
♦ NOTE: Depending on the context, this adjective may be used to mean "ready for sex."

stiffy (to have a) *n.* (humorous) to have an erect penis.

turned on (to be) *exp.* (mild) to be sexually aroused • (lit); to be activated.

wet (to be) *adj.* (vulgar) said of a woman or girl who is sexually excited.

woody (to have a) *n.* (humorous) to have an erect penis (which is as hard as wood).

A CLOSER LOOK (3):
Sexual Body Parts in Slang

Slang terms referring to body parts are colorful, many of them humorous, and unquestionably plentiful as seen in the next pages:

Breasts
(NOTE: All of the synonyms for "breasts" are mild).

balloons *n.pl.* (humorous) large breasts.

bazongas *n.pl.* (humorous) large breasts.

bazookas *n.pl.* (humorous) large breasts.

bazooms *n.pl.* (humorous) breasts.

❧ NOTE: This is a humorous transformation of the term "bosoms."

boobies *n.pl.* breasts.

boobs *n.pl.* breasts.

bumpers *n.pl.* (humorous).
❧ NOTE: This is a humorous term comparing the *"bumpers"* of a car with a woman's "breasts."

cans *n.pl.* large breasts.

coconuts *n.pl.* (humorous) large breasts.

endowed (to be) *adj.* to be large breasted.

grapefruits *n.pl.* (humorous) large breasts.

headlights *n.pl.* (humorous) large breasts.

hooters *n.pl.* (humorous) large breasts.

jugs *n.pl.* (humorous) large breasts.

knockers *n.pl.* (humorous) large breasts.

maracas *n.pl.* (humorous) large breasts.

melons *n.pl.* (humorous) large breasts.

milk bottles *n.pl.* (humorous) large breasts.

mosquito bites *n.pl.* (humorous) small breasts.

tits *n.pl.* (very popular) breasts.

titties *n.pl.* breasts.

watermelons *n.pl.* (humorous) very large breasts.

Buttocks

ass *n.* (vulgar) • **1.** buttocks • **2.** despicable person.

behind *n.* (mild) • *Get your behind over here;* Come here.
❧ VARIATION: **heinie** *n.* (mild) an abbreviation of *"behind."*

bottom *n.* (mild).

bum *n.* (mild).

buns *n.* (not vulgar and extremely popular) • *He's got cute buns!;* He has cute buttocks!

can *n.* (mild).

cheeks *n.* (mild).

derriere *n.* a euphemistic replacement for *"buttocks"* (See NOTE) • *Put your derriere right here;* Sit down right here.
❧ NOTE: Some people feel that to use the actual terms

for any intimate body part is in bad taste. Although the word *"buttocks"* is perfectly acceptable, there are those who prefer to use a less direct term such as *"derriere."* Since Americans feel that French is such a beautiful and romantic language, French synonyms for certain body parts are commonly used as tasteful replacements.

duff *n.* (mild).

fanny *n.* (mild).
♦ NOTE: It's important to note that the term *"fanny,"* which is an innocent word used in America meaning "buttocks," is an extremely vulgar term in England meaning "vagina."

keester *n.* (humorous).
♦ VARIATION: **keister.**

moon someone (to) *exp.* to expose one's buttocks by pulling down one's pants and bending over • *Those guys over there just mooned us!;* Those guys over there just exposed their buttocks to us!

prat *n.* (mild).

rear end *n.* (mild).

rump *n.* (mild).

seat *n.* (humorous).

sweet cakes *n.* attractive buttocks.

sweet cheeks *n.* attractive buttocks.

tail *n.* (mild).

tush *n.* (mild).
♦ NOTE: This popular term comes from Yiddish.
♦ VARIATION: **tushy** *n.*

wazoo *n.* (mild).
♦ NOTE: This term is commonly used in the expression *"up the wazoo"* meaning "in great quantity": *I've got homework up the wazoo tonight!;* I've got lots of homework tonight!

ying yang *n.* (mild).
♦ NOTE: This term is commonly used in the expression *"up the ying yang"* meaning "in great quantity": *I don't need another dress. I've got dresses up the ying yang;* I don't need another dress. I've got lots of dresses.

Penis
(See: "male genitals" & "penis")

basket *n.* (mild and popular) genitals.

battering ram *n.* (mild).
♦ NOTE: This term is used

due to its similarity in shape and action of a penis during sex.

bazooka *n.* (mild).
⟩ NOTE: This term is used due to its similarity in shape to a penis. This is also used to mean large protruding breasts, depending on the context.

bone *n.* (crude).
⟩ NOTE: This term signifies an erect penis which is as hard as a bone. In addition, a common term for an erect penis is a *"boner."*

cock *n.* (extremely vulgar).
⟩ NOTE: Due to its extreme vulgarity, many people refer to the word *"cock"* as the "C-word." The female counterpart of *"cock"* is the extremely vulgar term *"cunt"* which is also referred to by many as the "C-word."

cucumber *n.* (crude).
⟩ NOTE: This term is used due to its similarity in shape to a penis.

cyclops *n.* (crude).
⟩ NOTE: This humorous term is used to describe a penis which looks like it has one eye (like a cyclops).

dick *n.* (extremely popular, yet crude).
⟩ NOTE (1): This is one of the most popular slang terms

for "penis."
⟩ NOTE (2): This term is also commonly used to mean "a despicable person."

Dickie and the boys *exp.* a humorous expression meaning the "penis and testicles."

dink *n.* (mild).

dong *n.* (mild).

equipment *n.* (mild).

family jewels *n.* (mild).
⟩ NOTE: This is a very popular euphemism for one's genitals.

hose *n.*
⟩ NOTE: This term is used due to its similarity in shape to a penis.

hung (to be) *adj.* (mild) to be endowed with a large penis • *That guy's really hung!;* That man has a really large penis!

joy-stick *n.* (mild).
⟩ NOTE: This is a humorous term comparing the joy-stick used to control computer games to the shape of a penis which causes "joy" when stimulated.

junior *n.* (mild).

love muscle *n.* (somewhat crude).

meat and two vegetables *exp.* a humorous, yet somewhat

crude, description of a penis and testicles.

middle leg *n.* (crude).
‣ NOTE: This is a light-hearted term comparing the penis with a leg.
‣ VARIATION: **third leg** *n.*

Mr. Happy *n.* (humorous, mild).
‣ NOTE: This term signifies the happiness or good feeling that is experienced when the penis is stimulated.

one-eyed monster *n.* (humorous, mild).
‣ NOTE: This is a humorous term for penis which is compared to a monster with one eye.

one-eyed wonder *n.* (humorous, mild).
‣ NOTE: This is a humorous term for penis which is compared to a miracle with one eye.

pecker *n.* (humorous, mild).
‣ NOTE: This term signifies a penis which looks like it's pecking during sex. It's important to note that in England, the term *"pecker"* simply means "chin."

pee-pee *n.* (baby talk, mild).
‣ NOTE: This term comes from the verb *"to pee"* which means "to urinate."

peenie *n.* (baby talk, mild).
‣ NOTE: This is a diminutive form of "penis."

peter *n.* (mild).

pisser *n.* (vulgar).
‣ NOTE: This comes from the verb *"to piss,"* meaning "to urinate," which is considered vulgar.

pistol *n.* (somewhat crude).
‣ NOTE: A pistol can be compared to a penis since both have cylindrical shafts and can both shoot; the pistol shoots bullets and the penis shoots semen during orgasm.

pole *n.* (mild).
‣ NOTE: This noun is used to signify "penis" since both are long and cylindrical.

prick *n.* (vulgar) • **1.** penis • **2.** despicable person.

private parts *exp.* (mild).
‣ NOTE: A very popular euphemism describing one's genitals.

privates *n.pl.* (mild).
‣ NOTE: A popular euphemism describing one's genitals.

putz *n.* (mild) • **1.** penis • **2.** despicable person.
‣ NOTE: This term comes from Yiddish meaning "penis."

rammer *n.* (crude).
  ♦ NOTE: This term signifies the "penis" due to its ramming action during sex.

ramrod *n.* (crude).
  ♦ NOTE: This term signifies the "penis" due to its ramming action during sex.

rod *n.* (crude).
  ♦ NOTE: This term signifies the "penis" since both are long and cylindrical.

rod of love *n.* (crude).
  ♦ NOTE: This term signifies the "penis" since both are long and cylindrical.

salami *n.* (crude).
  ♦ NOTE: This term signifies the "penis" since both are long and cylindrical.

sausage *n.* (crude).
  ♦ NOTE: This term signifies the "penis" since both are long and cylindrical.

shlong *n.* (humorous).

spear *n.* (mild).
  ♦ NOTE: This term signifies the "penis" since both are long and cylindrical and perform acts of penetration.

staff *n.* (mild).
  ♦ NOTE: This term signifies the "penis" since both are long and cylindrical.

sword *n.* (mild).
  ♦ NOTE: This term signifies the "penis" since both are long and cylindrical and perform acts of penetration.

thing *n.* (mild).

tool *n.* (mild).

trouser snake *n.* (mild).

trouser trout *n.* (mild).

wiener *n.* (humorous).
  ♦ NOTE: This term signifies the "penis" since both are long and cylindrical.
  ♦ VARIATION: **ween** *n.*
  ♦ VARIATION: **weenie** *n.*

Testicles

balls *n.pl.* (very popular yet vulgar).

basket *n.* (mild) penis and testicles together, genitalia.

family jewels *n.pl.* (mild) penis and testicles together, genitalia.

nuts *n.pl.* (vulgar).

rocks *n.pl.* (mild).

Rocky Mountain oysters *n.pl.* a southern delicacy of cooked pig testicles.

Vagina
(NOTE: All synonyms for "vagina" are considered crude).

bearded clam *n.* a somewhat humorous, yet crude, comparison of the vagina to a *"bearded clam."*

beaver *n.* a popular, yet crude, synonym for *vagina* due to its fur.

box *n.* (crude).

box lunch *exp.* (humorous, yet crude).
 ‣ NOTE: This is a play-on-words since this term has the traditional meaning of "a prepared lunch taken to work, school, etc. in a box" as well as the slang connotation of "a sexually active vagina."

crack *n.* (crude).
 ‣ NOTE: This term signifies "vagina" due to its similarity to a *"crack."*

cunt *n.* (probably the most vulgar synonym for "vagina").
 ‣ NOTE: Due to the vulgarity of this term, it is often referred to as the "C-word."

fur pie *n.* (vulgar).

furburger *n.* (vulgar).

hole *n.* (vulgar)

muff *n.* (crude).
 ‣ NOTE: **muff diver** *n.* one who enjoys oral sex with women.

muffin *n.* (crude).

pussy *n.* (popular, yet vulgar).
 ‣ NOTE: In England, this term has only one definition: "a small cat" whereas in America, it has the additional definition of "vagina."

snatch *n.* (vulgar).

the Y *n.*
 ‣ NOTE: This is a humorous, yet vulgar, description of a woman lying on her back with her legs spread apart forming the letter "Y."

twat *n.* (vulgar).

PROSTITUTION, DRUGS, & POLICE SLANG/JARGON

– Taking a Stroll –

Dialogue in slang

Taking a Stroll...

DIALOGUE

Susie and Larry are taking a stroll after dinner.

Susie: Larry, I think we walked out of our neighborhood. That looks like a **whorehouse**. We must be in the **red-light district**!

Larry: You're right. I thought she looked like a **madam**. Wow! There are **hookers** all over this block. I guess we're on their **turf**.

Susie: Look at her **cruising** that guy. She must be looking for a **trick**.

Larry: Don't you know anything? That guy's a **mack** and probably her **source**, too. Can't you tell by his clothes? She's probably **scoring** some **nose candy** or some **smack** from him or something. Look how **burnt out** she is! She's got to be a **cokehead**.

Susie: I'm surprised the **cops** haven't set up a **sting** and **busted** everyone. There's even the smell of **pot** in the air and **roaches** all over the ground! They all probably have **rap sheets** a mile long.

LESSON SIX

Translation of dialogue in standard American-English

Taking a Stroll...

DIALOGUE

Susie and Larry are taking a stroll after dinner.

Susie: Larry, I think we walked out of our neighborhood. That looks like a **brothel**. We must be in the **prostitution area**!

Larry: You're right. I thought she looked like the **owner of the brothel**. Wow! There are **prostitutes** all over this block. I guess we're in their **territory**.

Susie: Look at her **soliciting** that guy. She must be looking for a **client**.

Larry: Don't you know anything? That guy's a **pimp** and probably her **drug seller**, too. Can't you tell by his clothes? She's probably **buying** some **cocaine** or some **heroin** from him or something. Look how **overdosed** she is! She's got to be a **cocaine addict**.

Susie: I'm surprised the **police** haven't set up a **trap** and **arrested** everyone. There's even the smell of **marijuana** in the air and **marijuana cigarettes** all over the ground! They all probably have **police records** a mile long.

LESSON SIX

Dialogue in slang as it would be heard

Taking a Stroll...

DIALOGUE

Susie 'n Larry 'r taking a stroll after dinner.

Susie: Larry, I think we walked out of our neighborhood. That looks like a **whorehouse**. We must be in the **red-light district**!

Larry: Yer right. I thought she looked like a **madam**. Wow! There 'r **hookers** all over this block. I guess we're on their **turf**.

Susie: Lookit 'er **cruisin'** that guy. She must be looking fer a **trick**.

Larry: Don' chew know anything? That guy's a **mack** n' prob'ly 'er **source**, too. Can' cha tell by 'is clothes? She's prob'ly **scorin'** s'm **nose candy** 'r s'm **smack** from 'im 'r something. Look how **burn' out** she is! She'z gotta be a **cokehead**.

Susie: I'm saprized the **cops** haven't sed up a **sting** 'n **busded** ev'ryone. There'z even the smell of **pot** 'n the air 'n **roaches** all over the ground! They all prob'ly have **rap sheets** a mile long.

122

Vocabulary

burnt out (to be) *adj.* (mild and very popular) • **1.** to be overdosed with drugs • **2.** to be exhausted.
  ◆ VARIATION: **to be burned out**

bust (to) *v.* (mild and very popular) to arrest.
  ◆ NOTE: **to get busted** *adj.* **1.** to get arrested and be given a citation or be taken to jail • **2.** to get in trouble.

cokehead *n.* (mild) cocaine addict.

cop *n.* (mild and very popular) police officer.
  ◆ VARIATION: **copper** *n.* (derogatory).
  ◆ NOTE: This term is associated with the lingo of thugs or gangsters.

cruise (to) *v.* (mild and very popular) to journey up and down a street in search of a sexual conquest.
  ◆ NOTE: This verb is commonly used to refer to someone who is looking for a sexual partner as well as a prostitute who is looking for a client.

hooker *n.* (extremely popular and mild) prostitute.
  ◆ NOTE: This term applies to a male or female prostitute.
  ➤ ORIGIN: During the civil war, troops under the command of Major General Joseph Hooker began visiting prostitutes while on leave. As their visits became more and more regular, the prostitutes were soon referred to as *"hookers."*

mack *n.* (mild) one who finds customers for prostitutes, a pimp.
  ◆ VARIATION (1): **mackerel** *n.* (mild).
  ◆ VARIATION (2): **mackman** *n.* (mild).
  ◆ VARIATION (3): **macko man** *n.* (mild).

madame *n.* (mild) the female director of a brothel.

nose candy *n.* (mild and popular) cocaine.
  ‣ VARIATION: **candy** *n.*

pot *n.* (mild and very popular) marijuana.
  ‣ NOTE: **pothead** *n.* marijuana addict.

rap sheet *n.* (mild) a police record on a criminal.

red-light district *n.* (mild) the neighborhood where prostitution takes place.
  ‣ NOTE: The neighborhood or location where prostitutes are known to congregate is called the *"red-light district"* due to the traditional red light in front of each brothel.
  ‣ ALSO: **red lighterie** *n.*

roach *n.* (mild) a marijuana cigarette.

score (to) *v.* (mild and popular) to buy drugs.

smack *n.* (mild and popular) heroin.

source *n.* (mild) drug supplier.

sting *n.* (mild) a carefully and secretly planned entrapment of those who are in the process of doing an unlawful act.
  ‣ VARIATION: **sting operation** *n.* (mild).

trick *n.* (mild) a prostitute's client.
  ‣ NOTE: **to turn a trick** *n.* to have sex with a client (said of a prostitute).
  ‣ SYNONYM: **john** *n.* (mild).

turf *n.* (mild) a prostitute's territory where she solicits clients.

whorehouse *n.* (mild and popular) brothel.

PRACTICE THE VOCABULARY

[Answers to Lesson 6, p. 169]

A. Underline the word that best completes each phrase.

1. Look how burnt (**in**, **out**, **over**) she is! That's what happens when you overdose on drugs.

2. The (**cops**, **tops**, **chops**) stopped them just as they were about to rob the bank.

3. Another name for a pimp is a (**jack**, **yack**, **mack**).

4. The female director of a brother is called a (**madame**, **mademoiselle**, **directrice**).

5. Look at all these prostitutes! This must be the (**blue**, **red**, **yellow**)-light district.

6. A popular slang term for heroin is (**punch**, **slap**, **smack**).

7. A prostitute's territory where she solicits clients is called her (**turf**, **surf**, **serf**).

8. My father just got (**shattered**, **busted**, **smashed**) for speeding.

9. A slang term for prostitute is a (**hooker**, **cooker**, **booker**).

10. A roach is a (**cigar**, **cigarette**, **pipe**) made with marijuana.

11. The prostitute is (**sailing**, **cruising**, **surfing**) up and down the street looking for a client.

12. A slang term for brothel is a (**hothouse**, **doghouse**, **whorehouse**).

B. Match the two columns.

☐ 1. I got arrested by a police officer yesterday for speeding.

☐ 2. I wonder how many clients that prostitute gets in one day.

☐ 3. I think he's a cocaine addict.

☐ 4. That guy must be her pimp.

☐ 5. She's journeying up and down the street in search of a sexual conquest.

☐ 6. The police are planning a secret entrapment of all the prostitutes in this area.

☐ 7. How many drugs did he buy from his supplier?

☐ 8. This is the first time I've ever been to a neighborhood where prostitution takes place.

☐ 9. The brothel is run by a young female director.

☐ 10. That looks like heroin.

☐ 11. Marijuana is actually prescribed for certain patients.

☐ 12. She's so hyperactive. I wonder if she uses cocaine.

A. **The cops are planning a sting on all the hookers in this area.**

B. **I wonder how many tricks that hooker turns in one day.**

C. **She's cruising.**

D. **I think he's a cokehead.**

E. **How many drugs did he score from his source?**

F. **She's so hyperactive. I wonder if she uses nose candy.**

G. **That guy must be her mack.**

H. **This is the first time I've ever been to the red-light district.**

I. **Pot is actually prescribed for certain patients.**

J. **I got busted by a cop yesterday for speeding.**

K. **That looks like smack.**

L. **The whorehouse is run by a young madame.**

A CLOSER LOOK (1):
Prostitution Slang

Prostitution has long been known as the world's oldest profession. Due to its long tenure, slang terms for various aspects of prostitution have certainly had ample time to develop.

The following list will provide you with an inside look at some of the most imaginative slang synonyms relating to the world of prostitution such as *brothel, pimp, prostitute,* and *to solicit:*

Brothel

body shop *n.* (mild).

bordello *n.* (mild).

call house *n.* (mild).
♦ NOTE: This signifies a house, or establishment, where men call on prostitutes.

call joint *n.* (mild).
♦ NOTE: The term *"joint"* is slang for "establishment." Therefore, a *"call joint"* is an establishment where men call on prostitutes.

cathouse *n.* (mild).

chicken ranch *n.* (mild).

den of iniquity *n.* (mild) • (lit); sanctuary of immorality.

hook shop *n.*

house of delight *n.* (mild).
♦ NOTE: This refers to a brothel, which commonly looks like a large home, where men experience delight due to the prostitutes.

house of ill fame *n.* (mild) • (lit); house of bad reputation (due to the often illegal sexual activity which occurs within its walls).

house of ill repute *n.* (mild) • (lit); house of bad reputation (due to the often illegal sexual activity which occurs within its walls).

house of joy *n.* (mild).
♦ NOTE: This refers to a brothel, which commonly looks like a large home, where men experience joy due to the prostitutes.
♦ VARIATION: **joy house** *n.*

massage parlor *n.* (mild).
♦ NOTE: In states where prostitution is illegal, many brothels represented

themselves as *"massage parlors"* which are legal.

meat market *n.* (mild).
‣ NOTE: This refers not only to brothels, but any establishment where people gather to look for sexual conquests.

service station *n.* (humorous).
‣ NOTE: This comes from the verb *"to service"* which has the slang connotation of "to satisfy (someone) sexually."

whorehouse *n.* (extremely popular).

Pimp

driver *n.* (mild).

flesh peddler *n.* (mild).
• **1.** pimp • **2.** prostitute.

maggot *n.* (mild).

rack salesman *n.* (mild).
‣ NOTE: This comes from the term "meat rack" since the word "meat" may be used to refer to a person.

run a stable (to) *v.* (mild) said of a pimp who has a string of *"working girls."*

Prostitute

ass peddler *n.* (vulgar) • (lit); buttocks seller.
‣ NOTE: This term refers to a male or female prostitute.

bimbo *n.* (mild) • **1.** prostitute • **2.** foolish girl.
‣ NOTE: This terms refers to a female prostitute.

call girl *n.* (mild) • (lit); a prostitute one calls on the phone to arrange a meeting.
‣ NOTE: This terms refers to a female prostitute only.

flesh peddler *n.* (mild) • (lit); one who sells one's body.

‣ NOTE: This terms refers to a male or female prostitute.

floozie *n.* (mild) a prostitute or girl of easy morals.
‣ NOTE: This terms refers to a female prostitute only.

ho *n.* (mild and humorous).
‣ NOTE: In many parts of the south, the term "whore" is pronounced *"ho."*

hustler *n.* (extremely popular and mild).
‣ NOTE: This term applies to a male or female prostitute.

lady of the evening *exp.* (mild).

slut *n.* a very derogatory and common term for a prostitute or girl of easy morals.

streetwalker *n.* (mild).
‣ NOTE: This term refers to a male or female prostitute.

visit the red-light district (to) *exp.* to look for a prostitute.
‣ NOTE: The neighborhood where prostitutes are known to congregate is called the *"red-light district"* due to the traditional red light in front of each brothel.

whore *n.* derogatory term for "prostitute."
‣ NOTE: This term is often pronounced in jest with a southern accent, *"ho."*
‣ NOTE: This term refers to a male or female prostitute.

working girl *n.* a euphemism for "prostitute."

Solicit (to)

hustle (to) *v.* (mild and very popular).
‣ NOTE: **hustler** *n.* (mild) male or female prostitute.

on the make (to be) *exp.* (mild).
‣ NOTE: This expression is used to refer to someone who is looking for a sexual partner as well as a prostitute who is looking for a client.

on the streets (to be) *exp.* (mild) said of a prostitute who is working on the streets.
‣ VARIATION: **to walk the streets** *exp.* (mild).

on the turf (to be) *exp.* (mild).
‣ NOTE: The term *"turf"* is used to refer to the area where prostitutes work.

peddle ass (to) *exp.* (vulgar) • (lit); to sell buttocks.

trick (to) *v.* (mild) to trade sexual favors for money.
‣ VARIATION: **to turn a trick** *exp.*
‣ NOTE: **trick** *n.* a prostitute's client.

whore (to) *v.* • **1.** to work as a prostitute • **2.** to look for sex.
‣ VARIATION: **to whore around** *exp.* (mild).

A CLOSER LOOK (2):
Drug Slang

Prostitution and drugs often seem to mix. This could be due to the fact that many prostitutes are already drugs users and find that in order to support their drug habits, they must turn to a quick and seemingly easy way to make money. In addition, prostitutes are under great pressure to make certain quotas for their pimps even if this means severe sleep deprivation. Consequently, they rely heavily on drugs for artificial stimulation.

Drug slang is common to any user of drugs. When I was 15 years old, I was at a party where someone offered me a cigarette filled with tobacco and *"elephant tranquilizer."* Not being a smoker, I turned it down. After quizzing several people the next day, I learned that *"elephant tranquilizer"* is a slang term for "phencyclidine" or *"PCP"* as it is commonly known. This is an extremely potent narcotic which causes violent behavior and occasionally death to the user.

It is clear that studying the following list could be an important step in self-defense for any unsuspecting victim:

Cocaine

big C *n.*

blow *n.*

coke *n.*
    ▶ NOTE: Since this is the same name for the popular soft drink as well, the difference in connotation simply depends on the context.

cokeland *n.* the locale where cocaine is bought.

cola *n.*

eightball *n.* 3.5 grams of cocaine.

gold dust *n.*

happy dust *n.*

heaven dust *n.*

hit *n.* an amount of ingested cocaine (or marijuana) • *Wanna hit?;* Do you want to take some cocaine?

jam house *n.* the locale where cocaine is bought.

joy flakes *n.*

joy powder *n.*

line *n.* a dosage of cocaine since it is traditionally sniffed in *"rows"* or *"lines."*

powder *n.*

rock house *n.* the locale where cocaine is bought.
  ♦ NOTE: A common slang term for "cocaine" is *"rock."*

row *n.* a dosage of cocaine since it is traditionally sniffed in *"rows"* or *"lines."*

sleigh ride *n.*

sniff (to) *v.* to use cocaine.

snort (to) *v.* (very popular) to use cocaine.

snow *n.*

snowball *n.*

stash house *n.* the locale where cocaine is bought.

talc *n.*

toot *n.*

toot (to) *v.* (very popular) to use cocaine.

white *n.*

white Christmas *n.*

white cross *n.*

white lady *n.*

Cocaine and Heroin

C and H *n.*

cold and hot *n.*

dynamite *n.*

horse *n.*

speedball *n.*

whizbang *n.*

Cocaine User

cokie *n.*

jammer *n.*

sniffer *n.*

snifter *n.*

snow snifter *n.*

snow snorter *n.*

snowbird *n.*

tooter *n.*

Crack Cocaine
(a potent form of cocaine)

crack *n.*

cube *n.*

ice *n.*

rock *n.*

Drug Overdose (to)

freak out (to) *v.*

O.D. (to) *v.*

overamp (to) *v.*

overcharge (to) *v.*

overjolt (to) *v.*

overvamp (to) *v.*

rock out (to) *v.*

space out (to) *v.*

zone out (to) *v.*

Drug Supplier

bagman *n.*

beat artist *n.*

big man *n.*

broker *n.*

candy man *n.*

dealer *n.*

dope peddler *n.*

drug pusher *n.*

fixer *n.*

house connections *exp.*

juggler *n.*

junker *n.*

missionary *n.*

operator *n.*

peddler *n.*

pusher *n.*

reefer man *n.*

scagman *n.*

shover *n.*

tea man *n.*

trafficker *n.*

viper *n.*

Drugs (to be on)

blown away (to be) *adj.*

blown out (to be) *adj.*

caught in a snowstorm (to be) *exp.* to be on cocaine (since a slang word for "cocaine" is "*snow*").

charged up (to be) *adj.*

coked (to be) *adj.* to be drugged from cocaine.

coked up (to be) *adj.* to be drugged from cocaine.

contact high (to have a) (to be) *adj.* to get drugged simply by being in close contact with others who are smoking (referred to as "second-hand smoke").

floating (to be) *adj.*

flying (to be) *adj.*

freaked out (to be) *adj.*

geezed up (to be) *adj.* (popular).

goofed (to be) *adj.*

have a buzz (to) *adj.* to be slightly intoxicated (from alcohol or drugs).

high (to be) *adj.*

high as a kite (to be) *adj.* • **1.** to be highly intoxicated (from alcohol or drugs) • **2.** to be extremely joyful.

hopped up (to be) *adj.*

hype *n.* drug user.

in orbit (to be) *adj.*

junked up (to be) *adj.*

loaded (to be) *adj.*

on a cloud (to be) *adj.*

on the needle (to be) *adj.*

on the weed (to be) *adj.* to be on marijuana.

out of it (to be) *adj.* • **1.** to be intoxicated (from alcohol or drugs) • **2.** to be in a state of oblivion (due to fatigue or meditation).

ripped (to be) *adj.* • **1.** on drugs • **2.** drunk.

sleigh riding (to be) *adj.*
to be on cocaine.

smashed (to be) *adj.*

snowed (to be) *adj.* to be
on cocaine.

snowed in (to be) *adj.* to
be on cocaine.

snowed up (to be) *adj.*
to be on cocaine.

spaced (to be) *exp. adj.*
• **1.** to be intoxicated
(from alcohol or drugs)
• **2.** to be in a state of
oblivion (due to fatigue
or meditation).
♦ VARIATION: **to be
spaced out** *exp.*

stoned (to be) *adj.*

**stoned out of one's
gourd (to be)** *adj.*

**stoned out of one's
head (to be)** *adj.*

**stoned out of one's
mind (to be)** *adj.*

strung out (to be) *adj.*

tea'd up (to be) *adj.*

torn up (to be) *adj.*

tripping (to be) *adj.*

twisted (to be) *adj.*
(popular).

wasted (to be) *adj.* (very
popular).

way out (to be) *adj.*

wigged out (to be) *adj.*

wiped out (to be) *adj.*
• **1.** to be drugged •
2. to be exhausted.

wired (to be) *adj.* to be
dynamic and lively
naturally or due to
drugs.

zonked out (to be) *adj.*
to be drugged or tired.

Heroin

angel *n.*

antifreeze *n.*

Big Harry *n.*

black tar *n.*

brown sugar *n.* bad
heroin.

cadillac *n.*

Chinese red *n.*

chiva *n.*

doojee *n.*

dynamite *n.*

eye opener *n.*

flea powder *n.*

H. *n.*

hard stuff *n.*

Harry *n.*

horse *n.*

joy powder *n.*

Lady H. *n.*

Mexican brown *n.* bad
  heroin.

poison *n.*

powder *n.*

red chicken *n.*

salt *n.*

scag *n.*

scramble *n.*

shit *n.* (vulgar).

stuff *n.*

sugar *n.*

the big H *n.*

the tragic magic *n.*

witch hazel *n.*

Heroin Addict

Scag Jones *n.*

smack slammer *n.*

smackhead *n.*

Lysergic Acid Diethylamide (L.S.D.)

25 *n.*

acid *n.*

barrels *n.pl.*

big D *n.*

blotters *n.pl.*

blue acid *n.*

blue cheer *n.*

blue flag *n.*

blue heaven *n.*

cube *n.*

dots *n.pl.*

flats *n.pl.*

flight *n.*

peace *n.*

sunshine *n.*

trip *n.* a positive or
  negative mental
  experience while on
  drugs.

♦ ALSO: **acid trip** *n.* a positive or negative mental experience while on lysergic acid diethylamide.

windowpane *n.*

yellow *n.*

yellow sunshine *n.*

Marijuana

buds *n.pl.*

Colombian *n.*

dope *n.*

drag *n.* dosage • *to take a drag;* to inhale a dosage of marijuana.

gage *n.*

gold *n.*

grass *n.*

hash *n.*

hemp *n.*

hit *n.* a dosage • *Wanna hit?;* Do you want a dosage of marijuana?

jay *n.* a marijuana cigarette.

joint *n.* a marijuana cigarette.

lid *n.* one ounce of marijuana.
♦ NOTE: This term was extremely popular in the 1960s and is now outdated.

lone weed *n.*

Mary *n.*

Mary Jane *n.*
♦ NOTE: The letters "M" and "J" in *"Mary Jane"* represent "marijuana."

Mary Wanna *n.*
♦ NOTE: *"Mary Wanna"* and "marijuana" are similar in pronunciation.

Mary Warner *n.*
♦ NOTE: *"Mary Warner"* and "marijuana" are similar in pronunciation.

Maui-wowee *n.* a strong marijuana coming from Hawaii.

Mexican brown *n.*

Mexican red *n.*

pot *n.* (extremely popular).
♦ NOTE: **pothead** *n.* marijuana addict.

reefer *n.* a marijuana cigarette.

shit *n.* (vulgar).

smoke *n.*
  ▸ VARIATION: **Smokes** *n.pl.*

tea *n.*

Thai stick *n.*

toke *n.* a portion of marijuana.

weed *n.* (very popular especially in the 1960s).
  ▸ ALSO: **evil weed** *n.*

Take Drugs (to)

blast (to) *v.*

blow (to) *v.*

blow coke (to) *v.*

blow snow (to) *v.*

cook (to) *v.*

do a blow (to) *v.*

do a toot (to) *v.*

do drugs (to) *v.*

dope (to) *v.*

dope up (to) *v.*

dose (to) *v.*

dose up (to) *v.*

drop (to) *v.*

fix (to) *v.*

freebase (to) *v.*

get high (to) *v.*

get off (to) *v.*

hit (to) *v.*

hit the needle (to) *v.*

hit the pipe (to) *v.*

joy pop (to) *v.*

mainline (to) *v.*

pop (to) *v.*

shoot (to) *v.*

shoot up (to) *v.*

sniff (to) *v.*

snort (to) *v.*

speedball (to) *v.*

toke (to) *v.*

trip (to) *v.*

A CLOSER LOOK (3):
Jail & Police Slang

Since prostitution is illegal throughout most of America, there is probably not a prostitute on the *"turf"* who is unfamiliar with the following terms:

Arrest (to)

book (to) *v.* (mild) to arrest and process.

catch red-handed (to) *v.* (mild) to discover someone in the act of committing a crime or prohibited act.

come down on someone (to) *v.* (mild) • **1.** to arrest someone and issue a citation or escort to jail • **2.** to reprimand someone.

haul in (to) *v.* (mild) to escort to jail.

nab (to) *v.* (mild) to arrest someone and issue a citation or escort to jail.

nail (to) *v.* (mild and very popular) to arrest someone and issue a citation or escort to jail.

pick up (to) *v.* (mild and very popular) to arrest someone and issue a citation or escort to jail.

pull in (to) *v.* (mild) to escort to jail.

put the bite on (to) *v.* (mild) to arrest someone and issue a citation or escort to jail.

put the cuffs on someone (to) *v.* (mild) to escort someone to jail.
♦ VARIATION: **to slap the cuffs on someone** *exp.* (mild).

run in (to) *v.* (mild) to escort to jail.

take in (to) *v.* (mild) to escort to jail.

throw in the clink (to) *v.* (mild) to put someone in jail.

throw the book at one (to) *v.* (mild) to arrest someone for several infractions.

Police Officer

badge *n.* (mild).

black and white *n.*
(mild) police car.
♦ NOTE: This term
refers to the
traditional black and
white colors of a police
car.

C.H.P. *n.* (mild) a
popular abbreviation
for "California
Highway Patrol."

cop *n.* (mild and
extremely popular)
♦ NOTE: This is an
abbreviation of the
slang term *"copper,"*
used only in old
gangster movies and
in jest, due to the
copper badges worn by
police officers.

dick *n.* (mild) detective.

flatfoot *n.* (mild).
♦ NOTE: This term
refers to a police
officer who patrols on
foot.

flathead *n.* (derogatory
yet humorous).
♦ NOTE: This term
signifies the old
traditional flat-top
haircuts of police
officers.

fuzz *n.* (derogatory).
♦ NOTE: This term was
very popular during
the 1960s and is still
heard in jest and in
movies of the period.

law *n.* (mild, used
primarily in westerns)
• *He's the law around
here;* He's the sheriff
around here.

long arm *n.* (mild).

long arm of the law *exp.*
(mild).

narc *n.* (mild) narcotics
officer.

nightcrawler *n.* (mild) a
police officer who
patrols at night.

ocifer *n.* (derogatory).
♦ NOTE: This term was
particularly popular in
the 1960s.

pig *n.* (derogatory).
♦ NOTE: This term was
particularly popular in the
1960s but is still heard
today.

Prison
(NOTE: None of the synonyms for "prison" are vulgar).

big cage *n.*

big house *n.* (used primarily in old gangster movies).

clink *n.* (used primarily in old gangster movies).

cooler *n.* (used primarily in old gangster movies).

cooped up (to be) *adj.* to be in prison • (lit); to be confined to a small area like a chicken coop.

graybar hotel *n.*
  ♦ NOTE: This signifies the gray steel bars used in jail cells.

hoosegow *n.* (used primarily in old gangster movies and westerns).

locked up (to be) *adj.* to be in prison.
  ♦ ALSO: **to lock up** *exp.* to put in jail.

pen *n.* a common abbreviation for "penitentiary."

  ♦ ALSO: **State Pen** *n.* State Penitentiary.

pokey *n.* (used primarily in old gangster movies and westerns).

put away (to be) *exp.* to be put in jail.
  ♦ ALSO: **to put away** *exp.* to put in jail.

put on ice (to be) *exp.* to be put in jail.
  ♦ ALSO: **to put on ice** *exp.* to put in jail.

sent up the river (to get) *exp.* to be put in jail.
  ♦ ALSO: **to send up the river** *exp.* to put in jail.

slammer *n.* (used primarily in old gangster movies).
  ♦ NOTE: This term signifies the slamming sound a prison door makes when closed.

throw the book at (to) *exp.* to find someone guilty on several counts and put in jail for an extended period of time.

BEING OBSCENE UNINTENTIONALLY

– American-English versus British-English –

Dialogue Between Two Americans

DIALOGUE

Mr. Edwards and his new employee are sitting in a restaurant.

Mr. Edwards: You've got lots of **spunk**. I like that in a new employee. Well, I'm **stuffed**. Wanna go **Roger**?

Employee: **Roger**? I'm **Randy**!

Same Dialogue as Heard by the British

Mr. Edwards: You've got lots of **sperm**. I like that in a new employee. Well, I've **just had intercourse**. **Do you want to go have sex**?

Employee: **Have sex**? I am **feeling lustful**!

Dialogue Between Two Brits

DIALOGUE

Jim and Eric are attending a party.

Jim: Excuse me, old **cock**. If you have a **rubber** handy, could you kindly **hump** it here?

Eric: No problem. Keep your **pecker** up! I always have one handy. By the way, every time I get **screwed**, I seem to crave a **fag**! Do you happen to have one I could borrow?

Same Dialogue as Heard by Americans

Jim: Excuse me, old **penis**. If you have a **condom** handy, could you kindly **rub your genitals on it** here?

Eric: No problem. Keep your **penis** erect! I always have one handy. By the way, every time I have **sexual intercourse**, I seem to crave a **homosexual**! Do you happen to have one I could borrow?

(Same Dialogue in American-English)

Jim: Excuse me, old **friend**. If you have an **eraser** handy, could you kindly **bring it** here?

Eric: No problem. Keep your **chin** up! I always have one handy. By the way, every time I get **intoxicated**, I seem to crave a **cigarette**! Do you happen to have one I could borrow?

American-English vs. British-English

Preparing for a trip to a foreign country where you don't know the language can lead to a great deal of anxiety and hassle. Many travelers submerge themselves in intensive language courses prior to departure, some dash off to bookstores in order to find appropriate pocket-sized dictionaries, and others buy expensive miniature computerized translators.

For the native-born American, it's very simple preparing to go to another English-speaking country like England, Australia, or Ireland, for example. After all, we all speak the exact same language, right? *Wrong!*

Although our languages are basically the same, there are some dangerous differences that could easily lead the speaker into great embarrassment, misunderstanding and even peril. For example, if an American were to attend a soccer game in Australia and announce that he was "rooting" for a certain player, he may find himself surrounded by some rather stunned Aussies since the verb *"to root"* means "to have sexual intercourse." Furthermore, if a native of Ireland were to visit the U.S. and declare that she went to a party and had "some great crack," her American friends would assume that she is a drug addict since *"crack"* is a very popular American slang term for "cocaine." However, in Ireland, *"to have some great crack"* simply means "to have a great time."

The following list offers translations of many common terms and expressions which have completely different meanings depending on whether or not they are used in America or England:

Have you ever seen so much spunk?

What an American hears:
Have you ever seen so much boldness?

What a Brit hears:
Have you ever seen so much sperm?

I'm stuffed!

What an American hears:
I'm extremely full!

What a Brit hears:
I've had sexual intercourse!

Do you want to go, Roger?

What an American hears:
Do you want to leave, Roger?

What a Brit hears:
Do you want to go have sex?

Hello. I'm Randy.

What an American hears:
Hello. I'm Randy.

What a Brit hears:
Hello. I'm extremely horny.

Do you have a rubber I could borrow?

What an American hears:
Do you have a condom I could borrow?

What a Brit hears:
Do you have an eraser I could borrow?

Why are you humping that?

What an American hears:
Why are you rubbing your genitals against that?

What a Brit hears:
Why are you carrying that?

Keep your pecker up!

What an American hears:
Keep your penis erect!

What a Brit hears:
Keep your chin up!

It certainly didn't take you long to get screwed at the party!

What an American hears:
It certainly didn't take you long to have sexual intercourse at the party!

What a Brit hears:
It certainly didn't take you long to get intoxicated at the party!

Still indulging in fags, I see.

What an American hears:
Still indulging in homosexuals, I see.

What a Brit hears:
Still indulging in cigarettes, I see.

I'll knock you up tomorrow morning.

What an American hears:
I'll get you pregnant tomorrow morning.

What a Brit hears:
I'll stop by your house tomorrow morning.

How about a ride?

What an American hears:
How about passage in your car?

What a Brit hears:
How about sex?

What balls!

What an American hears:
What testicles!

What a Brit hears:
What nonsense!

Wanna banger?

What an American hears:
Do you want to have sexual intercourse with her?

What a Brit hears:
Do you want a sausage?

♦ NOTE: *"Banger"* is the colloquial American pronunciation of *"Bang her"* meaning "to have sexual intercourse with her."

I'll be over soon to beat you up.

What an American hears:
I'll be over soon to batter you.

What a Brit hears:
I'll be over soon to pick you up.

The play was a bomb!

What an American hears:
The play was a huge failure!

What a Brit hears:
The play was a huge success!

I've never seen such a cock-up in my life!

What an American hears:
I've never seen such an erect penis in my life!

What a Brit hears:
I've never seen such a muddled situation in my life!

My sister slipped in the snow and fell on her fanny!

What an American hears:
My sister slipped in the snow and fell on her buttocks!

What a Brit hears:
My sister slipped in the snow and fell on her vagina.

▶ NOTE: In England, the term *"fanny"* is one of the worst obscenities one can use. It is comparable to the American term *"cunt"* and should therefore be used with extreme caution.

He's very fruity.

What an American hears:
He's very effeminate.

What a Brit hears:
He's very sexy.

My boss gave me the bird today!

What an American hears:
My boss gestured "Fuck you!" to me today!

What a Brit hears:
My boss fired me today!

Go to bed!

What an American hears:
Go to bed!

What a Brit hears:
Shut up!

I hear your mother is very homely.

What an American hears:
I hear your mother is very ugly.

What a Brit hears:
I hear your mother is very domestic.

He honked for me when he arrived.

What an American hears:
He tooted his horn for me when he arrived.

What a Brit hears:
He threw up for me when he arrived.

I've never seen such big hooters!

What an American hears:
I've never seen such big breasts!

What a Brit hears:
I've never seen such big noses!

He wouldn't stop poking me during the entire movie!

What an American hears:
He wouldn't stop jabbing me in the ribs with his finger during the entire movie!

What a Brit hears:
He wouldn't stop having sexual intercourse with me during the entire movie!

Does he look queer to you?

What an American hears:
Does he look homosexual to you?

What a Brit hears:
Does he look troubled to you?

As soon as I got home, I shot the cat.

What an American hears:
As soon as I got home, I killed the cat with a gun.

What a Brit hears:
As soon as I got home, I threw up.

What's that sod doing here?

What an American hears:
What's that dirt and grass doing here?

What a Brit hears:
What's that bastard doing here?

VULGAR GESTURES

– Handy Hand Gestures from a Safe Distance –

VULGAR GESTURES
Handy-Hand Gestures from a Safe Distance

Since learning a language is the only way a non-native speaker can fully integrate into a particular society, language courses both spoken and sign are offered all over the world. One of the most common and important languages that seems to have been overlooked is the language of gestures.

For the perpetrator of a vulgar gesture who does not want to be attacked physically, one quick gesture is usually all it takes to convey a pointed message. This also ensures the messenger a hasty retreat.

The next illustrated list will demonstrate some of the most popular obscene gestures known by any native-born American:

– The Finger –
(also known as "The Bird" & "The One Finger Salute")

This is perhaps the most widely used obscene gesture in America which is used to represent the male genitalia. It effectively symbolizes the vulgar expression *"Fuck you!"* and is usually used when there is sufficient distance between the sender and recipient to avoid possible physical confrontation.

Interestingly enough, this gesture is used in many parts of the world and takes on a different look as we travel from the west coast of America and onward:

WEST COAST

EAST COAST

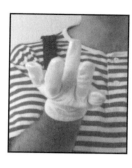

FRANCE

MIDDLE EAST

◆ NOTE: *(It is interesting to note that in Europe, it is common to point to something on paper by using the middle finger which seems to surprise Americans who visit abroad.)*

This basic gesture is also commonly enlarged to a grandiose maneuver using the entire arm:

Another descriptive way of gesturing *"Fuck you!"* is to make a circle with the thumb and index finger of one hand and inserting the index finger of the other hand back and forth through the circle:

– The "Groin Grab" –

This is a common gesture signifying *"I don't believe a word you're saying!"* It merely consists of putting one's hand on one's own groin and rubbing up and down. It is also common to take the most unbelievable part of the speaker's story and fit it into the phrase, *"I've got your _____ right here!"* while executing the gesture:

For example:

"If you do me this favor, I'll give you a million dollars."

"I've got your million dollars right here!"

– The "Stop Trying to Deceive Me" Gesture –

This is probably one of the most crude gestures in the American repertoire yet it has become extremely popular. The gesture represents the vulgar slang expression, *"Stop trying to jack me off"* (literally meaning "Stop trying to masturbate me") which is used to signify "Stop trying to deceive me" or more accurately, "Stop telling me lies in order to make me feel good."

The gesture is achieved by pretending to hold a large imaginary penis in one's hand and stroking it up and down:

1.

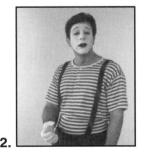

2.

A CLOSER LOOK
How to Insult Virtually Everyone... Unintentionally!

Learning gestures is a necessity for any traveler since many gestures have completely different meanings outside the United States. Many American gestures which are humorous, light, and simply second nature can be interpreted as offensive, malicious, and even combative in other countries.

The following examples may surely save you from great embarrassment, condemnation and very possibly assault:

– The "OKAY" Gesture –

This is an extremely popular American gesture which simply means *"Everything is fine"* or *"Well done!"* It is executed by forming a circle with the thumb and index finger leaving the other three fingers straight up. However, in Brazil and Greece this circle represents the anal sphincter and consequently, symbolizes *"You asshole!"*

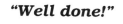

U.S.A.   CANADA

BRAZIL   GREECE

– Indicating "Two" –

Even before we learn the alphabet, we are taught how to count using our fingers. Holding up fingers to indicate numbers 1 through 5 seems to be especially second nature. If we order 2 pastries at a bakery, we may instinctively hold up 2 fingers. However, if you do this same seemingly innocent gesture in England, instead of receiving your 2 pastries, you may receive 2 black eyes!

In England, to hold up 2 fingers with the back of the hand facing the other person means only one thing, *"Up yours!"* or *"Fuck you!"* since both fingers represent 2 phallic symbols:

U.S.A.

CANADA

ENGLAND

"I'd like two of those please."   **"Fuck you!"**

In England, the correct way to gesture "2" is to hold up your thumb and index finger. Unlike Americans who start counting with the index finger, Europians begin with the thumb:

ENGLAND

"Two please."

– *The Hitchhiking Gesture* –

Hitchhiking can be more dangerous than you think. An American traditionally stands on the curb with his arm held out straight toward the street, fist clenched and thumb extended upward.

In Nigeria however, this gesture symbolizes the male penis and means *"Fuck you!"* Americans who have traveled to Nigeria no doubt have felt that the natives are insensitive to hitchhikers due to their hostile response:

"Could you please give me a lift?!"

"Fuck you!"

U.S.A.   CANADA

NIGERIA

– *The Beckoning Gesture* –

When gesturing for someone to approach, it is common in America to use the index finger. However, it would certainly not be advisable to use this gesture when inviting a Yugoslavian or Malaysian to join you since this gesture is only used with animals and would cause great offense.

Most importantly, if you were to use this gesture with a woman in Indonesia or Australia, you would either be slapped or find yourself with a companion for the evening as this is the gesture for summoning prostitutes:

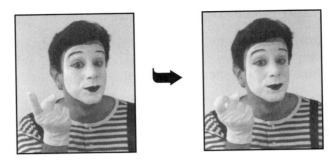

      "Come here."

U.S.A.   CANADA

      "I'd like to buy your
                              services for the evening."

AUSTRALIA   INDONESIA

In many European and Latin American countries the correct way to beckon someone is to turn the hand upside-down with the palm facing the ground. The thumb is held still while the other four fingers extend straight then curl several times:

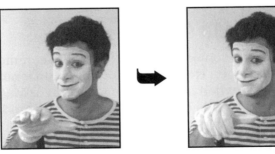

"Come here."

Beckoning a waiter can be potentially hazardous for a Mexican who is unfamiliar with American gestures. In Mexico it is customary to make a kissing sound with the mouth aimed at the server. This is identical to the American gesture for "Kiss my ass!" which is an extremely abusive expression of contempt:

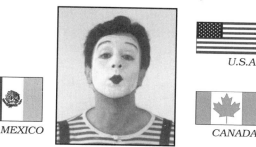

MEXICO
U.S.A.
CANADA

"Come here."   **"Kiss my ass!"**

– The "Stop" Gesture –

Near elementary schools, it is common to see a crossing guard assisting children across the screen. The crossing guard will typically extend his arm out straight with his hand open and palm facing the traffic. American drivers understand this gesture and come to a stop to allow the pedestrians to cross.

However, if the crossing guard were to make the same gesture in Greece, the drivers would undoubedtly not stop; quite the contrary. They would most likely speed up and aim! The reason for this is because in Greece this gesture symbolizes pushing fecal matter into the face of the other person. In can be compared to the American expression, *"Eat shit!"*:

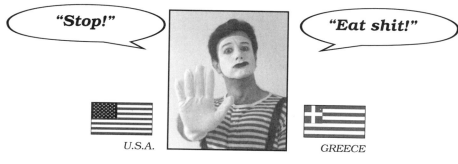

"Stop!"   **"Eat shit!"**

U.S.A.   *GREECE*

– The "Stand-There-and-Wait" Gesture –

Often when we are in a position of waiting, we occupy ourselves in various ways such as by doing something physical like swinging our arms and hitting the open palm of one hand with the fist of the other as the arms meet in front of the body.

It would not be advisable however, to make such a gesture in public while visiting Chile or France unless, of course, you are purposely trying to signify "Up yours!":

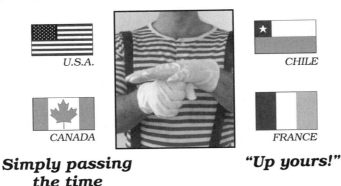

U.S.A.

CANADA

CHILE

FRANCE

Simply passing the time

"Up yours!"

– The "Thumbs Up" Gesture –

To convey agreement or satisfaction, it is common practice to give a *"thumbs up"* sign by making a fist and extending the thumb straight up. This gesture is also commonly followed by a slight upward jerk of the entire fist.

Any American who has used this gesture in Australia has learned quickly that it carries only one meaning... *"Up yours!"*:

"A-okay!"

"Up yours!"

U.S.A.

AUSTRALIA

– A Gesture of Greeting –

Many natives of Tibet must surely feel that Americans are extremely unfriendly upon first meeting. After all, when greeted by a Tibetan, many Americans seem aloof, annoyed, even disgusted. There is a simple reason for this. The Tibetan is unaware that his traditional greeting of sticking out his tongue as a gesture of friendship is interpreted by Americans as being rude and insolent:

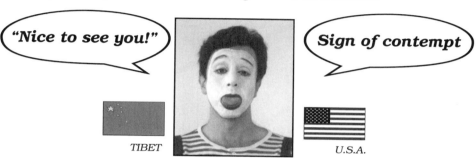

TIBET U.S.A.

– The "I Got Your Nose" Gesture –

American adults commonly play a game with little children whereby the adult slips his curled index and middle fingers on either side of the child's nose. Upon pulling the fingers away from the child, the adult quickly sticks his thumb between the two fingers and triumphantly shouts, *"I got your nose!"*

To do this to a Mexican child would be unwise, especially in front of his parents who would be shocked and furious. Innocently, the unsuspecting America has just made the Mexican gesture for *"Fuck you!"* since the thumb is used to represent the male penis:

U.S.A. MEXICO

– The European "Hand-In-The-Lap" Gesture –

In American families, we are told to keep our elbows off the table since it is considered bad manners. It is therefore quite common to eat with one hand resting in one's lap.

If you have ever done this in Europe, you have committed an obscene act since you may be suspected of either playing sexually with yourself or your neighbor!:

U.S.A.   FRANCE

– Gesturing Yes and No –

This can lead to great confusion and misunderstanding between Americans and Bulgarians. In America, we nod our heads up and down to signify "yes" and back and forth to signify "no." However, in Bulgaria it's just the opposite!:

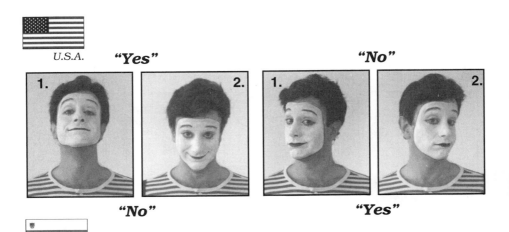

U.S.A.   *"Yes"*   *"No"*

"No"   *"Yes"*

BULGARIA

ANSWERS TO LESSONS 1-6

LESSON ONE - *Euphemisms*
(The Camp Out)

Practice the Vocabulary

A. 1. Guy
2. bleeping
3. crud
4. heck
5. Geez
6. P.O.'d
7. Shoot
8. friggin'
9. Darn
10. mother

B. 1. E
2. G
3. F
4. A
5. B
6. H
7. K
8. C
9. J
10. I
11. D

C. **WORD SEARCH**

1. Geez
2. you-know-what
3. arse
4. (the) heck
5. Shoot
6. Drat
7. darn
8. French
9. crud
10. mother
11. bleeping
12. B.I.T.C.H.

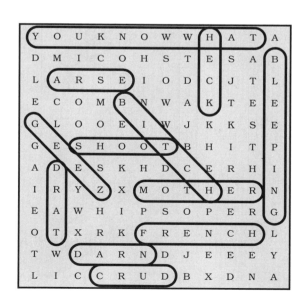

LESSON TWO - *Non-Vulgar Insults*
(At the Market)

Practice the Vocabulary

A. 1. She's so tall!
   2. He's rather ugly.
   3. He's a little bald.
   4. She's an extremely generous person.
   5. Have you ever met such a nice person?
   6. My brother's new girlfriend is really wonderful.
   7. She's a real beauty!
   8. The new librarian is a good driver!
   9. What a gourmet!
   10. That pretty girl forgot to pick me up at the airport.

B. 1. billiard
   2. uglies
   3. fish
   4. crazo
   5. motormouth
   6. tramp
   7. creep
   8. slob
   9. chicken
   10. runt
   11. stuck
   12. wheels

FIND-THE- WORD-CUBE

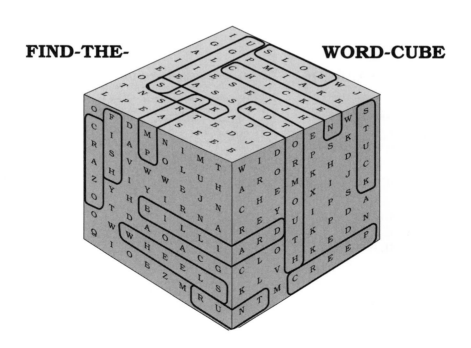

C. 1. b
  2. a
  3. b
  4. a

5. b
6. a
7. a
8. b

LESSON THREE - *Vulgar Insults*
(At School)

Practice the Vocabulary

A. 1. fucker
  2. pisser
  3. head
  4. rocks
  5. rag
  6. son

7. bull
8. up
9. ass
10. brains
11. asshole
12. bites

B. **"CUSSWORD" PUZZLE**

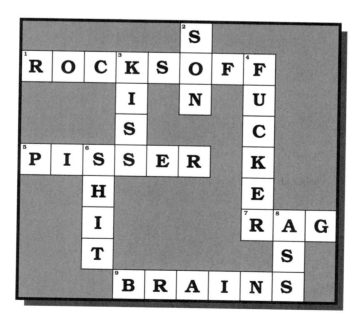

LESSON FOUR - *The Many Uses of Shit*
(The Hollywood Studio Tour)

Practice the Vocabulary

A. 1. the shit
   2. shittiest
   3. hot shit
   4. shitlist
   5. shit-faced
   6. for shit

   7. catch shit
   8. pulled some shit
   9. shit
 10. shit creek
 11. shit out of luck
 12. shitload

B. 1. L
   2. B
   3. J
   4. D
   5. K
   6. A

   7. E
   8. H
   9. F
 10. C
 11. G
 12. I

C. **"CUSSWORD" PUZZLE**

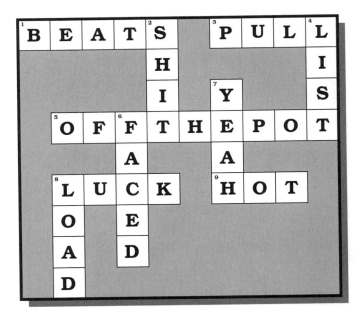

LESSON FIVE - *The Many Uses of Fuck*
(The New Car)

Practice the Vocabulary

A. 1. b
   2. a
   3. b
   4. b
   5. b

   6. a
   7. a
   8. a
   9. a
 10. a

B. 1. mother-fucking
   2. fucked with
   3. fucked
   4. fucked over
   5. dumbfuck

   6. Fuckin' A
   7. Fuck that noise
   8. fucked up
   9. what the fuck

LESSON SIX - *Prostitution, Drug, & Police Slang*
(Taking a Stroll)

Practice the Vocabulary

A. 1. out
   2. cops
   3. mack
   4. madame
   5. red
   6. smack

   7. turf
   8. busted
   9. hooker
 10. cigarette
 11. cruising
 12. whorehouse.

B. 1. J
   2. B
   3. D
   4. G
   5. C
   6. A

   7. E
   8. H
   9. L
 10. K
 11. I
 12. F

Glossary

The glossary contains all the slang, idioms, and expressions that were used in the dialogues.

-A-

a few miles on him/her (to have) *exp.* (humorous) to be old.
 ◆ NOTE: This is a common expression traditionally applied to an old car.

A.I.D.S. *n.* Acquired Immune Deficiency Syndrome.

absofuckin'lutely *adv.* absolutely • *Do I like her? Absofuckin'lutely!;* Do I like her? Absolutely!
 ◆ NOTE: The "-ing" ending in this expression is commonly reduced to "-in'."

acid *n.* lysergic acid diethylamide (L.S.D.)

airhead (to be an) *n.* (mild) an irresponsible and unthinking person • (lit); one who has nothing but air in the head.

all over each other (to be) *exp.* (mild) • **1.** said of two people who are kissing each other aggressively • **2.** said of two people who are having aggressive sex • *No matter where they are, they're always all over each other;* No matter where they are, they're always kissing each other aggressively (or having aggressive sex).
 ◆ NOTE: The difference between definitions **1.** and **2.** depend on the context.

Andy Gump *n.* (mild) a portable toilet devised by an inventor named Andy Gump.

angel *n.* heroin.

antifreeze *n.* heroin.

arse *n.* • **1.** idiot, fool, jerk • *Don't act like such an arse!;* Don't act like such a jerk! • **2.** buttocks • *When I went skiing yesterday, I kept falling on my arse;* When I went skiing yesterday, I kept falling on my butt.
 ◆ ORIGIN: This is commonly used as a euphemism for **"ass"** *n.* (lit); buttocks. The term *"ass"* is actually a shortened version of *"asshole"* meaning a "contemptible person" or literally "anus." For some reason, the shortened version, *"ass,"* is considered somewhat vulgar but not obscene. However, its complete form, *"asshole"* is indeed regarded as obscene and offensive. Both terms are extremely popular.

ass *n.* (vulgar) • **1.** buttocks • *That guy slapped me on my ass while I was standing on the bus!;* That man slapped me on my buttocks while I was standing on the bus! • **2.** imbecile • *Stop acting like such an ass;* Stop acting like such an imbecile. • **3.** despicable person.

ass backwards (to be) *exp.* said of something that was assembled backwards • *I think you put that*

170

bicycle together ass backwards. The handle bars should be in the front, not in the back!; I think you put that bicycle together backwards. The handle bars should be in the front, not in the back!
♦ NOTE: On occasion, you may even hear some people invert the word *"ass backwards"* to *"bass ackwards"* to stress humorously that the object is completely backwards.

ass hole *n.* (vulgar) a despicable person • (lit); anal sphincter.

ass licker (to be an) *exp.* said of someone who does anything to get in the good graces of one's superior • *Yesterday, Jim bought the boss lunch and even offered to drive him to the airport. That guy's such an ass licker!;* Yesterday, Jim bought the boss lunch and even offered to drive him to the airport. That man will do anything to get in the good grace of the boss.
♦ SYNONYM: See: **kiss-ass**.
♦ ALSO: **to lick someone's ass** *exp.* • *It's really obvious that you're trying to lick the teacher's ass;* It's really obvious that you're trying to get in the good graces of the teacher.

ass peddler *n.* (vulgar) prostitute • (lit); buttocks seller.
♦ NOTE: This term refers to a male or female prostitute.

ass wipe *n.* (vulgar) a despicable person • (lit); toilet paper.

asshole (to be an) *n.* (vulgar) to be a despicable person • (lit); to be an anal sphincter • *He lied and got me into trouble. Can you believe what an asshole he is?;* He lied and got me into trouble. Can you believe what a despicable person he is?

asswipe *n.* • (lit); toilet paper • *extremely despicable person • How can you like him? He's such an*

asswipe!; How can you like him? He's such a despicable person!

au naturel (to be) *adj.* (mild) to be naked.
♦ NOTE: This comes from French meaning "to be natural."

"Aunt Flo's here" *exp.* (somewhat crude yet humorous) to menstruate.
♦ NOTE: This is a play-on-words since the proper name *"Flo"* is a homonym of the verb *"flow"* referring to the flowing of one's blood during menstruation.

-B-

B.F. *n.* despicable person • *He's such a B.F.!;* He's such a despicable person.
♦ NOTE: This is a euphemistic abbreviation of *"butt fucker"* which is considered extremely vulgar.

B.F.D. *exp.* used to indicate great indifference • *I know you lost the contest but B.F.D. You'll try again next time;* I know you lost the contest but don't be concerned. You'll try again next time.
♦ NOTE: This is a euphemistic abbreviation of *"big fucking deal"* which is considered vulgar.

B.I.T.C.H. *n.* • (lit); female dog • **1.** unpleasant woman • *She's a real B.I.T.C.H.;* She's a really unpleasant woman. • **2.** extremely difficult • *This work is such a B.I.T.C.H!;* This work is extremely difficult!
♦ NOTE: To create a euphemism out of an obscene or coarse word, many people simply just spell it out. This tends to relieve the severity of the word since we don't actually hear the term in its entirety. The term *"bitch"* is considered only somewhat coarse to most people and is therefore commonly heard in most situations. There are some, however, who feel that it is still

unpleasant language and will only spell it out.

♦ NOTE: The use of *B.I.T.C.H.* in the examples above, are extremely popular in the "un-spelled" form of the term and are heard frequently: *She's a real bitch!* • *This work is such a bitch!*

B.J. *exp.* oral sex • *I heard she gave him a B.J. last night;* I heard she gave him oral sex last night.

♦ NOTE: This is a euphemistic abbreviation of *"blow job"* which is considered vulgar.

B.M. *n.* a common abbreviation of "bowel movement" • *The baby had a B.M. in her diapers;* The baby had a bowel movement in her diapers.

♦ ALSO: **to B.M.** *v.* • *Your little sister just B.M.'d on the floor;* Your little sister just defecated on the floor.

B.S. *exp.* nonsense • *That's a bunch of B.S.!;* That's a bunch of nonsense!

♦ NOTE: This is a euphemistic abbreviation of *"bullshit,"* (literally "bull excrement") which is considered vulgar.

baby (to be a) *n.* (mild) name given to a fearful person since babies are known for being easily frightened • *He's such a baby!;* He's such a fearful person!

♦ VARIATION: **big baby** *n.* an adult who acts like a baby.

back teeth floating (to have one's) *exp.* a humorous, yet crude, description of someone who has to urinate so badly it's as if the urine were rising to the level of one's back teeth • *My back teeth are floating!;* I have to urinate badly!

bad case of the uglies (to have a) *exp.* (humorous) to be extremely ugly • *He's got a bad case of the uglies!;* He's really ugly!

♦ SYNONYM: **to have a face that**

could stop a clock *exp.* (humorous).

badass (to be) *adj.* (teen slang) • **1.** bad and dangerous • *Don't get him mad. That guy's badass!;* Don't get him mad. That guy's bad and dangerous! • **2.** good and impressive • *I watched you play tennis yesterday. You're really badass!;* I watched you play tennis yesterday. You're really impressive!

♦ NOTE: The difference between definitions **1.** and **2.** depends on the context.

badge *n.* (mild) police officer.

bag of bones (to be a) *exp.* (mild) to be extremely thin.

bag of wind (to be a) *exp.* (humorous).

♦ NOTE: This expression is said of someone who talks so much that all they appear to be doing is exhaling.

♦ VARIATION: **to be a windbag** *n.*

bagman *n.* drug supplier.

bald as a billiard ball (to be as) *exp.* (humorous) to be extremely bald • *That guy's as bald as a billiard ball!;* That guy's totally bald!

♦ SYNONYM: **to be as bald as an eagle** *exp.* (humorous).

bald as an eagle (to be) *exp.* (mild) to be completely hairless on one's head.

baldy *n.* (mild) name given to a bald person • *Hey, Baldy!;* Hey, you bald person!

ball (to) *v.* (vulgar) to fornicate • *Did you ball her yesterday?;* Did you have sex with her yesterday?

♦ NOTE: This verb comes from the slang connotation of *"balls"* meaning "testicles."

balloons *n.pl.* (humorous) large breasts.

balls *n.pl.* (very popular yet vulgar) testicles.

baloney *n.* nonsense (may be used as a euphemistic replacement for *"bullshit"* which is considered vulgar) • *You actually believed that baloney?;* You actually believed that nonsense?

bananas (to be) *adj.*
  ▶ VARIATION: **to go bananas** *exp.* to go crazy • *He went bananas;* He went crazy.

bang (to) *v.* (vulgar) to fornicate • *Did you see them leave the party early? I bet they went to go bang in the car!;* Did you see them leave the party early? I bet they went to go have sex in the car!
  ▶ ALSO: **to gang bang** *exp.* to have sex with many partners at the same time; to have an orgy.

bare-assed (to be) *adj.* (crude yet very popular) to be naked • (lit); to have one's naked buttocks exposed.

barf (to) *v.* (extremely popular and mild) to vomit.

barrels *n.pl.* lysergic acid diethylamide (L.S.D.)

basket *n.* (mild) penis and testicles together, genitalia.

bastard *n.* (vulgar) a despicable person • (lit); an illegitimate son.
  ▶ NOTE: This applies to males only.

bats in the belfry (to have) *exp.* (humorous).
  ▶ NOTE: This is a humorous expression signifying that the subject has something wrong in his/her head.
  ▶ VARIATION: **to be batty** *adj.*

battering ram *n.* (mild) penis.
  ▶ NOTE: This term is used due to its similarity in shape and action of a penis during sex.

bazongas *n.pl.* (humorous) large breasts.

bazooka *n.* (mild) penis.
  ▶ NOTE: This term is used due to its similarity in shape to a penis. This is also used to mean large protruding breasts, depending on the context.

bazookas *n.pl.* (humorous) large breasts.

bazooms *n.pl.* (humorous) breasts.
  ▶ NOTE: This is a humorous transformation of the term "bosoms."

bean pole (to be a) *exp.* (humorous) to be very thin.

bearded clam *n.* a somewhat humorous, yet crude, comparison of the vagina to a *"bearded clam."*

beat artist *n.* drug supplier.

beat off (to) *v.* to masturbate • *He beats off to dirty magazines;* He masturbates to pornographic magazines.
  ▶ NOTE (1): This is probably the most common, yet vulgar, slang expression for "to masturbate."
  ▶ NOTE (2): This verbs comes from the beating motion associated with masturbation.

beat one's meat (to) *exp.* to masturbate • *He beats his meat every night;* He masturbates every night.
  ▶ NOTE: The term *"meat"* is commonly used in slang to mean "penis."

beat the shit out of someone (to) *exp.* to beat someone severely • *When I find him, I'm gonna beat the shit out of him!;* When I find him, I'm going to beat him severely!

beaten with the ugly stick (to be) *exp.* (humorous) said of someone who is extremely ugly.
  ▶ VARIATION: **to be hit with the ugly stick** *exp.* (humorous).

"Beats the shit out of me" *exp.* "I don't know"

beaver *n.* a popular, yet crude, synonym for *vagina* due to its fur.

been around (to have) *exp.* (mild) •
1. to be old • **2.** to have had sex
with a variety of people.

behind *n.* (mild) buttocks • *Get your*
behind over here; Come here.
  ◗ VARIATION: **heinie** *n.* (mild) an
  abbreviation of *"behind."*

big C *n.* cocaine.

big cage *n.* police officer.

big D *n.* lysergic acid diethylamide
(L.S.D.)

Big Harry *n.* heroin.

big house *n.* prison (used primarily
in old gangster movies).

big man *n.* drug supplier.

big mouth (to have a) *n.* (mild) to be
extremely talkative.

"Big Red dropped in" *exp.*
(somewhat crude yet humorous) to
menstruate.

"Big shit!" *exp.* "It's not a big
problem!" • *Why are you so upset*
about losing? Big shit!; Why are
you so upset about losing? It's not
a big problem!

bimbo *n.* (mild) • 1. prostitute • **2.**
foolish girl.
  ◗ NOTE: This terms refers to a
  female prostitute.

bird legs (to have) *exp.* (mild) said of
a person with extremely thin legs.

birdbrain (to be a) *n.* (humorous) to
be excessively dumb • *Can you*
believe she forgot where she
parked yesterday? What a
birdbrain!; Can you believe she
forgot where she parked
yesterday? She's so dumb!
  ◗ NOTE: This is said of someone
  whose brain appears to be the size
  of that of a bird.

bitch (to be a) *n.* (somewhat coarse) •
1. unpleasant woman • *You like*
her? She can be such a bitch!; You
like her? She can be so
unpleasant! • **2.** unpleasant man
(especially used among gays) •

What a bitch!; What an unpleasant
man! • **3.** difficult • *This job is a*
real bitch!; This job is really
difficult!
  ◗ NOTE (1): bitchy *adj.* (somewhat
  coarse) unpleasant (may be used
  for a man or woman) • *I asked her*
  a simple question and she got all
  bitchy with me!; I asked her a
  simple question and she became
  extremely unpleasant with me!
  ◗ NOTE (2): to bitch *v.* (somewhat
  coarse) to complain • *Stop bitching*
  and just try to enjoy yourself; Stop
  complaining and just try to enjoy
  yourself.

bitch on wheels (to be a) *exp.*
(humorous yet somewhat crude) to
be exceptionally shrewish • *Why is*
she being so nasty? What a bitch
on wheels!; Why is she being so
nasty? What a shrew!

bite (to) *v.* (vulgar) to be terrible • *It*
bites that she did that to you; It's
terrible that she did that to you.
  ◗ **CAUTION**: It is important to
  note that *"to bite"* is a variation on
  the popular expression *"to bite the*
  big one," *"the big one"* being a
  euphemism for "penis." Therefore,
  "to bite" should be used with
  caution due to its reference.
  ◗ SYNONYM: **to suck** *v.* (vulgar).
    ⇨ **CAUTION**: It is important to
    note that *"to suck"* is a shortened
    version of the popular expression
    "to suck dick," *"dick"* being a slang
    synonym for "penis." Therefore,
    "to suck" should be used with
    caution due to its reference.

blabbermouth (to be a) *n.* (mild).
  ◗ NOTE: to blabber *v.* to talk
  excessively.

black and white *n.* (mild) police car.
  ◗ NOTE: This term refers to the
  traditional black and white colors
  of a police car.

black tar *n.* heroin.

blast (to) *v.* to take drugs.

blazes *n.* used in surprise to add emphasis to a question (may be used as a euphemistic replacement for *"hell"* which is considered harsh) • (lit); fire • *What the blazes is he doing here?!*
♦ VARIATION: **blue blazes** *exp.* • (lit); extremely hot fire • *What in blue blazes did you do to my car?!*

bleed the weasel (to) *exp.* (humorous) to masturbate • *I can hear him bleeding the weasel next door;* I can hear him masturbating next door.
♦ NOTE: This is a humorous, yet crude, expression comparing the action of masturbating with that of *"bleeding a weasel."*

bleeping *adj.* This is commonly used as a euphemistic replacement for the adjective *"fucking"* which means "intense." (The term *"fuck"* will be discuss in depth in lesson five). Its origin comes from television and radio where a "bleep" sound is commonly used to replace obscene words.
♦ VARIATION: **bleepity bleep** *n.* • *That bleepity-bleep cop gave me a ticket!;* That fucking police officer gave me a ticket!

blimp (to be a) *exp.* • (lit); to be (as fat as) a dirigible.
♦ VARIATION: **to be a blimpo** *adj.*

blockhead (to be a) *n.* (mild) a ridiculous and unthinking person • (lit); one who has a block of wood (which has no brains) for a head.

blotters *n.pl.* lysergic acid diethylamide (L.S.D.)

blow (to) *exp.* (vulgar) • **1.** to perform oral sex • *Did you get blown last night?;* Did you have oral sex last night? • **2.** to have an orgasm • (lit); to explode • *I'm gonna blow!;* I'm going to have an orgasm! • **3.** to take drugs, primarily cocaine (known only in the drug world).

blow *n.* cocaine.

blow chow (to) *exp.* (crude, due to its descriptive nature) to vomit • (lit); to explode with food.
♦ NOTE (1): to blow *n.* to explode.
♦ NOTE (2): chow *n.* food.

blow chunks (to) *exp.* (very crude, due to its extreme descriptive nature) to vomit • (lit); to explode with chunks of food.
♦ NOTE: to blow *n.* to explode.

blow coke (to) *v.* to take drugs.

blow job (to give a) *exp.* to perform oral sex • *She gave him a blow job last night;* She performed oral sex on him last night.

blow snow (to) *v.* to take drugs.

blowhard (to be a) *n.* (mild) one who talks excessively about unrealistic ideas.

blown away (to be) *adj.*

blown out (to be) *adj.* to be on drugs.

blubberhead (to be a) *n.* (mild) an unthinking person • (lit); one who has nothing but blubber for a brain.

blue (to be) *adj.* (mild) to be pornographic • *The language in the movie was very blue;* The language in the movie was very vulgar.
♦ NOTE: When said of a person, the connotation of *"blue"* changes to "melancholy."

blue acid *n.* lysergic acid diethylamide (L.S.D.)

blue balls (to have) *exp.* to have gonorrhea.

blue cheer *n.* lysergic acid diethylamide (L.S.D.)

blue flag *n.* lysergic acid diethylamide (L.S.D.)

blue heaven *n.* lysergic acid diethylamide (L.S.D.)

body shop *n.* (mild) brothel.

boink (to) *v.* (humorous) to fornicate • *I think she wants to boink you;* I think she wants to have sex with you.

bone *n.* (crude) penis.
▶ NOTE: This term signifies an erect penis which is as hard as a bone. In addition, a common term for an erect penis is a "*boner.*"

bonehead (to be a) *n.* (mild) a nonsensical and unthinking person • (lit); one who has nothing but a bone for a head.

boner (to have a) *n.* (crude yet very popular) to be sexually aroused.
▶ NOTE: This term signifies a penis which is as erect and as hard as a bone.
▶ VARIATION: **to have a bone** *n.* (crude).

bonkers (to be) *adj.*
▶ VARIATION: **to go bonkers** *exp.* to become crazy • *When she lost the contest, she went bonkers;* When she lost the contest, she became crazy.

boob (to be a) *n.* (mild) an ridiculous and unthinking person, a fool.

boobies *n.pl.* breasts.

boobs *n.pl.* breasts.

book (to) *v.* (mild) to arrest and process.

bordello *n.* (mild) brothel.

both oars in the water (not to have) *exp.* (humorous) said of a slightly crazy person • *She doesn't have both oars in the water;* She's rather crazy.

bottom *n.* (mild) buttocks.

box *n.* (crude) vagina.

box lunch *exp.* (humorous, yet crude) vagina.
▶ NOTE: This is a play-on-words since this term has the traditional meaning of "a prepared lunch taken to work, school, etc. in a box" as well as the slang connotation of "a sexually active vagina."

break wind (to) *exp.* (mild) to have flatulence.

broad in the beam (to be) *exp.* (humorous) to be fat across the rear.

broker *n.* drug supplier.

brown sugar *n.* bad heroin.

buck naked (to be) *exp.* (mild) to be completely naked • (lit); to be as naked as a male deer.

buds *n.pl.* marijuana.

buffalo chips *n.pl.* (mild) dried excrement left on prairies by buffalos.
▶ ALSO: **cow chips** *n.pl.* dried excrement left by cows.

buick (to) *v.* (humorous) to vomit.
▶ NOTE: This verb, also the name of an American car, signifies the sound one makes when vomiting.

built like a brick shithouse (to be) *exp.* to be extremely solid and muscular (may be said of a man or woman) • *Your boyfriend is built like a brick shithouse!;* Your boyfriend is really solid and muscular!

bullshit (to be) *exp.* (vulgar) to be nonsense • (lit); to be bull excrement • *That's a bunch of bullshit!;* That's complete nonsense!
▶ NOTE: Any expression containing the term "*shit*" is vulgar.

bum *n.* (mild) buttocks.

bum-fuck *adj.* distant • *She wants me to drive to all the way to bum-fuck Idaho!;* She wants me to drive her all the way to distant Idaho!

bump (to) *v.* (humorous) to fornicate • *I know he asked you to go to the movies but I think all he wants to do is bump!;* I know he asked you to go to the movies but I think all he wants to do is have sex!

bump and grind (to) *exp.* (mild) to have aggressive sex • *They did a lot of bumping and grinding all night long!;* They had aggressive sex all night long.

bumpers *n.pl.* (humorous) large breasts.
 ♦ NOTE: This is a humorous term comparing the *"bumpers"* of a car with a woman's "breasts."

buns *n.* (not vulgar and extremely popular) buttocks • *He's got cute buns!;* He has cute buttocks!

burnt out (to be) *adj.* (mild and very popular) • **1.** to be overdosed with drugs • **2.** to be exhausted.
 ♦ VARIATION: **to be burned out**

business (to do one's) *exp.* a euphemism for "to defecate" • *Steve's in the bathroom doing his business;* Steve's in the bathroom defecating.
 ♦ NOTE: This expression is more commonly used with children than it is with adults.

bust (to) *v.* (mild and very popular) to arrest.
 ♦ NOTE: to get busted *adj.* **1.** to get arrested and be given a citation or be taken to jail • **2.** to get in trouble.

butt fuck (to) *exp.* to have sexual intercourse through the anus • *I think they're into butt fucking;* I think they enjoy sexual intercourse through the anus.
 ♦ ALSO: **butt fucker** *exp.* despicable person • *What a butt fucker!;* What a despicable person!

butt naked (to be) *exp.* (mild) to be completely nude.

butt ugly (to be) *exp.* (crude yet humorous) to be extremely ugly • (lit); to be as ugly as one's buttocks.

butt-head *n.* (humorous yet somewhat crude) a despicable person.

butt-hole n. (vulgar) a despicable person • (lit); anal sphincter.

butthead (to be a) *n.* (somewhat crude) • **1.** an unthinking person • **2.** a despicable person.

-C-

C and H *n.* cocaine and heroin.

C.H.P. *n.* (mild) a popular abbreviation for "California Highway Patrol."

C.Y.A. *exp.* a euphemistic replacement for *"Cover your ass!"* meaning "Protect yourself from possible blame!" • *Make sure to tell the boss in writing that the client was the one who changed the design, not you. Remember, C.Y.A.!;* Make sure to tell the boss in writing that the client was the one who changed the design, not you. Remember, protect yourself from possible blame!

caca • **1.** *n.* nonsense (may be used as a euphemistic replacement for *"shit"* which is considered vulgar) • (lit); excrement *That story she told you is nothing but caca;* That story she told you is nothing but nonsense. • **2.** *exclam.* used to convey moderate frustration and anger • *Caca! I lost again!*

cadillac *n.* heroin.

call girl *n.* (mild) prostitute • (lit); a prostitute one calls on the phone to arrange a meeting.
 ♦ NOTE: This terms refers to a female prostitute only.

call house *n.* (mild) brothel.
 ♦ NOTE: This signifies a house, or establishment, where men call on prostitutes.

call joint *n.* (mild) brothel.
 ♦ NOTE: The term *"joint"* is slang for "establishment." Therefore, a *"call joint"* is an establishment where men call on prostitutes.

can *n.* (mild) buttocks.

can (to go to the) *n.* (somewhat crude) to go to the bathroom (and defecate or urinate, depending on the context).
 ♦ VARIATION: **to go to the can, man** *exp.*

candy man *n.* drug supplier.

cans *n.pl.* large breasts.

cat box *n.* (mild) toilet • (lit); a plastic box that indoor cats use for urination and defecation • *I'll be right back. I have to go use the cat box;* I'll be right back. I have to go use the toilet.
◗ NOTE: This term is used among women only.
◗ VARIATION: **sandbox** *n.* (mild).

catch red-handed (to) *v.* (mild) to discover someone in the act of committing a crime or prohibited act.

catch shit from (to) *exp.* to get reprimanded by • *I'm gonna catch shit from my parents when they see what I did to the car;* I'm going to get reprimanded by my parents when they see what I did to the car.

cathouse *n.* (mild) brothel.

caught in a snowstorm (to be) *exp.* to be on cocaine (since a slang word for "cocaine" is *"snow"*).

chancres *n.pl.* syphilis.

charged up (to be) *adj.* to be on drugs.

cheap (to be) *adj.* (mild) said of one who only buys goods which are inexpensive regardless of the quality.
◗ VARIATION: **to be a cheapskate** *n.* (mild) a disdainful term for one who only buys goods which are inexpensive regardless of the quality.

cheeks *n.* (mild) buttocks.

chicken ranch *n.* (mild) brothel.

chickenshit (to be) • **1.** *adj.* to be afraid • *Just go up and talk to her. Don't be so chickenshit;* Just go up and talk to her. Don't be so afraid. • **2.** *n.* to be a coward • *He's such a chickenshit;* He's such a fearful person!

Chinese red *n.* heroin.

chiva *n.* heroin.

choke the chicken (to) *exp.* (humorous) to masturbate • *All he ever thinks about is choking the chicken;* All he ever thinks about is masturbating.
◗ NOTE: This is a humorous, yet crude, expression comparing the action of masturbating with that of *"choking a chicken."*

chump (to be a) *n.* (mild) an unthinking and gullible person.

chunky (to be) *adj.* to be somewhat fat.

circle jerk (to) *exp.* to stand in a circle an masturbate simultaneously • *Can you believe he's actually into circle jerking?;* Can you believe he actually enjoys group masturbation?

circle jerk *n.* (vulgar) a group of men who masturbate while standing in a circle.

clap *n.* gonorrhea.

clink *n.* police officer (used primarily in old gangster movies).

close to one's wallet (to be) *exp.* (mild) a figurative expression said of one who guards his/her wallet closely.

close-fisted (to be) *exp.* (mild) a figurative expression said of one who keeps the fist tightly closed around his/her money to keep from spending.

cock *n.* (extremely vulgar) penis.
◗ NOTE: Due to its extreme vulgarity, many people refer to the word *"cock"* as the "C-word." The female counterpart of *"cock"* is the extremely vulgar term *"cunt"* which is also referred to by many as the "C-word."

cock-sucker *n.* (extremely vulgar) a despicable person • (lit); one who is active in oral sex.
◗ NOTE: cock *n.* (extremely vulgar) penis.

coconuts *n.pl.* (humorous) large breasts.

codger (to be a) *n.* (mild) to be an old eccentric and irritable man.
▸ VARIATION: **to be an old codger** *n.*

coke *n.* cocaine.
▸ NOTE: Since this is the same name for the popular soft drink as well, the difference in connotation simply depends on the context.

coked (to be) *adj.* to be drugged from cocaine.

coked up (to be) *adj.* to be drugged from cocaine.

cokehead *n.* (mild) cocaine addict.

cokeland *n.* the locale where cocaine is bought.

cokie *n.* cocaine user.

cola *n.* cocaine.

cold and hot *n.* cocaine and heroin.

cold fish (to be a) *exp.* (mild) to be an unemotional and unfriendly individual • *I introduced myself to her, but she was such a cold fish;* I introduced myself to her, but she was extremely unemotional and unfriendly.

collar the cock (to) *exp.* (humorous) to masturbate • *I started collaring the cock when I was 13 years old;* I started masturbating when I was 13 years old.
▸ NOTE (1): This is a humorous, yet crude, expression comparing the action of masturbating with that of *"collaring a cock."*
▸ NOTE (2): This is a sexual play-on-words since the word *"cock"* means "a male chicken" in standard English as well as "penis" in American slang.

Colombian *n.* marijuana.

come down on someone (to) *v.* (mild) • **1.** to arrest someone and issue a citation or escort to jail • **2.** to reprimand someone.

come-fuck-me boots/dress/ etc. *exp.* said of any article of clothing that is sexually alluring • *Did you see that come-fuck-me dress she's wearing?;* Did you see that alluring dress she's wearing?
▸ VARIATION: **fuck-mes** *exp.* • *I'm wearing my fuck-mes tonight!*

contact high (to have a) (to be) *adj.* to get drugged simply by being in close contact with others who are smoking.

cook (to) *v.* to take drugs.

cook on all four burners (not to) *exp.* said of a person who is slightly crazy.

cooler *n.* police officer (used primarily in old gangster movies).

cooped up (to be) *adj.* to be in prison • (lit); to be confined to a small area like a chicken coop.

cop *n.* (mild and extremely popular) police officer.
▸ NOTE: This is an abbreviation of the slang term *"copper,"* used only in old gangster movies and in jest, due to the copper badges worn by police officers.

cow (to be a) *n.* to be as fat as a cow.
▸ ALSO: **to be a fat cow** *exp.*

cow patty *n.* (mild) dried excrement left by cows.
▸ VARIATION: **cow pie** *n.* (mild).

crabs *n.pl.* sexual disease.

crack *n.* • **1.** crack cocaine • **2.** (crude) vagina.
▸ NOTE: This term signifies "vagina" due to its similarity to a *"crack."*

cracked (to be) *exp.*
▸ ALSO: **to crack [up]** *v.* to become crazy.

crackpot (to be a) *n.* one who is crazy and unpredictable, an eccentric.

crap (to) • (vulgar) **1.** *v.* to defecate • *I gotta go crap;* I have to go defecate. • **2.** *interj.* used to indicate anger •

Crap! I locked myself out of my house!; I'm so angry! I locked myself out of my house!

▸ VARIATION: **to take a crap** *exp.* (extremely popular yet vulgar) • *I have to take a crap;* I have to defecate.

▸ ALSO (1): **the crap** *exp.* to the extreme • *With our current budget, we could publicize the crap out of this book!;* With our current budget, we could publicize this book to the extreme!

▸ ALSO (2): **to scare the crap out of someone** *exp.* (extremely popular yet vulgar) to scare someone greatly • *They scared the crap out of me when they all yelled "surprise!;" They scared really scared me when they all yelled "surprise!"*

crap • **1.** *n.* nonsense (may be used as euphemistic, yet rather crude, replacement for *"shit"*) • *Why do you keep listening to his crap?;* Why do you keep listening to his nonsense? • **2.** *n.* uncivil behavior • *I'm tired of putting up with his crap!;* I'm tired of tolerating his uncivil behavior! • **3.** *exclam.* used to convey great frustration and anger • *Crap! I can't find my wallet!*

crapper *n.* (vulgar) toilet.
▸ NOTE (1): This comes from the verb *"to crap,"* meaning "to defecate."
▸ NOTE (2): This term comes from the inventor of the first flush toilet, Sir John Crapper.

crazo (to be a) *n.* (mild) to be an excessively eccentric individual • *That guy's a real crazo!;* That man is a real eccentric individual!

cream (to) *v.* (vulgar) said of one who is sexually aroused and reaching orgasm • (lit); to orgasm.
▸ VARIATION: **to cream one's jeans** *exp.* (very vulgar) • (lit); to orgasm.

cream one's jeans (to) *exp.* (extremely vulgar) to have an orgasm • *I almost creamed my jeans when I saw her;* I almost had an orgasm when I saw her.
▸ NOTE: to cream *v.* to get sexually excited • *I'm creaming over her;* I'm getting really sexually excited over her.

creep (to be a) *n.* (mild) to be a despicable person • *My little brother lied to me so that I'd give him money. What a creep!;* My little brother lied to me so that I'd give him money. What a despicable person!

crock of shit (to be a) *exp.* to be nonsense • *You believed that crock of shit?;* You believed that nonsense?
▸ VARIATION: **a crock** *n.* • *That's a crock!;* That's nonsense!

crud • **1.** *n.* any unidentifiable or unusual substance • (lit); excrement • *What's that crud you're drinking?;* What's that bizarre substance you're drinking? • **2.** *exclam.* an exclamation used in surprise or anger • *Crud! I left my wallet at work!;* I'm so angry! I left my wallet at work! • **3.** *n.* excrement (when used in the following expression, this term takes on a more vulgar meaning) • *I have to go take a crud;* I have to go defecate.
▸ ORIGIN: This is commonly used as a euphemism for *"crap"* which is considered vulgar yet extremely popular.

cruise (to) *v.* (mild and very popular) to journey up and down a street in search of a sexual conquest.
▸ NOTE: This verb is commonly used to refer to someone who is looking for a sexual partner as well as a prostitute who is looking for a client.

cube *n.* • **1.** lysergic acid diethylamide (L.S.D.) • **2.** crack cocaine.

cuckoo (to be) *adj.* to be eccentric and unpredictable.

cucumber *n.* (crude) penis.
> NOTE: This term is used due to its similarity in shape to a penis.

cum (to) *v.* (extremely popular and mild) to have an orgasm • *I'm gonna cum!;* I'm going to reach orgasm!
> VARIATION: **to come** *v.*
> NOTE: The past participle of *"to cum"* and *"to come"* is *"came."*

cunt *n.* (probably the most vulgar synonym for "vagina").
> NOTE: Due to the vulgarity of this term, it is often referred to as the "C-word." This term may also be applied to an extremely despicable woman.

curly *n.* (mild) name given to a bald person • *How 'ya doin', curly?;* How are you, bald person?

cut one (to) *exp.* (mild) to have flatulence.

cut the cheese (to) *exp.* (mild) to have flatulence
> NOTE: This expression originated due to the strong offensive smell produced when certain cheeses are cut.

cyclops *n.* (crude) penis.
> NOTE: This humorous term is used due to describe a penis which looks like it has one eye (like a cyclops).

-D-

daffy (to be) *adj.*

"Dagnabbit!" *exclam.* may be used as a euphemistic replacement for *"God damn it!"* which is used to convey frustration and anger • *Dagnabbit! I lost my car keys again!*

daisy chain *n.* (mild) a group of men or women or both who are engaged in sex together

darn • **1.** *n.* unpleasant • *Do you have to play that darn music all day?;* Do you have to play that unpleasant music all day? • **2.** *exclam.* an exclamation used in astonishment and anger • *Darn! Look at that new car!;* I'm really astonished! Look at that new car! • *Darn! I locked myself out of the house again!;* I'm so angry! I locked myself out of the house again! (NOTE: When used in anger, the exclamation *"Darn it!"* is used as a common substitution) • **3.** *v.* to damn • *Darn you!;* May you be damned to hell!
> ORIGIN: This is a commonly used euphemism for the term *"damn"* which is not really considered vulgar as much as it is deemed harsh. As with many words coming from the church, many feel that the use of these terms is in bad taste and prefer to use euphemisms.

"Dash it all!" *exclam.* used to indicate anger and frustration (may be used as a euphemism for *"Damn it!"* which is considered harsh) • *Dash it all! I missed the last bus!* How frustrating! I missed the last bus!
> NOTE: *"Dash it all!"* is an exclamation which is used only by the English. It has been listed here due to its popular usage by English performers in American television and movies.

date with Rosy Palm and her five sisters (to have a) *exp.* (humorous) to masturbate • *I have a date with Rosy Palm and her five sisters tonight;* I'm going to masturbate tonight.
> NOTE: This expression comes from a play-on-words since the term "Rosy" is both a proper name as well as a synonym for the color "pink." Therefore, in this expression *"Rosy Palm"* represents one's own hand or "rosy palm"

along with one's fingers which will all be used in masturbation.

dealer *n.* drug supplier.

deed (the) *n.* (mild) sex • *Wanna go do the deed?*; Do you want to go have sex?
▸ VARIATION: **the dirty deed** *exp.* • *Let's go do the dirty deed*; Let's go have sex.

deep shit (to be in) *exp.* to be in serious trouble • *I'm gonna be in deep shit when my mother sees what I've done to the rug*; I'm going to be in serious trouble when my mother sees what I've done to the rug.

deep-throat (to) *exp.* to perform oral sex by taking the entire penis down one's throat • *She deep-throated him without gagging*; She perform oral sex on him by taking his entire penis down her throat without gagging.

den of iniquity *n.* (mild) brothel • (lit); sanctuary of immorality.

derriere *n.* a euphemistic replacement for *"buttocks"* (See NOTE) • *Put your derriere right here*; Sit down right here.
▸ NOTE: Some people feel that to use the actual terms for any intimate body part is in bad taste. Although the word *"buttocks"* is perfectly acceptable, there are those who prefer to use a less direct term such as *"derriere."* Since Americans feel that French is such a beautiful and romantic language, French synonyms for certain body parts are commonly used as tasteful replacements.

diarrhea of the mouth (to have) *exp.* (humorous yet crude).
▸ VARIATION: **to have verbal diarrhea** *exp.*

dick (to) *v.* (vulgar) to fornicate • *All he ever talks about is dicking her!*; All he ever talks about is having sex with her!

▸ NOTE: This comes from the slang noun *"dick,"* meaning "penis."

dick *n.* • **1.** (mild) detective • **2.** (extremely popular, yet crude) penis.
▸ NOTE (1): This is one of the most popular slang terms for "penis."
▸ NOTE (2): This term (as well as *"dickhead"*) is also commonly used to mean "a despicable male."

Dickie and the boys *exp.* a humorous expression meaning the "penis and testicles."

dimwit (to be a) *n.* (mild) a foolish and unthinking person, an idiot • (lit); one whose cleverness is dim or faint.

ding-a-ling (to be a) *adj.* to be a deranged person or an eccentric.

dingy (to be) *adj.* to be crazy or foolish.

dink *n.* (mild) penis.

dinky (to be) *adj.* (mild) to be exceptionally small.

dip shit (to be a) *exp.* to be a fool • *Did you see the stupid thing he did? What a dip shit!*; Did you see the stupid thing he did? What a fool!

dip stick (to be a) *n.* (mild) an unthinking person.
▸ VARIATION: **dip** *n.* • *What a dip!*; What a fool!
▸ NOTE: A *"dip stick"* is literally a stick which is used to verify the oil level in a car. Due to its similarity in sound, it is commonly used as a euphemism for the term *"dip shit"* meaning "fool."

dippy (to be) *adj.* to be slightly crazy.

dirtbag (to be a) *n.* (mild) to be a despicable person.

dirty (to be) *adj.* (mild and very popular) to be pornographic • *Are you reading this dirty book?*; Are you reading this porno- graphic book?

do a blow (to) *v.* to take drugs.

do a toot (to) *v.* to take drugs.

do drugs (to) *v.* to take drugs.

do it (to) *exp.* (mild) to fornicate.
‣ NOTE: In this expression, *"it"* refers to "sex."

do the do (to) *exp.* (a mild term from rap music slang) to fornicate • *I think Janice and Tim are out doin' the do somewhere;* I think Janice and Tim are out having sex somewhere.
‣ NOTE: It's extremely common in slang, especially rap slang, to reduce the *"-ing"* ending to *"-in'"* as seen in *"doin' the do."*

do the nasty (to) *exp.* (a mild term from rap music slang) to fornicate • *Are you going out tonight to do the nasty?;* Are you going out tonight to have sex?

do the wild thing (to) *exp.* (an acceptable term from rap music slang) to fornicate • *Do you think they did the wild thing last night?;* Do you think they had sex last night?

dode (to be a) *n.* (mild) fool.
‣ NOTE: This is one of the newest slang terms for "fool" and is used mainly by the younger generation.

dodo (to be a) *n.* (mild) fool.

"Does a bear shit in the woods?" *exp.* said in response to something obvious • *Do I think she's pretty? Does a bear shit in the woods?;* Do I think she's pretty? Obviously!

dog (to be a) *n.* (mild) to be an ugly person.
‣ VARIATION: **to be a bow-wow** (which is the sound made by a barking dog) *exp.* (humorous).

doggone *adj.* irritating (may be used as a euphemistic replacement for *"God damn"* which is considered irreverent) • *These doggone shoes*

are too tight!; These irritating shoes are too tight!
‣ ALSO: **"Doggone it!"** *exclam.* used to indicate anger or frustration (may be used as a euphemistic replacement for *"God damn it!"* which is considered irreverent) • *Doggone it! He's late again!;* How frustrating! He's late again!

dolt (to be a) *n.* (mild) a foolish person.

dong *n.* (mild) penis.

doojee *n.* heroin.

dope (to) *v.* to take drugs.

dope *n.* marijuana.

dope peddler *n.* drug supplier.

dope up (to) *v.* to take drugs.

dork (to be a) *n.* (very popular among the younger generation) an extremely foolish person, a stupid and awkward person.

dorky (to be) *adj.* to be idiotic and clumsy.
‣ NOTE: This adjective is primarily used by the younger generation.

dose (to) *v.* to take drugs.

dose up (to) *v.* to take drugs.

dots *n.pl.* lysergic acid diethylamide (L.S.D.)

douche bag (to be a) *exp.* (crude) despicable person • *I can't believe he did that to you. What a douche bag!;* I can't believe he did that to you. What a despicable person!

drag *n.* dosage • *to take a drag;* to inhale a dosage of marijuana.

"Drat!" *exclam.* an exclamation used in annoyance • *Drat! I can't find my glasses!*
‣ NOTE: This is a commonly used euphemism for the exclamation *"Damn!"*

drive the porcelain bus (to) *exp.* (humorous) to vomit.
‣ NOTE: This is a humorous description of someone who is

kneeling and holding the porcelain bowl of the toilet while vomiting.

driver *n.* (mild) pimp.

drop (to) *v.* to take drugs.

drug pusher *n.* drug supplier.

duff *n.* (mild) buttocks.

dumb bunny (to be a) *n.* an affectionate term for a foolish person.

dumb Dora (to be a) *n.* (mild) a foolish woman or girl.

dumb ox (to be a) *n.* (mild) an extremely foolish person.
♦ NOTE: This compares a person to an ox which is considered extremely slow and stupid.

dumb-fuck *n.* (vulgar) idiot.

dumbass (to be a) *n.* (crude) • an extremely foolish person.

dumbbell (to be a) *n.* (mild) a foolish person.

dumbfuck (to be a) *n.* to be an idiot • *Can you believe what a dumbfuck he is?;* Can you believe what an idiot he is?

dumbo (to be a) *n.* (mild) a foolish person.

dumdum (to be a) *n.* (mild) an affectionate term for a foolish person.

dummy (to be a) *n.* (mild) an affectionate term for a foolish person.

dump (to) *v.* (crude) to defecate • (lit); to unload • *The dog dumped on the rug;* The dog defecated on the rug.
♦ VARIATION (1): **to dump a load** *exp.* (crude) • *I have to go dump a load;* I have to go defecate.
♦ VARIATION (2): **to take a dump** *exp.* (extremely popular yet crude) • *He's been in there taking a dump for the past 15 minutes!;* He's been in there defecating for the past 15 minutes!

dunce (to be a) *n.* (mild) a foolish person.

dunderhead (to be a) *n.* (mild) a foolish and unthinking person.

dweeb (to be a) *n.* fool (mild and very popular among the younger generation) to be a despicable person.

dynamite *n.* cocaine and heroin.

-E-

easy (to be) *adj.* (mild) to be quick to have sex with a variety of partners.

easy lay (to be an) *n.* (very popular and somewhat crude) to be promiscuous.

eat face (to) *exp.* to kiss • *Did they eat face last night?;* Did they kiss last night?

"Eat shit!" *exp.* a strong reproach to a despicable comment • *How dare you say that to me! Eat shit!;* How dare you say that to me! You disgust me!

eightball *n.* 3.5 grams of cocaine.

endowed (to be) *adj.* to be large breasted.

equipment *n.* (mild) penis.

"Excuse the fuck outta me!" *exp.* "Well, excuse me!"

eye opener *n.* heroin.

-F-

"F.U!" *interj.* "Fuck you!"
♦ NOTE: This is a common reproach to a despicable person • *I can't believe you'd do such a rotten thing. F.U.!;* I can't believe you'd do such a rotten thing. Fuck you! • In this interjection, the letter "U" is used to represent "you" since the sounds are identical.

F-ing • **1.** *adj.* absolute, complete • *Our picnic was an F-ing disaster yesterday because of the rain;* Our picnic was a complete disaster yesterday because of the rain. • **2.** *adv.* absolutely, completely • *What an F-ing great stereo!;* What

an absolutely great stereo! • **3.** used before a verb to indicate great annoyance • *Why do you always F-ing come over here and bother me every two minutes?!* • **4.** used before a noun to indicate great annoyance • *I don't want to drive her to the airport but what F-ing choice do I have?!*
◆ ORIGIN: This is commonly used as a euphemism for the adjective/adverb *"fucking"* which is considered extremely vulgar yet very popular.
◆ SYNONYM: SEE: **Friggin'**.

F-word (the) *n.* a euphemism for the vulgar term *"fuck"* • *Mom! I just heard Barry use the F-word!;* Mom! I just heard Barry say "fuck!"
◆ ALSO: **the S-word** *n.* a euphemism for the vulgar term *"shit."*

face only a mother could love (to have a) *exp.* (humorous) to be extremely ugly.

face that could stop a clock (to have a) *exp.* (humorous) to be extremely ugly.

face that would crack a mirror (to have a) *exp.* (humorous) to be extremely ugly.

facilities *n.pl.* (mild) a euphemistic term for toilet.

family jewels *n.* (mild).
◆ NOTE: This is a very popular euphemism for one's genitals.

fanny *n.* (mild) buttocks.
◆ NOTE: It's important to note that the term *"fanny,"* which is an innocent word used in America meaning "buttocks," is an extremely vulgar term in England meaning "vagina."

fart (to) *v.* (extremely popular yet somewhat crude) to have flatulence or be flatulent • *Who farted?;* Who has flatulence?
◆ VARIATION: **fart** *n.* flatulence •

This noun is commonly used with *"to cut"* meaning "to release."

fat slob (to be a) *exp.* (mild) to be an inordinately piggish, heavy, and disgusting individual • *I'll never invite him to my party again. He was such an embarrassment. What a fat slob!;* I'll never invite him to my party again. He was such an embarrassment. What a pig!

fat stuff *n.* a fat person.

fathead (to be a) *n.* (mild) an extremely foolish person.
◆ NOTE: This describes someone who has nothing but fat in place of a brain.

fatso (to be a) *n.* a slang transformation of the adjective "fat."
◆ ALSO: **to be a fatty** *exp.*

filth *n.* (mild) indecency • (lit); dirt • *How can they show this kind of filth on television?;* How can they show this kind of indecency on television?

fink (to be a) *n.* (mild) to be a despicable person.
◆ NOTE: This is an older term used mainly in jest.

fix (to) *v.* to take drugs.

fixer *n.* drug supplier.

flaky (to be) *adj.* to be rather peculiar and unreliable.

flap one's gums (to) *exp.* (humorous) • (lit); to move one's mouth open and closed continuously due to excessive talking.

flatfoot *n.* (mild) police officer.
◆ NOTE: This term refers to a police officer who patrols on foot.

flathead *n.* (derogatory yet humorous) police officer.
◆ NOTE: This term signifies the old traditional flat-top haircuts of police officers.

flats *n.pl.* lysergic acid diethylamide (L.S.D.)

flea powder *n.* heroin.

flesh peddler *n.* (mild). • **1.** pimp • **2.** prostitute.

flight *n.* lysergic acid diethylamide (L.S.D.)

flip one's lid (to) *exp.* to become crazy.

flip one's wig (to) *exp.* to become crazy.

flip out (to) *exp.* • **1.** to become crazy • *He used to be a genius but he suddenly flipped out for no reason!;* He used to be a genius but he suddenly became crazy! • **2.** to became extremely excited • *She flipped out over her new car!;*. She became extremely excited over her new car!

flipped (to be) *adj.* to be crazy.
‣ VARIATION: **to be flipped out** *exp.*

float an air biscuit (to) *exp.* (humorous and mild) to have flatulence.

floating (to be) *adj.* to be on drugs.

flog the Bishop (to) *exp.* (humorous) to masturbate • *My new roommate flogs the Bishop three times a day!;* My new roommate masturbates three times a day!
‣ NOTE: This humorous, yet crude, expression was created since the head of the penis resembles the hat worn by the Bishop. The expression, therefore, compares the action of masturbating to *"flogging the Bishop"* or "flogging one's penis."

floozie *n.* (mild) a prostitute or girl of easy morals.
‣ NOTE: This terms refers to a female prostitute only.
‣ VARIATION: **floozy.**

flying (to be) *adj.* to be on drugs.

fogy (to be a) *n.* (mild) someone with outdated ideas.
‣ VARIATION: **to be an old fogy** *n.*
‣ NOTE: Also spelled *"fogey."*

"Fooey!" *exclam.* (also spelled "phooey") used to indicate anger or frustration (may be used as a euphemistic replacement for *"Fuck"* which is considered extremely vulgar) • *Fooey! I lost the contest for the third time!;* How frustrating! I lost the contest for the third time!
‣ VARIATION: **"Fooey on him/that!"** *exp.* used to indicate contempt for someone or something (may be used as a euphemistic replacement for *"Fuck him/that!"* which is considered extremely vulgar) • *She forgot to pick you up at the airport? Fooey on her!;* She forgot to pick you up at the airport? How contemptible!

fool around (to) *exp.* (mild) to fornicate or fondle sexually • *Wanna go fool around later?;* Do you want to go have sex later?

for shit (to be) *exp.* to be useless • *This car's for shit!;* This car's useless!

fossil (to be a) *n.* (humorous) refers to someone (or something) old and out-of-date.
‣ NOTE: This term is traditionally applied to old remnants or bones from a past geological era.
‣ VARIATION: **to be an old fossil** *n.*

four-letter word *n.* Since most of the worst obscene terms in the American-English language contain four letters, they have been nicknamed "four-letter words" • *My mother never uses four-letter words;* My mother never uses swear words.
‣ NOTE: It's interesting to note that the French equivalent of the American *"four-letter word"* is *"un mot à cinq lettres"* which means "a five-letter word." This is due to the fact that the most commonly used obscenity in France is *"merde,"* meaning "shit," containing five letters.

'fraidy cat (to be a) *n.* (mild) a fearful person.

freak out (to) *exp.* • **1.** to become completely crazy. • **2.** to drug overdose.

freaked out (to be) *adj.* to be on drugs.

freebase (to) *v.* to take drugs.

French kiss (to) *exp.* to kiss with the tongue • *Can you believe he actually tried to French kiss me?;* Can you believe he actually tried to kiss me with his tongue?
♦ SYNONYM: **to wet kiss** *exp.*

fried (to be) *adj.* said of someone who seems to have brain damage (usually due to drugs).

friggin' • **1.** *adj.* absolute, complete • **2.** *adv.* absolutely, completely • **3.** used before a verb to indicate great annoyance • **4.** used before a noun to indicate great annoyance.
♦ ORIGIN: This is commonly used as a euphemism for the adjective/adverb *"fucking"* which is considered extremely vulgar yet very popular.
♦ NOTE: It's very common in colloquial speech to reduce the *"-ing"* ending to *"-in'."* The term *"frigging"* is almost always used in its reduced form, *"friggin'."*
♦ SYNONYM: SEE: **F-ing.**

fruitcake (to be a) *n.* to be a crazy person.

fuck (to) *v.* • **1.** to have sex • *All he ever thinks about is fucking;* All he ever thinks about is having sex. • **2.** to cheat • *You paid way too much for your car. I'm afraid you got fucked!;* You paid way too much for your car. I'm afraid you got cheated.
♦ VARIATION (1): **to fuck one's brains out** *exp.* to have aggressive or prolonged sex with someone.
♦ VARIATION (2): **to fuck like a bunny** *exp.* to have aggressive, speedy, and frequent sex.

"Fuck a duck!" *exclam.* exclamation denoting surprise or disdain • *Fuck a duck! That's ridiculous!*

fuck around (to) *exp.* • **1.** to spend time idly • *We're just gonna go fuck around outside today;* We're just going to go spend time idly outside today. • **2.** to have sex • *He's out fucking around tonight;* He's out having sex tonight.
♦ NOTE: The difference between definitions **1.** and **2.** depend on the context.

"Fuck no!" *exp.* "Absolutely not!" • *"You like that food?" "Fuck no!;"* "You like that food?" "Absolutely not!"
♦ ANTONYM: **"Fuck yes!"** *exp.* "Absolutely!"

fuck off (to) *exp.* to shirk one's responsibilities and play • *I worked for two weeks on this project while my partner was out fucking off the whole time!;* I worked for two weeks on this project while my partner was out shirking his responsibilities and playing the whole time.
♦ ALSO: **"Fuck off!"** *interj.* **"Leave me alone!"**

fuck someone over (to) *exp.* • **1.** to cheat someone • *Every time I trust someone, I get fucked over;* Every time I trust someone, I get cheated. • **2.** to betray someone • *I got fucked over by my best friend;* I was betrayed by my best friend.
♦ VARIATION: **to fuck someone over royally** *exp.* to betray someone completely • *She royally fucked me over!* [or] *She fucked me over royally!;* She completely betrayed me!

fuck something up (to) *exp.* • **1.** to ruin something • *I totally fucked up my car* [or] *I totally fucked my car up;* I totally ruined my car. • **2.** to blunder • *I forgot to mail the letter which needed to arrive today! I guess I really fucked up;* I forgot to mail the letter which needed to

arrive today! I guess I really blundered. • **3.** to injure something • *I fucked up my back this morning* [or] *I fucked my back up this morning;* I injured my back this morning.
♦ ALSO: **fuck-up** *n.* one who always blunders.

"Fuck that noise!" *exp.* "That's ridiculous!" • *He wants me to take him to the airport at 1:00 in the morning?! Fuck that noise!;* He wants me to take him to the airport at 1:00 in the morning?! That's ridiculous!
♦ NOTE: In this expression, it is important to stress *"that"* by raising the pitch of the voice slightly.

fuck up (to) *exp.* (vulgar) to ruin; to bungle • *I fucked up my car;* I ruined my car.
♦ NOTE: This comes from the verb *"to fuck,"* meaning "to fornicate." This is one of the most vulgar yet popular obscenities in the American-English language.

fuck with someone (to) *exp.* to harass someone • *Don't fuck with him. He's dangerous!;* Don't harass him. He's dangerous!

fuck with something (to) *exp.* to toy with something • *I fucked with the car for an hour trying to repair it, but it's still not working;* I toyed with the car for an hour trying to repair it, but it's still not working.

"Fuck you/him/her/them/it etc.!" *exclam.* used in contempt • *I can't believe you tried to cheat me! I thought you were my friend. Well, fuck you!*

"Fuck!" *exp.* • **1.** used to signify anger or frustration • *Fuck! I just missed my flight!* **2.** used to signify amazement • *Fuck! She's beautiful!*

fuck-face *n.* (vulgar yet very popular) an extremely despicable person.

fuck-head *n.* (vulgar) a despicable person.

fucked (to be) *adj.* to be intolerable • *That's fucked that she could do such a mean thing to you!;* That's intolerable that she could do such a mean thing to you!

fucker (to be a) *n.* (vulgar) to be an extremely despicable person • (lit); to be a fornicator • *That guy stole my wallet! What a fucker!;* That guy stole my wallet! What an extremely despicable person!
♦ VARIATION: **to be a mother-fucker** *exp.*

fucker *n.* (vulgar yet extremely popular) an extremely despicable person.

fuckface (to be a) *n.* to be a despicable person • *Did you hear the derogatory way he was talking about you? What a fuckface!;* Did you hear the derogatory way he was talking about you? What a despicable person!

fuckhead (to be a) *n.* to be a despicable person • *How can you like that fuckhead?;* How can you like that despicable person?

fuckin' *adv.* absolute(ly), extreme(ly) • *I don't fuckin' know!;* I absolutely don't know! • *He's a fuckin' idiot!;* He's an absolute idiot!
♦ NOTE: The *"-ing"* ending in this adverb is commonly reduced to *"-in'."*

"Fuckin' A!" *exp.* "Absolutely!" • *"Do you think he's a jerk?" "Fuckin' A!;"* • "Do you think he's a fool?" "Absolutely!"
♦ NOTE: The *"-ing"* ending in this expression is commonly reduced to *"-in'."*
♦ VARIATION: **fuckin' A right** *exp.* absolutely correct.

fucking *adv.* • **1.** completely • *She fucking embarrassed me in front of all my friends!;* She completely embarrassed me in front of all my friends! • **2.** used to add emphasis to the verb that follows • *Don't fucking bother me!; Just don't bother me!* • *Don't even ask me if you can borrow my car. I'm not fucking lending it to you!; Don't* even ask me if you can borrow my car. I'm simply not lending it to you! • **3.** infuriating • *I spent $500 on this fucking washing machine and it doesn't even work!;* I spent $500 on this infuriating washing machine and it doesn't even work!

"Fudge!" *exclam.* used to indicate disappointment, anger, or frustration (may be used as a euphemistic replacement for *"Fuck!"* which is considered extremely vulgar) • *Fudge! I was so sure I was going to win;* What a disappointment! I was so sure I was going to win.

full of hot air (to be) *exp.* (mild) said of an arrogant person who thinks he/she knows the answer to every question • *You actually believed what he said? He's so full of hot air!;* You actually believed what he said? He's such an arrogant person who thinks he knows the answer to every question!

full of shit (to be) *exp.* to talk absolute nonsense • *He told you he owned three cars? He's full of shit!;* He told you he owned three cars? He's talking absolute nonsense!

fur pie *n.* (vulgar) vagina.

furburger *n.* (vulgar) vagina.

fuzz *n.* (derogatory) police officer.
  ♦ NOTE: This term was very popular during the 1960s and is still heard in jest and in movies of the period.

-G-

"Gad!" *exclam.* a commonly used euphemism for "God," used to denote excitement, surprise or annoyance • **1.** (excitement) *Gad! What a beautiful house!* • **2.** (surprise) *Gad! Did you see that shooting star?* • **3.** (annoyance) *Gad! Why doesn't he just leave me alone?!*
  ♦ VARIATION (1): **"Gadzooks!"** *exclam.* used primarily by the older generation or in jest.
    ⇨ ORIGIN: Originally pronounced, "God's hooks!" which referred to the nails on the cross.
  ♦ VARIATION (2): **"Egads!"** *exclam.* used primarily by the older generation or in jest.
    ⇨ ORIGIN: "Oh, God!"

gage *n.* marijuana.

gang bang *n.* (crude yet popular) group sex.
  ♦ NOTE: **to bang** *v.* (humorous) to fornicate.

gasbag (to be a) *n.* (humorous) to be extremely talkative.

"Gee!" *exclam.* a commonly used euphemism for *"Jesus,"* used to denote excitement, surprise, or annoyance. *"Gee!"* may be used in place of *"Gad!"* in all three instances.
  ♦ VARIATION (1): **"Gee whillikers!"** used primarily by the older generation or in jest.
  ♦ VARIATION (2): **"Gee whiz!"** *exclam.*
  ♦ VARIATION (3): **"Geez Louise!"** *exclam.*

geek (to be a) *n.* (extremely popular and mild) a dull and stupid person.
  ♦ NOTE: This was made popular by the younger generation but is becoming used more and more by the older generation. This term is commonly heard on television.

"Geez!" *exclam.* a commonly used euphemism for *"Jesus,"* used to denote excitement, surprise, or annoyance. *"Geez!"* may be used in place of *"Gad!"* in all three instances.
  ♦ VARIATION: **"Geez Louise!"** *exclam.*

geezed up (to be) *adj.* (popular in the drug world) to be on drugs.

get high (to) *v.* to take drugs.

get it on (to) *exp.* (somewhat crude) to fornicate • *She got it on with her boyfriend all weekend;* She had sex with her boyfriend all weekend.

get laid (to) *exp.* (somewhat crude) to fornicate • *I got laid last night for the first time;* I had sex last night for the first time. • *Did she lay you after the party?;* Did she have sex with you after the party?

get off (to) *exp.* (mild) • **1.** to reach orgasm • *Did you get off last night?;* Did you reach orgasm last night? • **2.** to enjoy greatly • *You really get off annoying people, don't you?;* You really enjoy annoying people, don't you? • **3.** to take drugs.

get one's rocks off (to) *exp.* (vulgar) • **1.** said of a man who relieves his testicles of semen by having sex • *I really got my rocks off last night;* I had some great sex last night. • **2.** to enjoy greatly • *He gets his rocks off by annoying people;* He really enjoys annoying people.

get some ass (to) *exp.* (vulgar) to fornicate • *So, did you get some ass tonight?;* So, did you have sex tonight?
♦ VARIATION: **to get a piece [of ass]** *exp.*

get the curse (to) *exp.* (mild) to menstruate • (lit); to get the affliction.

gets one's rocks off (to) *exp.* (vulgar) to enjoy greatly • (lit); said of a man who relieves his testicles ("rocks") of semen by having sex • *He gets his rocks off by singing;* He really enjoys singing.

give a fuck (not to) *exp.* not to care at all • *I don't give a fuck what you do!;* I don't care at all what you do!
♦ VARIATION: **not to give a flying fuck** *exp.*

give a shit (not to) *exp.* not to care at all • *I don't give a shit what you do;* I don't care at all what you do.

give head (to) *exp.* (very popular) to perform oral sex • *I could hear her giving him head last night!* I could hear her performing oral sex on him last night!

give someone shit (to) *exp.* • **1.** to lie to someone • *Don't give me that shit! That's not true and you know it!;* Don't give me those lies! That's not true and you know it! • **2.** to give someone opposition • *Don't give me shit. Just do what I tell you;* Don't hassle me. Just do what I tell you.

go (to) *v.* (mild) to urinate.

go all the way (to) *exp.* (mild) to get past foreplay and into sex • *Wanna go all the way now?;* Do you want to get past foreplay and into sex now?

go down on someone (to) *exp.* to perform oral sex on someone • *He went down on her on their first date!;* He performed oral sex on her on their first date!

go on (to) *exp.* (mild) to talk continuously.
♦ VARIATION: **to go on and on** *exp.*

go to the can (to) *exp.* (somewhat crude) to defecate • *I'll be right back. I have to go to the can;* I'll be right back. I have to go to the bathroom.
♦ VARIATION: **to go to the can man** *exp.* (rhyming slang and somewhat crude) • *I gotta go to the can man;* I have to go to the bathroom.

go to the john (to) *exp.* (extremely popular and mild) to defecate (or urinate) • *Why don't you go to the john before we leave on our trip?;* Why don't you go to the bathroom before we leave on our trip?

gold *n.* marijuana.

gold dust *n.* cocaine.

"Goldarnit!" *exclam.* (pronounced "galdarnit") used to indicate anger or frustration (may be used as a euphemistic replacement for *"God damn it!"* which is considered irreverent) • *Goldarnit! That guy just cheated me!;* I'm angry! That guy just cheated me!
  ♦ NOTE: This term is mainly used in old westerns and in jest.

golden apples *n.* (mild) dried excrement left on prairies.

"Golly!" *exclam.* a very mild and commonly used euphemism for *"God,"* used to denote excitement, surprise, or annoyance. *"Golly!"* may be used in place of *"Gad!"* in all three instances.
  ♦ VARIATION (1): **"Golly gee!"** *exclam.* used primarily in jest.
  ♦ VARIATION (2): **"Golly gee whillikers!"** *exclam.* used primarily in jest.

gone (to be) *adj.* to be crazy • (lit); to have left one's senses.

goob (to be a) *n.* (mild) an extremely foolish person.
  ♦ NOTE: This term is used primarily by the younger generation. It comes from a fictional character used in an old popular television show called "The Andy Griffith Show" where a character named Goober was known for being extremely foolish. Teens have simply shortened the name to *"goob"* and changed the first letter to lowercase.
  ♦ VARIATION: **goober** *n.*

good fuck (to be a) *exp.* to be a satisfying sex partner • *I hear she's a good fuck;* I hear she's a satisfying sex partner.

"Good grief!" *exclam.* used to indicate surprise and disbelief (may be used as a euphemistic replacement for *"Good God!"* which is considered, by some, to be irreverent) • *Good grief! How did*

you get the kitchen so dirty?; I can't believe it! How did you get the kitchen so dirty?
  ♦ VARIATION: **"Good gravy!"** *exclam.* used primarily in jest.

goof ball (to be a) *n.* (mild) a silly and amusing person.

goofed (to be) *adj.* to be on drugs.

goofus (to be a) *n.* (mild) a fool.

goon (to be a) *n.* (mild) a fool.

"Gosh!" *exclam.* a very mild and commonly used euphemism for *"God,"* used to denote excitement, surprise, or annoyance. *"Gosh!"* may be used in place of *"Gad!"* in all three instances.

gramps *n.* (mild) a disrespect- ful name given to an old man • *Hey, gramps!;* Hello, old man!

granny *n.* (mild) a disrespectful name given to an old woman • *Hurry up, granny!;* Hurry up, old woman!

grapefruits *n.pl.* (humorous) large breasts.

grass *n.* marijuana.

graybar hotel *n.* police officer.
  ♦ NOTE: This signifies the gray steel bars used in jail cells.

grease the bayonet (to) *exp.* (humorous) to masturbate • *I think I need to go grease the bayonet;* I think I need to go masturbate.
  ♦ NOTE: This is a humorous, yet crude, expression comparing the action of masturbating with that of *greasing a bayonet* which is long and hard like an erect penis.

grind (to) *v.* (crude) to pound one's sex organs into those of one's partner • *They were grinding all night;* They were having sex all night.

gross (to be) *adj.* (mild) to be hideously ugly or disgusting.

group grope *n.* (crude) group sex.
  ♦ NOTE: **to grope** *v.* to caress.

grunt (to) *v.* (humorous yet crude) to defecate • (lit); to make unintelligible animal noises • *I gotta go grunt;* I have to go defecate.
▸ NOTE: This verb is used to signify the grunting sounds made by someone who is defecating.

gutless (to be) *adj.* (mild).
▸ NOTE: In American slang, *"guts"* is used to mean "courage."
▸ ALSO: **gutless wonder** *n.* (mild) an extremely fearful person.
▸ ANTONYM: **gutsy (to be)** *adj.* (mild).

"Guy!" *exclam.* a mild and commonly used euphemism for *"God,"* used to denote excitement, surprise, or annoyance. *"Guy!"* may be used in place of *"Gad!"* in all three instances.

-H-

H. *n.* heroin.

H.I.V. *n.* Human Immunodeficiency Virus.

half-pint (to be a) *n.* (humorous) to be very short.
▸ VARIATION: **to be pint-sized** *adj.*

hand job (to give oneself a) *exp.* to masturbate • *He's probably in his room giving himself a hand job;* He's probably in his room masturbating.

happy dust *n.* cocaine.

hard on the eyes (to be) *exp.* (mild) to be extremely ugly.

hard stuff *n.* heroin.

hard-on (to have a) *n.* (crude yet extremely popular) said of a man with an erect penis.

hardcore (to be) *adj.* (mild) to be very pornographic and explicit • *That movie was real hardcore;* That movie was very pornographic and explicit.
▸ ANTONYM: **to be softcore** *adj.*

said of a sexy film which does not contain penetration.

Harry *n.* heroin.

hash *n.* marijuana.

haul ass (to) *exp.* to hurry • *If we don't haul ass, we're going to be late;* If we don't hurry, we going to be late.
▸ NOTE: This expression can also be used in reference to an object: *This train can really haul ass!;* This train can really move!

haul in (to) *v.* (mild) to escort to jail.

have a buzz (to) *adj.* to be slightly intoxicated (from alcohol or drugs).

have a nooner (to) *exp.* (mild) to have quick sex during lunch • *He always leaves the office during lunch. I think he has a nooner every day;* He always leaves the office during lunch. I think he has quick sex during lunch every day.

have a one-night stand (to) *exp.* (mild) to have a sexual affair with someone for just one night • *I don't even remember her name. She was just a one-night stand;* I don't even remember her name. She was just someone I had sex with one night.

have a quickie (to) *exp.* (mild) to have speedy sex • *We don't have time to leave for my house. How about a quickie right here?;* We don't have time to leave for my house. How about speedy sex right here?

have a visitor (to) *exp.* (mild and humorous) to menstruate.

have Montezuma's revenge (to) *exp.* (humorous and mild) to have diarrhea • *I think I caught Montezuma's revenge!* I think I caught a case of diarrhea.
▸ NOTE (1): Many people visiting the United States travel to Mexico during their stay. Unfortunately, these people often return with a severe case of diarrhea after having drunk the water which

contains parasites. It is said that this is Montezuma's revenge, the former emperor of Mexico (1480-1520), toward those who once invaded his country. This condition is also referred to as *"las touristas"* meaning "that which is acquired by tourists."

have one's nose in the air (to) *exp.* (mild) said of someone who walks around with the chin (or nose) held high as if to look down on others.

have one's period (to) *exp.* (mild and extremely popular) to menstruate • (lit); to have one's term (of menstruation).

have someone's ass (to) *exp.* to kill someone (figuratively) • *I'm gonna have his ass for what he tried to do to me!;* I'm gonna kill him for what he tried to do to me!

have the hots for (to) *exp.* (mild) to be so sexually excited by someone as to feel warm due to one's accelerated pulse.

head *n.* (crude) toilet.
    ♦ NOTE: This is a standard nautical term for "toilet." Oddly enough, when used outside of a ship, it is considered crude.

headlights *n.pl.* (humorous) large breasts.

heaven dust *n.* cocaine.

heck • **1.** *n.* used as *"the heck,"* this is a common euphemism for *"the hell"* denoting surprise, annoyance, or nonsense • (surprise) *It's great to see you! What the heck are you doing here?* • (annoyance) *What the heck do you want now?* • (nonsense) *He told you he was rich? The heck he is!;* He told you he was rich! That's nonsense! • **2.** *exclam.* used to denote excitement or annoyance • (excitement) *Heck! That's great news!* • (annoyance) *Heck! Why doesn't he just go away?!* • **3.** to add emphasis to "yes" and "no" •

Heck yes! I'd love to go with you to the carnival! • **4. like heck** *exp.* a lot • *My broken arm hurts like heck!;* My broken arm hurts a lot!
    ♦ NOTE (1): The term *"heck"* is also commonly used in the following expressions:
    • to have a heck of a lot of money; to have a lot of money.
    • the heck with it; to hell with it (said about something very irritating.
    • all heck broke loose; great chaos developed.
    • to be funny as heck; to be extremely funny.
    • a heck of a good show, speech, time, etc.; an extremely good show, speech, time, etc.
    ♦ NOTE (2): In all of the previous examples of *"heck," "hell"* is very commonly used. As with many words coming from the church, many feel that the use of these terms is in bad taste and prefer to use euphemisms.

hemp *n.* marijuana.

herpes *n.pl.* cold sores.

high (to be) *adj.* to be on drugs.

high and mighty (to be) *exp.* (mild) to think highly of oneself.
    ♦ NOTE: This is said of a powerful king or queen who sits on an elevated throne.

high as a kite (to be) *adj.* • **1.** to be highly intoxicated (from alcohol or drugs) • **2.** to be extremely joyful.

hippo (to be a) *adj.* to be as fat as a hippopotamus.
    ♦ NOTE: The term *"hippo"* is a common abbreviation for "hippopotamus."

hit (to) *v.* to take drugs.

hit *n.* an amount of ingested cocaine (or marijuana) • *Wanna hit?;* Do you want to take some cocaine?

hit the needle (to) *v.* to take drugs.

hit the pipe (to) *v.* to take drugs.

ho *n.* (mild and humorous) prostitute.
  ♦ NOTE: In many parts of the south, the term "whore" is pronounced *"ho."*

hog (to be a) *exp.* to be fat as a hog.

hoity-toity (to be) *exp.* (mild) to be pretentious.

hole *n.* (vulgar) vagina.

"Holy Cow!" *exclam.* used to indicate surprise and disbelief (may be used as a euphemistic replacement for *"Holy Christ!"* which is considered to be irreverent) • *Holy Cow! How did your little sister get way up there?;* What a surprise! How did your little sister get way up there?
  ♦ CAUTION: The expression *"Holy Cow!"* would be considered quite irreverent to natives from India where the cow is considered holy.

"Holy Cripes!" *exclam.* used to indicate surprise and disbelief (may be used as a euphemistic replacement for *"Holy Christ!"* which is considered to be irreverent) • *Holy Cripes! Did you hear what just happened?;* What a surprise! Did you hear what just happened?

"Holy Moley!" *exclam.* used to indicate surprise and disbelief (may be used as a euphemistic replacement for *"Holy Moses!"* which is considered to be irreverent) • *Holey Moley! How did you do that?;* What a surprise! How did you do that?

"Holy shit!" *exp.* "This is terrible!" • *Holy shit! I forgot to pick up my father from the airport!;* This is terrible! I forgot to pick up my father from the airport!

hook shop *n.* brothel.

hooker *n.* (extremely popular and mild) prostitute.
  ♦ NOTE: This term applies to a male or female prostitute.
  ♦ ORIGIN: During the civil war,

troops under the command of Major General Joseph Hooker began visiting prostitutes while on leave. As their visits became more and more regular, the prostitutes were soon referred to as *"hookers."*

hoosegow *n.* police officer (used primarily in old gangster movies and westerns).

hooters *n.pl.* (humorous) large breasts.

hop in the saddle (to) *exp.* (humorous) to fornicate • *He hops in the saddle with every girl he meets;* He has sex with every girl he meets.
  ♦ NOTE: This expression comes from westerns where a cowboy would commonly *"hop in the saddle"* with a beautiful girl and ride off into the sunset.
  ♦ VARIATION: **to hop in the sack** *exp.* (*"sack"* being a slang term for "bed").

hopped up (to be) *adj.* to be on drugs.

horny (to be) *adj.* (crude yet extremely popular) to be extremely sexually excited.
  ♦ ALSO: **to be a horn dog** *n.* to be an extremely sexual person.

horse *n.* cocaine and heroin.

horse shit *exp.* nonsense • (lit); horse excrement • *That's a bunch of horse shit!;* That's utter nonsense!

hose *n.* penis.
  ♦ NOTE: This term is used due to its similarity in shape to a penis.

hot (to be) *adj.* (mild) • **1.** to be sexually aroused • **2.** to be sexy.
  ♦ VARIATION: **to be hot to trot** *exp.* (mild) • **1.** to be sexually aroused • **2.** to be sexy.
  ♦ VARIATION: **to be hot and bothered** *exp.* to be sexually aroused.

hot for some (to be) *exp.* (mild) to be sexually aroused by someone.
  ♦ VARIATION: **to have the hots for someone** *exp.* (mild).

hot shit (to be) *exp.* to be impressive
• *He thinks he's such hot shit*; He thinks he so impressive.
♦ VARIATION: **"He thinks he's hot shit but he's just runny diarrhea"** *exp.*

house connections *exp.* drug supplier.

house of delight *n.* (mild) brothel.
♦ NOTE: This refers to a brothel, which commonly looks like a large home, where men experience delight due to the prostitutes.

house of ill fame *n.* (mild) brothel • (lit); house of bad reputation (due to the often illegal sexual activity which occurs within its walls).

house of ill repute *n.* (mild) brothel • (lit); house of bad reputation (due to the often illegal sexual activity which occurs within its walls).

house of joy *n.* (mild) brothel.
♦ NOTE: This refers to a brothel, which commonly looks like a large home, where men experience joy due to the prostitutes.
♦ VARIATION: **joy house** *n.*

hump (to) *v.* (somewhat crude) to rub one's sex organs against another person • *As soon as I walked into his house, his dog started humping my leg!*; As soon as I walked into his house, his dog started rubbing his sex organs against my leg!

hung (to be) *adj.* (mild) to be endowed with a large penis • *That guy's really hung!*; That man has a really large penis!

hurl (to) *v.* (humorous) to vomit.
♦ NOTE: This is one of the newest slang verbs for "to vomit" which was popularized in an American movie called "Wayne's World." This verb is now extremely popular among teenagers.

hustle (to) *v.* (mild and very popular) to solicit.
♦ NOTE: hustler *n.* (mild) male or female prostitute.

hustler *n.* (extremely popular and mild) prostitute.
♦ NOTE: This term applies to a male or female prostitute.

hype *n.* drug user.

-I-

ice *n.* crack cocaine.

in one's birthday suit (to be) *exp.* (humorous) naked, said of one who is in the same "clothing" as at birth.

in orbit (to be) *adj.* to be on drugs.

in the buff (to be) *exp.* (mild) to be nude.
♦ VARIATION: **to be buffo** *adj.*

in the gutter (to be) *exp.* (mild) to be indecent • *Your mind is always in the gutter*; Your mind is always focusing on indecent acts.
♦ NOTE: This is actually a parody on the term *"dirty,"* a synonym for "pornographic," since that which is found in the gutter is extremely dirty.

in the ozone (to be) *exp.* to have left one's senses and be as far away from them as the ozone layer.

in the raw (to be) *exp.* (humorous) to be nude; said of one who is exposing his/her "raw meat."

-J-

J.O. (to) *v.* masturbation • *I'm gonna go J.O.*; I'm going to go masturbate.
♦ NOTE: This is a euphemistic abbreviation of the verb to *"jack off"* which is considered vulgar.

jack off (to) *exp.* (very popular yet crude) to masturbate • *Is it true she jacked you off last night?*; Is it true she masturbated you last night?

jackass (to be a) *n.* (somewhat crude) • **1.** an imbecile • **2.** a despicable person.

jam house *n.* the locale where cocaine is bought.

jammer *n.* cocaine user.

jay *n.* a marijuana cigarette.

jellyfish (to be a) *n.* (mild) a meek and fearful person.

jerk (to be a) *n.* (mild) an extremely foolish, unthinking, and despicable person.

jerk the joint (to) *exp.* to masturbate • *My little brother just jerked the joint yesterday for the first time;* My little brother just masturbated for the first time.
 ♦ NOTE: This is a somewhat humorous, yet crude, expression comparing the action of masturbating with that of *"jerking a joint"* or more literally, "tugging one's attachment."

jerkin' the gherkin *exp.* (humorous) to masturbate • *He's been jerkin' the gherkin for an entire hour in there!;* He's been masturbating for an entire hour in there!
 ♦ NOTE (1): This is a humorous, yet crude, rhyming expression which compares the action of masturbating with that of *"jerking a gherkin pickle."*
 ♦ NOTE (2): gherkin *n.* penis (due to its similar shape to a pickle).

"Jiminy Cricket!" *exclam.* used to indicate surprise and disbelief (may be used as a euphemistic replacement for *"Jesus Christ"* which is considered to be irreverent) • *Jiminy Cricket! Where did you find all that money?;* What a surprise! Where did you find all that money?
 ♦ NOTE (1): This exclamation is based on a famous cartoon character whose initials are the same as Jesus Christ and consequently may be used as a euphemistic replacement.
 ♦ NOTE (2): This exclamation is used primarily in jest.
 ♦ SYNONYM: **"Jiminy**

Christmas!"** *exclam.* used primarily in jest.

john (to go to the) *n.* (mild) to go to the bathroom (and defecate or urinate, depending on the context).
 ♦ NOTE: This term comes from the inventor of the first flush toilet, Sir John Crapper.

joint *n.* a marijuana cigarette.

joy flakes *n.* cocaine.

joy pop (to) *v.* to take drugs.

joy powder *n.* • **1.** cocaine • **2.** heroin.

joy-stick *n.* (mild) penis.
 ♦ NOTE: This is a humorous term comparing the joy-stick used to control computer games to the shape of a penis which causes "joy" when stimulated.

juggler *n.* drug supplier.

jughead (to be a) *n.* (mild) a foolish and unthinking person • (lit); a person who has an empty jug in place of a head.

jugs *n.pl.* (humorous) large breasts.

jump (to) *v.* (mild) to attack sexually • *As soon as they got home, he jumped her!;* As soon as they got home, he attacked her sexually.

jump one's bones (to) *exp.* (somewhat crude) to fornicate • *He's not really interested in you. He just wants to jump your bones!;* He's not really interested in you. He just wants to have sex with you!

junior *n.* (mild) penis.

junked up (to be) *adj.* to be on drugs.

junker *n.* drug supplier.

-K-

keester *n.* (humorous) buttocks.
 ♦ VARIATION: **keister.**

kick ass (to) *exp.* to do something aggressively and extremely well • *I can't believe how fast they're constructing that new house. They're really kickin' ass!;* I can't believe how fast they're constructing that new house. They're really doing it aggressively and extremely well.

▶ ALSO: **to kick some ass** *exp.* to beat up or to reprimand (depending on the context) • *If those neighbors keep playing that loud music, I'm gonna go over there and kick some ass;* If those neighbors keep playing that loud music, I'm going to go over there and reprimand them.

kiss-ass (to be a) *exp.* (vulgar) said of someone who does anything to get in the good graces of someone • *He keeps buying the boss lunch all the time. What a kiss-ass;* He keeps buying the boss lunch all the time. He'll do anything to get in the boss's good graces.

▶ SYNONYM: **to brown-nose** *v.* (vulgar) said of someone who "kisses someone's ass" to such a degree as to get his/her nose brown.

knockers *n.pl.* (humorous) large breasts.

know enough to come in from the rain (not to) *exp.* said of a person who does not have the common sense to come inside to escape the rain.

know shit about something (not to) *exp.* not to know the slightest thing about something • *She doesn't know shit about cooking;* She doesn't know the slightest thing about cooking.

▶ VARIATION: **not to know jack shit about something** *exp.*

know-it-all (to be a) *exp.* (mild) one who boasts distastefully about the knowledge one has whether it is justified or not.

knucklehead (to be a) *n.* (mild) an affectionate term for a silly person.

kook (to be a) *n.* to be a peculiar and unpredictable person.

▶ VARIATION: **kooky (to be)** *adj.* to be peculiar and unpredictable.

-L-

Lady H. *n.* heroin.

lady of the evening *exp.* (mild) prostitute.

lamebrain (to be a) *n.* (mild) a foolish and unthinking person • (lit); a person with an impaired brain.

lard-ass (to be a) *exp.* to have fat buttocks.

▶ NOTE: ass *n.* (vulgar) buttocks.

lardo (to be a) *n.* to be a fat person.

▶ NOTE: The term *"lardo"* is a slang transformation of the noun "lard" meaning "fat."

last of the big spenders (to be the) *exp.* (mild) a facetious expression said of a miser.

▶ VARIATION: **to be the last of the big-time spenders** *exp.* (mild).

laugh at the lawn (to) *exp.* (humorous) to vomit.

▶ NOTE: This is a humorous expression, used in reference to an individual describing a cat vomiting after eating grass.

law *n.* (mild, used primarily in westerns) police officer • *He's the law around here;* He's the sheriff around here.

lay a log (to) *exp.* (a crude and very descriptive expression) to defecate.

▶ NOTE: **log** *n.* a bowel movement (due to its long cylindrical shape).

lay one on the lips (to) *exp.* to kiss • *She tried to lay one on my lips but I turned away;* She tried to kiss me but I turned away.

leak (to) *v.* (mild) to urinate • (lit); to dribble liquid.

▶ VARIATION: **to take a leak** *exp.* (extremely popular yet somewhat crude).

let one fly (to) *exp.* (mild) to have flatulence, to have gas.

let one go (to) *exp.* (mild) to have flatulence • *Who let one go?*; Who has flatulence?

lid *n.* one ounce of marijuana.
‣ NOTE: This term was extremely popular in the 1960s and is now outdated.

line *n.* a dosage of cocaine since it is traditionally sniffed in *"rows"* or *"lines."*

little boys'/girls' room *exp.* may be used as a euphemistic replacement for "bathroom" • *Excuse me, can you tell me where the little girls' room is?*; Excuse me, can you tell me where the bathroom is?
‣ NOTE: Some people feel that to use the word *"bathroom,"* (which is certainly an acceptable term) is rather crude and unrefined.

little girls' room *exp.* (mild) women's toilet.
‣ NOTE: This is a common term given to a public bathroom for little girls. This term is used euphemistically in reference to an adult in an attempt to soften the indelicacy of announcing a trip to the toilet.

loaded (to be) *adj.* to be on drugs.

locked up (to be) *adj.* to be in prison.
‣ ALSO: **to lock up** *exp.* to put in jail.

lone weed *n.* marijuana.

long arm *n.* (mild) police officer.

long arm of the law *exp.* (mild) police officer.

long in the tooth (to be) *exp.* (mild) said of someone who is getting old.

long-winded (to be) *exp.* (mild) said of someone whose excessive chatter produces large amounts of wind.

look like death warmed over (to) *exp.* (mild) to look ugly or sick.

loony (to be) *adj.* to be peculiar and unpredictable.

‣ NOTE: This comes from the noun "lunatic" meaning a "crazy person."

loony tune (to be a) *n.*
‣ NOTE: This is a common series of cartoons created by Warner Bros. studios and is used here as a play-on- words since it contains the word *"loony."*

loose (to be) *adj.* (mild) to be promiscuous.

loser (to be a) *n.* (mild) to be an unlucky, clumsy, and miserable person • *You're dating that loser?*; You're dating that miserable person?

loudmouth (to be a) *n.* (mild) to be a talkative and loud person.

love handles (to have) *exp.* an affectionate expression referring to the ring of fat around one's midsection.

love muscle *n.* (somewhat crude) penis.

low-down no-good (to be) *adj.* (mild) vile, contemptible.
‣ NOTE: This is a very popular adjective used in conjunction with any one of the nouns in this section.

low-life (to be a) *n.* (mild) a very low individual.

lunkhead (to be a) *n.* (mild) a foolish and unthinking person.

Lysergic Acid Diethylamide (L.S.D.)

-M-

M.F. (to be an) *n.* a euphemistic abbreviation for *"mother-fucker,"* an extremely vulgar synonym for a "despicable person."
‣ VARIATION: **mo-fo** *n.*

M.F. *exp.* despicable person • *He's such an M.F.!*; He's such a despicable person!
‣ NOTE: This is a euphemistic

abbreviation of *"mother fucker"* which is considered vulgar.

mack *n.* (mild) one who finds customers for prostitutes, a pimp.
 ♦ VARIATION (1): **mackerel** *n.* (mild).
 ♦ VARIATION (2): **mackman** *n.* (mild).
 ♦ VARIATION (3): **macko man** *n.* (mild).

mad as a hatter (to be) *exp.* • (lit); to be as crazy as one who sells hats.
 ♦ NOTE: Many decades ago, hat sellers were known for being crazy since the hats they made (and wore) contained lead-based dyes which would be absorbed by the skin and cause insanity.

madame *n.* (mild) the female director of a brothel.

maggot (to be a) *n.* • **1.** (mild) to be a despicable person • (lit); fly larva • **2.** pimp (known only among the world of prostitution).

mainline (to) *v.* to take drugs.

make (to) *v.* (mild) to defecate • *The baby looks like he's about to make in his pants;* The baby looks like he's about to defecate in his pants.

make a pit stop (to) *exp.* (mild) to stop one's routine temporarily and go to the bathroom.
 ♦ NOTE: This expression comes from the sport of auto racing where drivers will temporarily exit the race in order to make car repairs which are performed in the *"pit."* This is commonly called *"making a pit stop."*

make whoopie (to) *exp.* (mild) to fornicate • *Let's go home and make whoopie;* Let's go home and have sex.

maracas *n.pl.* (humorous) large breasts.

Mary *n.* marijuana.

Mary Jane *n.* marijuana.
 ♦ NOTE: The letters "M" and "J" in *"Mary Jane"* represent "marijuana."

Mary Wanna *n.* marijuana.
 ♦ NOTE: *"Mary Wanna"* and "marijuana" are similar in pronunciation.

Mary Warner *n.* marijuana.
 ♦ NOTE: *"Mary Warner"* and "marijuana" are similar in pronunciation.

massage parlor *n.* (mild) brothel.
 ♦ NOTE: In states where prostitution is illegal, many brothels represented themselves as *"massage parlors"* which are legal.

Maui-wowee *n.* a strong marijuana coming from Hawaii.

mean shit (not to) *exp.* nothing • *This contract doesn't mean shit!;* This contract doesn't mean anything!

meat and two vegetables *exp.* a humorous, yet somewhat crude, description of a penis and testicles.

meat market *n.* (mild) brothel, bar, gym, etc.
 ♦ NOTE: This refers not only to brothels, but any establishment where people gather to look for sexual conquests.

meathead (to be a) *n.* (mild) a foolish and unthinking person • (lit); a person with nothing but a big piece of meat in place of a head.

melons *n.pl.* (humorous) large breasts.

meshuga (to be) *adj.* to be crazy.
 ♦ NOTE: This comes from Yiddish.
 ♦ VARIATION: **meshungina** *adj.*

Mexican brown *n.* • **1.** bad heroin • **2.** marijuana.

Mexican red *n.* marijuana.

middle leg *n.* (crude) penis.
 ♦ NOTE: This is a light-hearted term comparing the penis with

a leg.

▶ VARIATION: **third leg** n.

milk bottles n.pl. (humorous) large breasts.

milk the chicken (to) exp. (humorous yet crude) to masturbate • *If I milk the chicken before I go to work, I get too tired*; If I masturbate before I go to work, I get too tired.

▶ NOTE: This is a humorous, yet crude, expression comparing the action of masturbating and reaching orgasm with that of *"milking a chicken."* The *"chicken"* in this expression refers to a penis which resembles the shape of a chicken's neck.

milktoast (to be a) n. (mild) to be a spineless person.

▶ NOTE: Also spelled "milquetoast."

mindfuck (to) v. to mislead • *You actually believe what he's saying? I'm telling you, he's mindfucking you*; You actually believe what he's saying? I'm telling you, he's misleading you.

missing a few marbles (to be) exp. to be slightly crazy.

▶ VARIATION (1): **not to have all one's marbles** exp.

▶ VARIATION (2): **to lose one's marbles** exp. to become crazy.

missionary n. drug supplier.

moon someone (to) exp. to expose one's buttocks by pulling down one's pants and bending over • *Those guys over there just mooned us!*; Those guys over there just exposed their buttocks to us!

mosquito bites n.pl. (humorous) small breasts.

mother • **1.** n. despicable person (may be used as a euphemistic replacement for *"mother fucker"* which is considered extremely vulgar • *That guy's a real mother!*; That guy's a real despicable person! • **2.** adj. extremely difficult

• *What a mother of a homework assignment!*; What a difficult homework assignment!

mother-fucking exp. extremely infuriating • *I'm so tired of my mother fucking car breaking down every week!*; I'm so tired of my infuriating car breaking down every week!

▶ NOTE: Adding *"mother"* before *"fucking"* makes this a stronger expression: *fucking* = contemptible • *mother fucking* = extremely contemptible.

mother-fucker n. (extremely vulgar yet popular) an exceedingly despicable person.

mother • **1.** adj. extremely difficult • *This bicycle is a real mother to ride!*; This bicycle is extremely difficult to ride! • **2.** n. a despicable person • *He's a real mother!*; He's a real despicable person!

▶ ALSO: **a mother of a** exp. an extremely difficult • *This is a mother of a homework assignment!*; This is an extremely difficult homework assignment.

▶ ORIGIN: This is a commonly used euphemism for the adjective and noun *"fuck"* which is considered to be one of the crudest, yet most popular, obscenities in the American-English language. The term *"fuck"* is also a popular, yet vulgar, verb meaning "to have sexual intercourse." This term will be discussed in depth in lesson five.

motherfucker (to be a) exp. to be a despicable person • **1.** n. despicable person (a euphemistic replacement for "mother fucker" which is considered extremely vulgar) • *That guy's a real mother!*; That guy's a real despicable person! • **2.** adj. extremely difficult • *What a mother of a homework assignment!*; What a difficult homework assignment!

♦ VARIATION (1): **to be an M.F.** *exp.* a euphemistic abbreviation of *"to be a mother fucker."*

♦ VARIATION (2): **to be a mo-fo** *exp.* a euphemistic abbreviation of *"to be a mother fucker."*

motormouth (to be a) *n.* (humorous) to be an extremely talkative person (who chatters incessantly as if his/her mouth were motorized) • *I didn't say one word when I was with her today. She's such a motormouth!;* I didn't say one word when I was with her today. She talks incessantly!

Mr. Happy *n.* (humorous, mild) penis.
♦ NOTE: This term signifies the happiness or good feeling that is experienced when the penis is stimulated.

muff *n.* (crude) vagina.
♦ NOTE: **muff diver** *n.* one who enjoys oral sex with women.

muffin *n.* (crude) vagina.

-N-

nab (to) *v.* (mild) to arrest someone and issue a citation or escort to jail.

nail (to) *v.* (mild and very popular) to arrest someone and issue a citation or escort to jail.

naked as a jaybird (to be) *exp.* (mild) to be completely naked.

narc *n.* (mild) narcotics officer.

nature's call *exp.* (mild) time to go to the bathroom • *I'll be right back. It's nature's call;* I'll be right back. I have to go to the bathroom.
♦ VARIATION: **"Nature's calling"** *exp.* "I have to go to the bathroom."

"Nature's calling" *exp.* (mild) "I have to go to the bathroom."
♦ NOTE: This expression refers to either urination or defecation, depending on the context.

nerd (to be a) *n.* (mild) to be a foolish-looking person.

♦ VARIATION (1): **to be nerdy** *adj.*
♦ VARIATION (2): **to be nerded out** *exp.*

nightcrawler *n.* (mild) a police officer who patrols at night.

nincompoop (to be a) *n.* (humorous) a fool.
♦ NOTE: This term is primarily used in cartoons or in jest.

ninny (to be a) *n.* (humorous) a fool.
♦ NOTE: This term is primarily used in cartoons or in jest.

nitwit (to be a) *n.* (mild) a foolish and unthinking person.

"No shit!" *exp.* "You're not serious!" • *She married Jeff yesterday? No shit!;* She married Jeff yesterday? You're not serious!
♦ VARIATION: **"Shit no!"** *exp.* "Absolutely not!"

No shit! *exp.* • *"You're not kidding!"*.
♦ VARIATION: **"Shit no!"** *exp.* "Absolutely not!" • *–Did you like the dinner he made last night? –Shit no!;* –Did you like the dinner he made last night? –Absolutely not!
♦ ANTONYM: **"Shit yes!"**

no spring chicken (to be) *exp.* (mild) said of a person who is well past his/her prime.
♦ NOTE: This expression comes from farms where the *"spring chicken"* was considered to be the most desirable, young, tender, and flavorful.

nookie *n.* (humorous) sex • *How about a little nookie?;* How about having a little sex?

nose candy *n.* (mild and popular) cocaine.
♦ VARIATION: **candy** *n.*

not all there (to be) *exp.* to be slightly crazy.

not playing with a full deck (to be) *exp.* (humorous) said of someone who is slightly crazy.
♦ NOTE: This expression comes

from card playing where an incomplete deck of cards results in an inconsistent and unusual game. Here, the lack of a full deck refers to the lack of a complete set of brains.
> ♦ VARIATION: **to be a few cards short of a desk** *exp.*

nothing upstairs (to have) *exp.*
> ♦ NOTE: In this expression, *"upstairs"* refers to one's head.

number one *exp.* may be used as a euphemistic replacement for "urination" • *I have to go number one;* I have to urinate.

number two *exp.* may be used as a euphemistic replacement for "defecation" • *The little baby went number two in his diapers;* The little baby defecated in his diapers.

numbskull (to be a) *n.* (somewhat humorous) an affectionate term for a foolish and unthinking person.

nut case (to be a) *n.* to be crazy.

nuts (to be) *adj.* (very popular).
> ♦ VARIATION: **to be just plain nuts** *exp.*

nuts *n.pl.* (vulgar) testicles.

nutty (to be) *adj.* to be nonsensical.
> ♦ VARIATION: A common play-on-words of this expression is *"to be nuttier than a fruitcake"* which is known for being full of nuts.

-O-

O.D. (to) *v.* to drug overdose.

O.P.P. *exp.* one's sexual organs • *He got into O.P.P. last night;* He had sex last night.
> ♦ NOTE: These are some of the newest slang initials in the American repertory and are known only by the younger generation. Unbeknownst to most parents, *"O.P.P."* comes from rap music and stands for "other people's pussy" (*"pussy"* is a vulgar slang synonym

for vagina) or "other people's penis."

O.T.R. *exp.* in a terrible mood • *Don't talk to her now. She's O.T.R.;* Don't talk to her now. She's in a terrible mood.
> ♦ NOTE: This is a euphemistic abbreviation of *"on the rag"* which is a vulgar expression applied to women who are menstruating. Although the term *"rag"* is used in slang to mean "sanitary napkin," this expression is occasionally applied to a male who is in a bad mood as well.

ocifer *n.* (derogatory) police officer.
> ♦ NOTE: This term was particularly popular in the 1960s.

off one's nut (to be) *exp.* (humorous) crazy.

off one's rocker (to be) *exp.* (humorous) crazy.

off one's trolley (to be) *exp.* (humorous) crazy.

off the deep end (to go) *exp.* to became completely crazy.

off-color (to be) *adj.* (mild) to be somewhat pornographic.

old coot (to be an) *exp.* (mild) a foolish and cantankerous person.

old fart (to be an) *n.* (somewhat crude yet humorous) • **1.** said of someone with outdated ideas • **2.** said of someone with no enthusiasm for physical activity • (lit); to be an old flatulence.

old poop (to be an) *n.* (humorous) • **1.** said of someone with outdated ideas • **2.** said of someone with no enthusiasm for physical activity • (lit); to be an old bowel movement.

old-timer (to be an) *n.* to be old • (lit); (mild) one who has been living for a long time.

older than dirt (to be) *exp.* (humorous) to be extremely old.
> ♦ VARIATION (1): **to be older than Methusela** *exp.* (mild).

♦ VARIATION (2): **to be older than Moses** *exp.* (mild).

♦ VARIATION (3): **to be older than the hills (to be)** *exp.* (mild).

oldster (to be an) *n.* (mild) to be old.

on a cloud (to be) *adj.* to be on drugs.

on an ego trip (to be) *exp.* (mild) to be completely self-impressive and self-absorbed.

on one's high horse (to be) *exp.* (mild) to be self-impressed.

on one's last legs (to be) *exp.* (mild) to be so old as to be close to death.

♦ NOTE: This term is also commonly applied to an old appliance which is about to cease functioning.

on someone's ass (to be) *exp.* to harass someone • *I'll do it when I'm ready! Just get off my ass!;* I'll do it when I'm ready! Just stop harassing me!

on the make (to be) *exp.* (mild) to solicit.

♦ NOTE: This expression is used to refer to someone who is looking for a sexual partner as well as a prostitute who is looking for a client.

on the needle (to be) *adj.* to be on drugs.

on the rag (to be) *exp.* (vulgar) to be in a bad mood • (lit); to be menstruating • *You're sure on the rag today!;* You're sure in a bad mood today!

♦ NOTE: In this expression, *"rag"* refers to a woman's sanitary napkin used during menstruation. Oddly enough, this expression is now also heard in reference to a man who is in a bad mood.

♦ VARIATION: **to be O.T.R.** *adj.* a common abbreviation and euphemism of the expression *"to be on the rag."*

on the streets (to be) *exp.* (mild) said of a prostitute who is working on the streets.

♦ VARIATION: **to walk the streets** *exp.* (mild).

on the turf (to be) *exp.* (mild) to solicit.

♦ NOTE: The term *"turf"* is used to refer to the area where prostitutes work.

on the weed (to be) *adj.* to be on marijuana.

one foot in the grave (to have) *exp.* (mild) to be close to death.

one-eyed monster *n.* (humorous, mild) penis.

♦ NOTE: This is a humorous term for penis which is compared to a monster with one eye.

one-eyed wonder *n.* (humorous, mild) penis.

♦ NOTE: This is a humorous term for penis which is compared to a miracle with one eye.

operator *n.* drug supplier.

out of it (to be) *adj.* • **1.** to be intoxicated (from alcohol or drugs) • **2.** to be in a state of oblivion (due to fatigue or meditation).

out of one's gourd (to be) *exp.* to have left one's senses.

♦ NOTE: **gourd** *n.* (humorous) head.

out of one's head (to be) *exp.* to have left one's senses.

out of one's mind (to be) *exp.* to have left one's senses.

out of one's skull (to be). *exp.* to have left one's senses.

out of one's tree (to be) *exp.* to have left one's senses.

out there (to be) *exp.* to be very bizarre.

out to lunch (to be) *exp.* (humorous) to have left one's senses.

♦ VARIATION: **to be O.T.L.** *exp.* a common abbreviation of *"to be out to lunch."*

over the edge (to be) *exp.* to have fallen into a state of madness.

over the hill (to be) *exp.* (mild) to be old.
> ♦ NOTE: In this expression, *"the hill"* represents youth.

overamp (to) *v.* to drug overdose.

overcharge (to) *v.* to drug overdose.

overjolt (to) *v.* to drug overdose.

overvamp (to) *v.* to drug overdose.

-P-

P.O.'d (to be) *adj.* to be extremely angry • *I'm really P.O.'d because my brother borrowed my shirt without asking!;* I'm really angry because my brother borrowed my shirt without asking!
> ♦ NOTE: This is a commonly used euphemism for the expression *"to be pissed off."* This expression is considered somewhat crude since it contains the verb *"to piss"* which is vulgar for "to urinate."

P.W.'d (to be) *exp.* to be subserviant to one's wife • *His wife does nothing but yell at him all the time and he does everything she tells him to do! He sure is P.W.'d!;* His wife does nothing but yell at him all the time and he does everything she tells him to do! He sure is subserviant to his wife!
> ♦ NOTE: This is a euphemistic abbreviation of the extremely vulgar expression *"to be pussy-whipped;" "pussy"* being a vulgar slang synonym for "vagina."

"Pardon my French" *exp.* "Forgive my use of obscenities."
> ♦ NOTE: This is a common apology used by the speaker for having just used an obscenity. The word *"French"* is used facetiously and ironically since Americans regard the language as being beautiful and romantic; quite the opposite of a vulgarism or obscenity.

pass gas (to) *exp.* (mild) to have flatulence.

peace *n.* lysergic acid diethylamide (L.S.D.)

pecker *n.* (humorous, mild) penis.
> ♦ NOTE: This term signifies a penis which looks like it's pecking during sex. It's important to note that in England, the term *"pecker"* simply means "chin."

peddle ass (to) *exp.* (vulgar) to solicit • (lit); to sell buttocks.

peddler *n.* drug supplier.

pee (to) *v.* (extremely popular yet somewhat crude) to urinate.

pee-pee (to go) *v.* (mild) to urinate.
> ♦ NOTE: This verb is commonly used with children as a diminutive form of the verb *"to pee."*

pee-pee *n.* (baby talk, mild) penis.
> ♦ NOTE: This term comes from the verb *"to pee"* which means "to urinate."

peenie *n.* (baby talk, mild) penis.
> ♦ NOTE: This is a diminutive form of "penis."

peewee (to be a) *n.* (mild) an abusive name given to a short person.

pen *n.* a common abbreviation for "penitentiary."
> ♦ ALSO: **State Pen** *n.* State Penitentiary.

penny-pinching (to be) *adj.* (mild) a figurative expression signifying one who has difficulty spending as little money as a penny to which he/she holds on tightly.
> ♦ ALSO: **to be a penny- pincher** *n.*

peter *n.* may be used as a euphemistic replacement for "penis" • *That guy's bathing suit is so tight, you can see his peter!;* That guy's bathing suit is so tight, you can see his penis!

pick up (to) *v.* (mild and very popular) • **1.** to arrest someone and issue a citation or escort to jail • **2.** to find a sexual partner.

piddle (to) *v.* (humorous) to urinate.
  ‣ NOTE: This verb is primarily used with children.

piece of shit (to be a) *exp.* to be a despicable person • *I can't believe you deceived me like that, you piece of shit!*; I can't believe you deceived me like that, you despicable person!

pig (to be a) *n.* (mild) • **1.** to be an ugly and dirty person. • **2.** to be very fat.
  ‣ ALSO: **to be a fat pig** *exp.*

piker (to be a) *n.* to be miserly.

pinch a loaf (to) *exp.* (crude) to defecate.
  ‣ NOTE: **loaf** *n.* a bowel movement • (lit); a mass of meat.
  ‣ NOTE: This expression signifies the pinching action of the anal sphincter when a bowel movement is released.

pinhead (to be a) *n.* (somewhat humorous) a foolish and unthinking person • (lit); one who has a head the size of that of a pinhead with a brain to match.

piss (to) *v.* (vulgar) to urinate.
  ‣ VARIATION: **to take a piss** *exp.* (very popular yet vulgar).

pisser (to be a) *n.* (vulgar) to be aggravating • *I got yelled at again by the teacher. What a pisser!*; I got yelled at again by the teacher. How aggravating!
  ‣ NOTE: **to be pissed [off]** *exp.* (crude) to be angry.

pisser *n.* (vulgar) penis.
  ‣ NOTE: This comes from the verb "to piss," meaning "to urinate," which is considered vulgar.

pistol *n.* (somewhat crude) penis.
  ‣ NOTE: A pistol can be compared to a penis since both have cylindrical shafts and can both shoot; the pistol shoots bullets and the penis shoots semen during orgasm.

play bouncy-bouncy (to) *exp.* (humorous) to fornicate • *I think they're playing bouncy-bouncy upstairs;* I think they're having sex upstairs.
  ‣ NOTE: This expression comes from the bouncing noise which comes from the springs of a bed during sex.

play the skin flute (to) *exp.* • **1.** a humorous, yet crude expression signifying oral sex with a male • *So, did you play the skin flute last night?;* So, did you perform oral sex with him last night? • **2.** to masturbate.
  ‣ NOTE: **skin flute** *exp.* penis.

play with oneself (to) *exp.* (extremely popular and mild) to masturbate or toy with one's genitals • *It's very natural for children to start playing with themselves at an early age;* It's very natural for children to play with their genitals at an early age.

poison *n.* heroin.

poke (to) *v.* (crude yet humorous) to fornicate • *Are you gonna poke her tonight?;* Are you going to have sex with her tonight?

pokey *n.* police officer (used primarily in old gangster movies and westerns).

pole *n.* (mild) penis.
  ‣ NOTE: This noun is used to signify "penis" since both are long and cylindrical.

polish the lance (to) *exp.* (humorous) to masturbate • *I'm so turned on now! I think I need to go polish the lance;* I'm so sexually excited now! I think I need to go masturbate.
  ‣ NOTE: This is a humorous, yet crude, expression comparing the action of masturbating with that of *"polishing a lance"* which is long and hard like a penis.

poo-poo (to go) *v.* (mild) to defecate.
  ◆ NOTE: This is a common euphemism used with children • *Do you have to go poo-poo?*; Do you have to defecate?

poop *n.* may be used as a euphemistic replacement for "defecation" • *I have to go poop*; I have to go defecate.
  ◆ ALSO (1): **poop** *n.* • **1.** specifics • *So, give me the poop on the new neighbors! What are they like?*; So, give me the specifics on the new neighbors! What are they like? • **2.** gossip • *Did you hear the poop about our new teacher?*; Did you hear the gossip about our new teacher? • **3.** a term of affection • *I love you, you old poop!* • **4.** a malcontent, a grouch • *He never wants to do anything with us. He's such an old poop!*; He never wants to do anything with us. He's such a malcontent!

pop (to) *v.* to take drugs.

pops *n.* a name given to an old man (and can be disrespectful depending on the context).
  ◆ NOTE: This is also an affectionate term for one's father.

porker (to be a) *n.* to be extremely fat as well as an overzealous eater.
  ◆ VARIATION: **pig** *adj.* to be fat as a pig.

porn *n.* (mild) pornography • *That film is nothing but porn!*; That film is nothing but pornography!
  ◆ VARIATION: **porno** *adj.* (mild)

pot *n.* • **1.** (somewhat crude) toilet.
  ◆ NOTE: This term comes from the obsolete "chamber pot" which was simply a portable bowl used for urination and defecation.
  ◆ VARIATION: **potty** *n.* Used only with children, this is a mild diminutive of *"pot"*. • **2.** (mild and very popular) marijuana.
  ◆ NOTE: **pothead** *n.* marijuana addict.

powder *n.* • **1.** heroin • **2.** cocaine.

powder one's nose (to) *exp.* (mild).
  ◆ NOTE: This is an excuse a woman may give for having to go the bathroom to either defecate or urinate, since to be completely truthful would be considered crude.

prat *n.* (mild) buttocks.

pray to the porcelain god (to) *exp.* (humorous) to vomit.
  ◆ NOTE: This is a humorous description of someone kneeling in front of the toilet vomiting.

prick *n.* (vulgar) • **1.** penis • **2.** despicable person.

private parts *exp.* (mild) penis.
  ◆ NOTE: A very popular euphemism describing one's genitals.

privates *n.pl.* (mild) penis.
  ◆ NOTE: A popular euphemism describing one's genitals.

pruneface (to be a) *n.* (humorous) a name given to an old person whose face is wrinkled like a prune.

psycho (to be) *adj.* to be extremely crazy.
  ◆ NOTE: This is a common abbreviation of "psychotic."

pucker up (to) *exp.* to prepare to give a kiss • *Pucker up 'cause I'm gonna give you a big kiss!*; Get prepared because I'm going to give you a big kiss!

puke (to) *v.* (extremely popular yet crude) to vomit.

pull in (to) *v.* (mild) to escort to jail.

pull some shit on someone (to) *exp.* to do something nasty to someone • *I'm not talking to him anymore because he pulled some shit on me yesterday*; I'm not talking to him anymore because he did something nasty to me yesterday.

puny (to be) *adj.* (mild) to be very short.

pusher *n.* drug supplier.

pussy *n.* (popular, yet vulgar) vagina.
 ♦ NOTE: In England, this term has only one definition: "a small cat" whereas in America, it has the additional definition of "vagina."

put away (to be) *exp.* to be put in jail.
 ♦ ALSO: **to put away** *exp.* to put in jail.

put on airs (to be) *exp.* (mild) to be pretentious and phoney.

put on ice (to be) *exp.* to be put in jail.
 ♦ ALSO: **to put on ice** *exp.* to put in jail.

put out (to) *exp.* (mild) to engage someone in sex • *If you're hoping to have sex with her, forget it. She doesn't put out;* If you're hoping to have sex with her, forget it. She doesn't engage in sex.

put the bite on (to) *v.* (mild) to arrest someone and issue a citation or escort to jail.

put the cuffs on someone (to) *v.* (mild) to escort someone to jail.
 ♦ VARIATION: **to slap the cuffs on someone** *exp.* (mild).

putz *n.* (mild) • **1.** penis • **2.** despicable person.
 ♦ NOTE: This term comes from Yiddish meaning "penis."

-R-

rack salesman *n.* (mild) pimp.
 ♦ NOTE: This comes from the term "meat rack" since the word "meat" may be used to refer to a person.

Ralph (to) *v.* (humorous) to vomit.
 ♦ NOTE: This humorous verb signifies the sound one makes while vomiting.

rammer *n.* (crude) penis.
 ♦ NOTE: This term signifies the "penis" due to its ramming action during sex.

ramrod *n.* (crude) penis.
 ♦ NOTE: This term signifies the

"penis" due to its ramming action during sex.

rap sheet *n.* (mild) a police record on a criminal.

rat (to be a) *n.* (mild) to be a despicable person.

rat fink (to be a) *n.* (mild).
 ♦ NOTE: This is an older term used mainly in jest.

rattle on (to) *exp.* (mild) to talk nonstop.

raunchy (to be) *adj.* (mild) to be pornographic and somewhat rough • *He's into raunchy sex;* He enjoys rough sex.
 ♦ VARIATION: **to be into raunch** *exp.* (mild) to enjoy rough and even painful sex.

raw (to be) *adj.* (mild) to be pornographic and unrefined.

ready (to be) *adj.* (mild).
 ♦ NOTE: Depending on the context, this adjective may be used to mean "ready for sex."

rear end *n.* (mild) buttocks.

red chicken *n.* heroin.

red-light district *n.* (mild) the neighborhood where prostitution takes place.
 ♦ NOTE: The neighborhood or location where prostitutes are known to congregate is called the *"red-light district"* due to the traditional red light in front of each brothel.
 ♦ ALSO: **red lighterie** *n.*

reefer *n.* a marijuana cigarette.

reefer man *n.* drug supplier.

regular (to be) *adj.* (mild) to have regular bowel movements (without the displeasure of constipation).

relic (to be a) *n.* (humorous) • (lit); to be an artifact from a past era.
 ♦ VARIATION: **to be an old relic** *n.*

retch (to) *v.* (humorous) to vomit.
 ♦ NOTE: This humorous verb

signifies the sound one makes while vomiting.

rip someone a new asshole (to) *exp.* to reprimand someone severely • *I can't believe that he'd do something so mean! I'm gonna go rip him a new asshole!*; I can't believe that he'd do something so mean! I'm going to go reprimand him severely!

ripped (to be) *adj.* • **1.** on drugs • **2.** drunk.

roach *n.* (mild) a marijuana cigarette.

road apple *n.* (mild) humorous term for "excrement" found in the road.

rock *n.* crack cocaine.

rock house *n.* the locale where cocaine is bought.
  ◗ NOTE: A common slang term for "cocaine" is *"rock."*

rock out (to) *v.* to drug overdose.

rocks *n.pl.* (mild) testicles.

Rocky Mountain oysters *n.pl.* a southern delicacy of cooked pig testicles.

rod *n.* (crude) penis.
  ◗ NOTE: This term signifies the "penis" since both are long and cylindrical.

rod of love *n.* (crude) penis.
  ◗ NOTE: This term signifies the "penis" since both are long and cylindrical.

roll in the hay (to) *exp.* (humorous) to fornicate • *How about a roll in the hay?*; How about some sex?

roll the fuzzy dice (to) *exp.* (humorous, yet crude) to masturbate • *I'm gonna go roll the fuzzy dice*; I'm going to go masturbate.
  ◗ NOTE: This is a humorous, yet crude, expression based on gambling slang, to *"roll the dice"* which has been altered since *"fuzzy dice"* refer to the testicles.

romp (to) *v.* (mild) to fornicate • (lit); to frolic • *Let's go romp in the basement*; Let's go have sex in the basement.

round heels (to have) *exp.* (mild) said of a girl who is always on her back with her heels dragging on the ground, being passed from one to the other.

row *n.* a dosage of cocaine since it is traditionally sniffed in *"rows"* or *"lines."*

rub the rod (to) *exp.* (humorous) to masturbate • *Is he rubbing the rod upstairs again?*; Is he masturbating upstairs again?
  ◗ NOTE: This is a humorous, yet crude, expression comparing the action of masturbating with that of *"rubbing a rod"* which is long and hard like a penis.

rump *n.* (mild) buttocks.

run a stable (to) *v.* (mild) said of a pimp who has a string of *"working girls."*

run in (to) *v.* (mild) to escort to jail.

run like shit (to) *exp.* to run quickly • *Run like shit! They're after us!*; Run quickly! They're after us!

runt (to be a) *n.* (mild) an abusive name given to a short person • *He may look like a runt, but he's very strong*; He may look very small and frail, but he's very strong.

-S-

S.B.D. *exp.* (humorous) silent, yet potent, flatulence • *Who cut the S.B.D.?*; Who has the silent flatulence?
  ◗ NOTE: This is a euphemistic abbreviation of "silent but deadly" which is considered humorous.

S.E.X. *n.* may be used as a euphemistic replacement for the word "sex" which is considered, by some, to be improper to say unless spelled • *I think they're finally going to have S.E.X.*

S.O.B. *exp.* a despicable person • *I'm gonna kill that S.O.B.!;* I'm going to kill that despicable person!
♦ NOTE: This is a euphemistic abbreviation of *"son of a bitch"* which is considered vulgar.

S.O.L. *exp.* extremely unfortunate • *I'm sorry but you missed dinner because you're so late. I guess you're just S.O.L.;* I'm sorry but you missed dinner because you're so late. I guess you're just extremely unfortunate.
♦ NOTE: This is a euphemistic abbreviation of *"shit out of luck"* which is considered vulgar.

S.O.S. *exp.* an army term for "chipped beef on toast" which was referred to as *"shit on a shingle"* or "S.O.S."

S.T.D. *n.* sexually transmitted disease.

salami *n.* (crude) penis.
♦ NOTE: This term signifies the "penis" since both are long and cylindrical.

salt *n.* heroin.

sausage *n.* (crude) penis.
♦ NOTE: This term signifies the "penis" since both are long and cylindrical.

scag *n.* heroin.

Scag Jones *n.* heroin addict.

scagman *n.* drug supplier.

scare the shit out of someone (to) *exp.* to scare someone terribly • *You scared the shit out of me when you jumped out of the closet!;* You scared me terribly when you jumped out of the closet!
♦ ALSO: **to be scared shitless** *exp.* to be scared terribly • (lit); to be so scared that one defecates.

scaredy-cat (to be a) *n.* (mild) coward.

♦ NOTE: This term is commonly used among children.

scatterbrain (to be a) *n.* (mild) one who is forgetful and unreliable.

schizo (to be) *adj.* to have two personalities.
♦ NOTE: This is a common abbreviation of "schizophrenic."
♦ VARIATION (1): **to be schizoid** *adj.*
♦ VARIATION (2): **to be schized out** *exp.*

schmo (to be a) *n.* (mild) a fool.
♦ NOTE: This comes from Yiddish.

score (to) *v.* • **1.** (mild) to fornicate • *Did you finally score with Anne?;* Did you finally have sex with Anne? • **2.** to buy drugs.

scramble *n.* heroin.

screw (to) *v.* (vulgar) to fornicate • *All she ever wants to do is screw;* All she ever wants to do is have sex.
♦ NOTE: This verb comes from the image of a screw penetrating an object.

screw loose (to have a) *exp.* to be slightly crazy.
♦ NOTE: It would be less common to hear *"to have a loose screw."*
♦ VARIATION: **to have a few screws loose** *exp.*

screwball (to be a) *n.* to be a crazy person.

screwy (to be) *adj.* to be peculiar.

seat *n.* (humorous) buttocks.

sent up the river (to get) *exp.* to be put in jail.
♦ ALSO: **to send up the river** *exp.* to put in jail.

service station *n.* (humorous) brothel.
♦ NOTE: This comes from the verb *"to service"* which has the slang connotation of "to satisfy (someone) sexually."

shake hands with the governor (to) *exp.* (humorous) to masturbate • *I*

think he's shaking hands with the governor; I think he's masturbating.
♦ NOTE: The term *"governor"* is a humorous, yet uncommon, term for "penis" since one's sex organs tend to "govern" the actions of many people.

shift gears (to) *exp.* (humorous) to masturbate • *He's a little young to be shifting gears, isn't he?;* He's a little young to be masturbating, isn't he?
♦ NOTE: This is a humorous expression comparing the action of masturbating with that of *"shifting gears"* in a car.

shit • (vulgar) 1. *v.* to defecate • *I gotta go shit;* I have to go defecate. • **2.** *n.* one's personal belongings • *Go get your shit and let's leave;* Go get your belongings and let's leave. • **3.** *adv.* nothing • *He gave me shit for my birthday;* He didn't give me anything for my birthday. • **4.** *n.* grief, trouble • *Why are you giving me so much shit?;* Why are you giving me so much trouble? • **5.** *n.* a despicable person • *She's such a shit!;* She such a despicable person! • **6.** heroin • **7.** marijuana.

shit a brick (to) *exp.* to be extremely frightened or shocked • *When I saw my girlfriend walk in the door, I thought I was gonna shit a brick!;* When I saw my girlfriend walk in the door, I became shocked!

shit ass *n.* (extremely vulgar) a despicable person.

shit for brains (to have) *exp.* (vulgar) to be extremely stupid • (lit); to have excrement for brains • *Can you believe what he did? He must have shit for brains!;* Can you believe what he did? He must be a complete idiot!
♦ VARIATION: **shit-for-brains** *exp.* an incredibly stupid person • *Hey, shit-for-brains!;* Hey, stupid!

shit from shinola (not to know) *exp.* not to know anything • *He doesn't know shit from Shinola about football;* He doesn't know a thing about football.
♦ NOTE: Shinola is a brand name for shoe polish.

shit head *n.* (vulgar yet very popular) a despicable person • (lit); one with a head full of excrement.

shit hole *n.* (extremely vulgar) a despicable person • (lit); anal sphincter.

shit-kicker *n.* • **1.** farmer • *I'm tired of the city. Maybe I should just spend the rest of my life being a shit-kicker;* I'm tired of the city. Maybe I should just spend the rest of my life being a farmer. • **2.** boot • *I'm gonna go put on my shit-kickers;* I'm gonna go put on my boots.
♦ NOTE: This expression originated from farmers who spend a great deal of time with animals and, consequently, pass many hours cleaning up excrement.

shit on someone (to) *exp.* to betray someone • *I couldn't believe that my best friend could shit on me like that;* I couldn't believe that my best friend could betray me like that.

shit or get off the pot (to) *exp.* to take action or abandon the project • (lit); to defecate or get out of the bathroom • *Why are you taking so long to do something about resolving this situation? Shit or get off the pot!;* Why are you taking so long to do something about resolving this situation? Take action or abandon the project!

shit out of luck (to be) *exp.* to be extremely unfortunate • *I tried to get tickets for the concert, but they were sold out. I guess I'm just shit out of luck;* I tried to get tickets for the concert, but they were sold out. I guess I'm just unfortunate.

shit someone (to) *exp.* to tease someone • *Are you shitting me?;* Are you teasing me?

"Shit, yeah!" *exp.* "Absolutely!"

shit-eating grin (to have a) *exp.* to have an expression of gloating • *Look at him with his shit-eating grin!;* Look at him gloating!

shit-faced (to be) *adj.* to be intoxicated • *I got shit-faced last night;* I got intoxicated last night.

shit-head (to be a) *n.* (vulgar) a despicable person • *What a mean thing he did to you! What a shit-head!;* What a mean thing he did to you! What a despicable person!

shit • **1.** *n.* unidentifiable substance • *What's that shit you're drinking?;* What's that substance you're drinking? • **2.** *adv.* extremely • *He's shit stupid!;* He's really stupid!

shitfit (to have a) *exp.* to have a tantrum • *When my father sees what I did to his new tie, he's gonna have a shitfit!;* When my father sees what I did to his new tie, he's going to have a tantrum!

shithead (to be a) *exp.* to be a despicable person • *Your brother won't let you borrow his tennis racket? What a shithead!;* Your brother won't let you borrow his tennis racket? What a despicable person!

shithouse *n.* (vulgar yet extremely popular) toilet.
 ‣ NOTE: This comes from the verb *"to shit"* which is vulgar for "to defecate."
 ‣ VARIATION: **shitter** *n.* (vulgar).

shitlist *n.* a mental or physical roster of people that one dislikes • *If you get on the boss's shitlist, you'll be sorry;* If you become one of the people that the boss doesn't like, you'll be sorry.

shitload (a) *adv.* a lot • *I have a shitload of work to do today;* I have a lot of work to do today.

shitter *n.* toilet • *I have to go to the shitter;* I have to go to the toilet.

shittiest *adj.* worst • *He did the shittiest job painting his house;* He did the worst job painting his house.

shitty (to be) *adj.* to be disgraceful • *He did a shitty job decorating the house for the party;* He did a disgraceful job decorating the house for the party.

shlong *n.* (humorous) penis.

shmuck *n.* (vulgar) a despicable person • (lit); penis.
 ‣ ORIGIN: Yiddish.

shoot (to) *v.* (mild) • **1.** to have an orgasm • (lit); to discharge • **2.** to take drugs.

shoot one's load (to) *exp.* (vulgar) to have an orgasm • (lit); to discharge one's cargo.
 ‣ NOTE: This expression is considered to be vulgar due to the descriptive nature of *"load."*
 ‣ VARIATION: **to shoot one's wad** *exp.* (vulgar) • (lit); to discharge one's mass (of semen).

shoot the shit (to) *exp.* to chat • *I'm going over to Barry's to shoot the shit;* I'm going over to Barry's house to have a chat.

shoot up (to) *v.* to take drugs.

"Shoot!" a commonly used euphemism for *"Shit!"* used to denote excitement, surprise, or annoyance. *"Shoot!"* may be used in place of *gad, darn, etc.*

shorty (to be a) *n.* (mild) an abusive name given to a short person.

shout at one's shoes (to) *exp.* (humorous) to vomit.
 ‣ NOTE: This humorous expression describes someone who is bending over vomiting toward one's shoes.

shover *n.* drug supplier.

shrimp (to be a) *n.* (mild) an abusive name given to a short person.
♦ NOTE: The term *"shrimp"* is literally a very small crustacean which is used to mean "a very short person" due to its small size.

shtup (to) *v.* (humorous) to fornicate
• *They shutupped the first day they met;* They had sex the first day they met.
♦ NOTE: This verb, coming from Yiddish, is considered humorous due to the pronunciation.

"Shucks!" a commonly used euphemism for *"Shit!"* used to denote disappointment • *Shucks! I lost the contest!*
♦ NOTE: The uses of *"shit"* will be discussed in depth in lesson four.

sick (to be) *adj.* (extremely popular and mild) to vomit • *I'm gonna be sick;* I'm going to throw up.
♦ NOTE: Although the adjective *"sick"* simply means "ill," when preceded by *"going to be,"* the connotation changes to "sick and vomiting."

sickie (to be a) *n.* to be an extremely crazy or perverted person.

sicko (to be a) *n.* to be an extremely crazy or perverted person.

sissy (to be a) *n.* • **1.** (mild) to be a fearful person • **2.** (derogatory) a homo- sexual male.

sixty-nine (to) *exp.* to perform mutual oral sex at the same time by both partners inverting their positions much like the transposed digits "6" and "9" in the number *"sixty-nine."*

skank *n.* (mild) an extremely promiscuous person.
♦ NOTE: This term is popular mainly among the younger generation.

skin and bones (to be) *exp.* (mild) to be extremely thin.

♦ VARIATION: **to be nothing but skin and bones** *exp.*

skin head (to be a) *n.* (mild) to be a bald person.
♦ NOTE: This is also the name given to a member of one of the Neo-Nazi organizations.

skinflint (to be a) *n.* to be miserly.

slammer *n.* police officer (used primarily in old gangster movies)
♦ NOTE: This term signifies the slamming sound a prison door makes when closed.

slap the snake (to) *exp.* (humorous) to masturbate • *All he ever thinks about is slapping the snake!;* All he ever thinks about is masturbating.
♦ NOTE: This is a humorous, yet crude, expression comparing the action of masturbating with that of *"slapping a snake"* which is long and cylindrical like a penis.

slaphappy (to be) *n.* to be in a euphoric state where everything seems hilarious; giddy.

sleaze ball (to be a) *n.* (mild) an extremely low and contemptible person.
♦ VARIATION: **sleazy** *adj.* low and contemptible.

sleigh ride *n.* cocaine.

sleigh riding (to be) *adj.* to be on cocaine.

slime (to be) *n.* (mild) a low and despicable person • (lit); thick slippery liquid.

slime ball (to be a) *n.* (mild) a low and despicable person • (lit); a ball of thick slippery liquid.
♦ VARIATION: **slimebucket** *n.* • (lit); a bucket of thick slippery liquid.

slip someone the big wet one (to) *exp.* (crude) to kiss with one's tongue.
♦ NOTE: In this expression, *"the big wet one"* refers to "the tongue."

slow on the draw (to be) *exp.*
(humorous) to be dull-witted.
♦ NOTE: This is a humorous
expression coming from westerns
where cowboys would duel with
guns. The cowboy with the slowest
reflexes, or slowest at drawing his
gun, would inevitably lose. This
expression is now commonly used
to indicate someone who is slow at
reasoning.

slow on the uptake (to be) *exp.* to be
slow at common reasoning.

slow-ass (to be a) *exp.* to be
extremely slow • *That driver in
front of me is such a slow-ass!;*
That driver in front of me is so
slow!

slut *n.* a very derogatory and
common term for a prostitute or
girl of easy morals.

slutty (to be) *n.* (somewhat crude) to
act like a prostitute and have
frequent sex.
♦ VARIATION: **to be a slut** *n.* •
(lit); to be a prostitute.

smack slammer *n.* heroin addict.

smack *n.* (mild and popular) heroin.

smackhead *n.* heroin addict.

small fry (to be a) *exp.* (mild) • **1.** an
abusive name given to a very short
person • **2.** an affectionate term
used to describe a child.

smart ass (to be a) *exp.* (crude yet
very popular) to be arrogant.

smashed (to be) *adj.* to be on drugs.

smoke *n.* marijuana.
♦ VARIATION: **smokes** *n.pl.*

smooch (to) *v.* to kiss • *I saw mom
and dad smooching in the living
room today;* I saw mom and dad
kissing in the living room today.

smutty (to be) *adj.* (mild) to be
pornographic.

snake (to be a) *n.* (mild) said of a
person who is as low as a snake.

♦ VARIATION: **snake in the grass**
exp.

snap one's twig (to) *exp.* to become
suddenly crazy.
♦ VARIATION: **to snap** *v.*

snatch *n.* (vulgar) vagina.

sniff (to) *v.* to use cocaine.

sniffer *n.* cocaine user.

snifter *n.* cocaine user.

snooty (to be) *adj.* (mild) to be
pretentious.

snort (to) *v.* (very popular) to use
cocaine.

snow *n.* cocaine.

snow snifter *n.* cocaine user.

snow snorter *n.* cocaine user.

snowball *n.* cocaine.

snowbird *n.* cocaine user.

snowed (to be) *adj.* to be on cocaine.

snowed in (to be) *adj.* to be on
cocaine.

snowed up (to be) *adj.* to be on
cocaine.

social disease *n.* gonorrhea.

son of a bitch (to be a) *exp.* (vulgar)
an extremely despicable person •
(lit); to be a son of a female dog •
I'm gonna kill that son of a bitch!;
I'm going to kill that despicable
person!
♦ VARIATION: **to be an S.O.B.**
exp. a common euphemistic
abbreviation of *"son of a bitch."*

source *n.* (mild) drug supplier.

space cadet (to be a) *n.* to be an
oblivious and irresponsible person.
♦ VARIATION: **to be a space case**
exp.

space out (to) *v.* to drug overdose.

spaced (to be) *exp. adj.* • **1.** to be
intoxicated (from alcohol or drugs)
• **2.** to be in a state of oblivion (due
to fatigue or meditation).
♦ VARIATION: **to be spaced out**
exp.

spacey (to be) *adj.* to be oblivious and irresponsible.

spare tire (to have a) *exp.* to have a ring of fat all around one's midsection, resembling the shape of a tire.

spaz (to be a) *n.* (mild) a very foolish and dull person.
  ♦ NOTE: This is an abbreviation of the term "spastic" meaning "one who has muscle spasms due to due to injury or illness."

spear *n.* (mild) penis.
  ♦ NOTE: This term signifies the "penis" since both are long and cylindrical and perform acts of penetration.

speedball (to) *v.* to take drugs.

speedball *n.* cocaine and heroin.

squat (to) *v.* (crude) to defecate • (lit); to crouch.
  ♦ NOTE: When used to signify "to defecate," the verb *"to squat"* is considered somewhat crude.

squirt (to be a) *n.* (mild) a abusive name given to a very short person.

staff *n.* (mild) penis.
  ♦ NOTE: This term signifies the "penis" since both are long and cylindrical.

stash house *n.* the locale where cocaine is bought.

steamy (to be) *adj.* (mild) to be sexy • *That's a steamy dance she's doing;* That's a sexy dance she's doing.

stick (to be a) *n.* (mild) to be very thin.

stiffy (to have a) *n.* (humorous) to have an erect penis.

sting *n.* (mild) a carefully and secretly planned entrapment of those who are in the process of doing an unlawful act.
  ♦ VARIATION: **sting operation** *n.* (mild).

stinker (to be a) *n.* (mild) • (lit); one who smells repulsively.

stoned (to be) *adj.* to be on drugs.

stoned out of one's gourd (to be) *adj.* to be on drugs.

stoned out of one's head (to be) *adj.* to be on drugs.

stoned out of one's mind (to be) *adj.* to be on drugs.

streetwalker *n.* (mild) prostitute.
  ♦ NOTE: This term refers to a male or female prostitute.

stroke oneself (to) *exp.* to masturbate • *He likes to stroke himself in front of people;* He likes to masturbate in front of people.

strung out (to be) *adj.* to be on drugs.

stuck on oneself (to be) *exp.* (mild) said of a person who is self-impressed and whose thoughts are, therefore, *"stuck on himself/herself."*

stuck up (to be) *adj.* (mild) to be conceited and arrogant • *I can't stand her. She's so stuck up!;* I don't like her at all. She's so arrogant.

stuff *n.* heroin.

stuffed shirt (to be a) *exp.* (mild) said of someone who walks arrogantly as if wearing a stuffed shirt.

stupe (to be a) *n.* (mild) a foolish and unthinking person.
  ♦ NOTE: This is a shortened version of "stupid."

suck [off] (to) *v.* to perform oral sex • *Can you believe he actually offered her money to suck him [off]?;* Can you believe he actually offered her money to perform oral sex on him?

suck face (to) *v.* to kiss • *I'm not going out with him. All he ever wants to do is to suck face;* I'm not going out with him. All he ever wants to do is to kiss.

sugar *n.* heroin.

sunshine *n.* lysergic acid diethylamide (L.S.D.)

sweet cakes *n.* attractive buttocks.

sweet cheeks *n.* attractive buttocks.

swinger (to be a) *n.* (mild) to be ready for all types of recreational sex at any moment.

sword *n.* (mild) penis.
  ♦ NOTE: This term signifies the "penis" since both are long and cylindrical and perform acts of penetration.

-T-

T and A *exp.* (mild) a common abbreviation and euphemism for "tits and ass" used to signify "nudity" • *There's a lot of T and A in that movie;* There's a lot of nudity in that movie.

T.S. *exp.* a shame • *I know you don't want to do your homework, but T.S.! You have no choice!;* I know you don't want to do your homework, but that's a shame! You have no choice!
  ♦ NOTE: This is a euphemistic abbreviation of *"tough shit"* which is considered vulgar.

tail *n.* (mild) buttocks.

take a shit (to) *exp.* to defecate • *The dog took a shit right on the rug;* The dog defecated right on the rug.

take in (to) *v.* (mild) to escort to jail.

take shit (to) *exp.* to accept abuse • *Why do you keep taking shit from him?;* Why do you keep accepting abuse from him?

talc *n.* cocaine.

talk to Huey on the big white phone (to) *exp.* (humorous) to vomit.
  ♦ NOTE: This humorous expression describes someone who is vomiting, and making a "Huey" sound into the toilet which looks like a large white telephone receiver.

talker (to be a) *n.* (mild) to be a talkative person.

tea *n.* marijuana.

tea man *n.* drug supplier.

tea'd up (to be) *adj.* to be on drugs.

technicolor yawn (to have a) *n.* (humorous) to vomit.
  ♦ NOTE: This describes one's mouth opening to reveal a variety of multicolored foods being vomited.

Thai stick *n.* marijuana.

than shit *adv.* to the extreme • *He's funnier than shit;* He's extremely funny • *She's meaner than shit!;* She's extremely mean!

that time of the month (to be) *exp.* (mild and very popular) to menstruate • *You don't look well. Is it that time of the month?;* You don't look well. Are you menstruating?

the big H *n.* heroin.

the dirty deed *exp.* may be used as a euphemistic replacement for "sex" • *Do you think they did the dirty deed last night?;* Do you think they had sex last night?

the elevator doesn't go all the way to the top *exp.* (humorous).
  ♦ NOTE: This is a humorous expression inferring that the subject doesn't use his/her entire brain.

the fuck *exp.* used to denote surprise, annoyance, or "nonsense" • (surprise) *It's great to see you! What the fuck are you doing here?* • (annoyance) *What the fuck do you want now?* • ("nonsense") *He told you he was rich? The fuck he is!;* He told you he was rich! That's nonsense!

the lights are on but nobody's home *exp.* (humorous).
  ♦ NOTE: This is a humorous expression describing a person who is awake but completely unaware.

"The red flag's up" *exp.* (somewhat crude yet humorous) to menstruate.
 ‣ NOTE: In this expression the *"red flag"* refers to "blood."

"The Red Sea's in" *exp.* (crude yet humorous) to menstruate.
 ‣ NOTE: In this expression, the *"red sea"* refers to "blood."

the runs (to have) *exp.* (mild) to have diarrhea.

"The shit rolls downhill" *exp.* "The blame is passed down to the person with the least amount of influence."

"The shit's gonna hit the fan!" *exp.* "A great disturbance is about to occur!" • *When my father comes home and sees what I did to his car, the shit's gonna hit the fan!;* When my father comes home and sees what I did to his car, a great disturbance is going to occur.

the shit *exp.* used to modify interrogative pronouns *who, what, where, when, why, how* • *Who the shit is that?;* Who could that possibly be? • *What the shit did I spill on myself?;* What could I have possibly spilled on myself?

the shits (to have) *exp.* to have diarrhea • *I must have eaten something spoiled because I've been having the shits all day;* I must have eaten something spoiled because I've been having diarrhea all day.
 ‣ VARIATION: **to have the runny shits** *exp.*

the tragic magic *n.* heroin.

the Y *n.* vagina.
 ‣ NOTE: This is a humorous, yet vulgar, description of a woman lying on her back with her legs spread apart forming the letter "Y."

thick (to be) *adj.* to be dull-witted.
 ‣ NOTE: This adjective describes a person who's head is so thick that information can not penetrate.

thin as a rail (to be) *exp.* (mild) to be extremely thin.

thing *n.* (mild) penis.

think one's shit doesn't stink (to) *exp.* to think unrealistically highly of oneself • *She's so arrogant! She thinks her shit doesn't stink!;* She's so arrogant! She thinks unrealistically highly of herself!

throne *n.* (humorous) toilet.
 ‣ NOTE: This term is a humorous comparison of a toilet to a royal throne.

throw in the clink (to) *v.* (mild) to put someone in jail.

throw the book at (to) *exp.* to find someone guilty on several counts and put in jail for an extended period of time.

throw up (to) *n.* (extremely common and mild) to vomit.
 ‣ NOTE: This is perhaps one of the most common synonyms for "to vomit" and is used by everyone.

tickle the tiger (to) *exp.* (humorous) to masturbate • *He tickles the tiger whenever he goes to bed;* He masturbates whenever he goes to bed.
 ‣ NOTE: The word *"tiger"* is used to mean "penis" in this expression due to the similarity between the large head of the tiger and the large head of the penis.

tight (to be) *adj.* (mild) to be rigid with one's money.
 ‣ VARIATION: **to be as tight as a drum** *exp.* to be very rigid with one's money.
 ‣ VARIATION: **to be a tightwad** *n.* (mild).

tight-ass (to be a) *exp.* uptight, tense • *She's not a very relaxed person. What a tight-ass!;* She's not a very relaxed person. She's so uptight!

tight-fisted (to be) *adj.* (mild) a figurative expression signifying one who has difficulty spending money which he/she holds onto tightly.

tightwad (to be a) *n.* (mild) to be extremely miserly • *He refused to buy me a cup of coffee because he said it was too expensive. What a tightwad!*; He refused to buy me a cup of coffee because he said it was too expensive. He's so miserly.

tinkle (to) *v.* (mild) to urinate.
‣ NOTE: This verb, primarily used with children, signifies the tinkling sound that is produced when one urinates in the toilet.

tits *n.pl.* (very popular) breasts.

titties *n.pl.* breasts.

toke (to) *v.* to take drugs.

toke *n.* a portion of marijuana.

tool *n.* (mild) penis.

toot (to) *v.* • **1.** (mild and humorous) to have flatulence • **2.** (very popular) to use cocaine.

toot *n.* cocaine.

tooter *n.* cocaine user.

torn up (to be) *adj.* to be on drugs.

touched in the head (to be) *exp.* to be eccentric and unpredictable.

tough shit (to be) *exp.* • **1.** used to signify "that's a shame" with a feeling of indifference and hostility from the speaker • *If you don't like the way I drive, tough shit!*; If you don't like the way I drive, too bad! • **2.** to be menacing; "cool" • *That guy's tough shit!*; That guy is menacing!

trafficker *n.* drug supplier.

tramp (to be a) *n.* (mild) to be a promiscuous person • (lit); to be like a vagabond who rarely sleeps in the same place twice • *Look, there's Donna. She's the school tramp*; Look, there's Donna. She's the school nymphomaniac.

trampy (to be) *adj.* (mild) to act like a prostitute and have frequent sex.
‣ VARIATION: **to be a tramp** *exp.* to be like a vagabond who rarely sleeps in the same place twice.

treat someone like shit (to) *exp.* to treat someone with great disrespect • *Why did you treat her like shit last night?*; Why did you treat her with such disrespect last night?

trick (to) *v.* (mild) to trade sexual favors for money.
‣ VARIATION: **to turn a trick** *exp.*

trick *n.* (mild) a prostitute's client.
‣ SYNONYM: **john** *n.* (mild).

trip (to) *v.* to take drugs.

trip *n.* a positive or negative mental experience while on drugs.
‣ ALSO: **acid trip** *n.* a positive or negative mental experience while on lysergic acid diethylamide.

tripping (to be) *adj.* to be on drugs.

troll (to be a) *n.* (mild) to be an ugly person.

trots (to have the) *exp.* (mild) to have diarrhea.

trouser snake *n.* (mild) penis.

trouser trout *n.* (mild) penis.

tub of lard (to be a) *exp.* to be an extremely fat individual • (lit); to be a container of fat.
‣ VARIATION: **to be a tub** *adj.*

tune one's organ (to) *exp.* (humorous) to masturbate • *I think I need to go tune my organ*; I think I need to go masturbate.
‣ NOTE: This expression is a play-on-words since the term "organ" refers to a musical instrument as well as a "penis."

turd *n.* (mild) • **1.** excrement • *Your dog just laid a turd on the couch*; Your dog just defecated on the couch. • **2.** despicable person • *That guy's such a turd!*; That guy's such a despicable person!
‣ ALSO: **bird turd** *n.* (humorous rhyming slang) bird excrement • *There are bird turds all over my car!*; There's bird excrement all over my car!

turf *n.* (mild) a prostitute's territory where she solicits clients.

turkey (to be a) *n.* (mild) an extremely foolish and unthinking person.

turned on (to be) *exp.* (mild) to be sexually aroused • (lit); to be activated.

tush *n.* (mild) buttocks.
◗ NOTE: This popular term comes from Yiddish.
◗ VARIATION: **tushy** *n.*

twat *n.* (vulgar) vagina.

tweek out (to) *v.* to take drugs.

twerp (to be a) *n.* (mild) to be a despicable person.

twisted (to be) *adj.* (popular in the drug world) to be on drugs.

twit (to be a) *n.* (mild) a foolish and worthless person.

-U-

ugly as sin (to be) *exp.* (mild) to be extremely ugly.

ugo (to be) *adj.* (humorous) a slang transformation of the adjective "ugly."

undies *n.* may be used as a euphemistic replacement for "underwear" • *I just bought some new undies;* I just bought some new underwear.
◗ NOTE: The word *"undies"* is considered infant language and is, therefore, occasionally borrowed by adults in order to desexualize the original term.

up shit creek (to be) *exp.* to be in a big predicament • *If I don't get this work done in five minutes, I'm gonna be up shit creek;* If I don't get this work done in five minutes, I'm going to be in a big predicament.
◗ NOTE: Although it's incorrect, many people transform this expression to *"to be up shit's creek."*

upchuck (to) *v.* (very common and mild) to vomit.
◗ NOTE: It would be incorrect to say *"to chuck up."*

uppity (to be) *adj.* (mild) said of someone who feels that he/she is superior or above, everyone else.

use (to) *v.* to take drugs.

-V-

V.D. *n.* venereal disease, syphilis.

viper *n.* drug supplier.

visit the red-light district (to) *exp.* to look for a prostitute.
◗ NOTE: The neighborhood where prostitutes are known to congregate is called the *"red-light district"* due to the traditional red light in front of each brothel.

-W-

wacky (to be) *adj.* to be eccentric and unpredictable.

walrus (to be a) *n.* to be as fat as a walrus.

wasted (to be) *adj.* (very popular) to be on drugs.

watermelons *n.pl.* (humorous) very large breasts.

way out (to be) *adj.* to be on drugs.

wazoo *n.* (mild) buttocks.
◗ NOTE: This term is commonly used in the expression *"up the wazoo"* meaning "in great quantity": *I've got homework up the wazoo tonight!;* I've got lots of homework tonight!

wee (to go) *v.* (mild) to urinate.
◗ NOTE: This verb is primarily used with children.
◗ ALSO: **to go wee-wee** *exp.* (a very popular expression used with children).

weed *n.* (very popular especially in the 1960s) marijuana.
♦ ALSO: **evil weed** *n.*

wet (to be) *adj.* (vulgar) said of a woman or girl who is sexually excited.

whack off (to) *exp.* (popular yet crude) to masturbate • *Did you know he whacks off all the time in his car?*; Did you know he masturbates all the time in his car?
♦ NOTE: This verb may also be spelled *"wack off."*

whacko (to be) *adj.* to be extremely eccentric and unpredictable.
♦ NOTE: The adjective *"whacko"* is considered slightly more extreme than *"wacky."*

whale (to be a) *n.* to be as fat as a whale.
♦ VARIATION: **to be a beached whale** *exp.* to be extremely fat and motionless such as after eating a huge meal.

wham bam, thank you ma'am *exp.* quick sex (humorous and popular) • *Our date last night was nothing but wham bam, thank you ma'am!;* Our date last night was nothing but quick sex.
♦ VARIATION: **slam bam thank you ma'am** *exp.*

"What the fuck" • **1.** *exclam.* (as a question) "How is this possible?" • *What the fuck? I can't remember where I put my keys!;* How is this possible? I can't remember where I put my keys! • **2.** *exp.* (as a statement) "It's not a big issue" • *What the fuck. If you don't want to go to her party, just don't!;* It's not a big issue. If you don't want to go to her party, just don't!

whip the weenie (to) *exp.* to masturbate • *It sounds like he's upstairs whipping the weenie;* It sounds like he's upstairs masturbating.
♦ NOTE: The term *"weenie,"*

literally meaning "sausage," is used to signify "penis" in slang.

whip the worm (to) *exp.* (humorous) to masturbate • *I know where you're going. You're gonna go whip the worm, aren't you?;* I know where you're going. You're going to go masturbate, aren't you?
♦ NOTE: In this expression, the term *"worm"* is used to mean "penis" due to its long cylindrical shape.

white *n.* cocaine.

white Christmas *n.* cocaine.

white cross *n.* cocaine.

white lady *n.* cocaine.

whiz (to) *v.* (vulgar) to urinate.
♦ VARIATION: **take a whiz (to)** *exp.* (very popular yet vulgar).

whizbang *n.* cocaine and heroin.

whore (to) *v.* • **1.** to work as a prostitute • **2.** to look for sex.
♦ VARIATION: **to whore around** *exp.* (mild).

whore *n.* derogatory term for "prostitute."
♦ NOTE: This term is often pronounced in jest with a southern accent, *"ho."*
♦ NOTE: This term refers to a male or female prostitute.

whorehouse *n.* (extremely popular) brothel.

wiener *n.* (humorous) penis.
♦ NOTE: This term signifies the "penis" since both are long and cylindrical.
♦ VARIATION: **ween** *n.*
♦ VARIATION: **weenie** *n.*

wigged out (to be) *adj.* to be on drugs.

windbag (to be a) *n.* (mild) said of someone whose excessive chatter produces large amounts of wind.

windowpane *n.* lysergic acid diethylamide (L.S.D.)

wiped out (to be) *adj.* • **1.** to be drugged • **2.** to be exhausted.

wired (to be) *adj.* to be dynamic and lively naturally or due to drugs.

witch hazel *n.* heroin.

without a stitch of clothing (to be) *exp.* (mild) to be completely naked.

woody (to have a) *n.* (humorous) to have an erect penis (which is as hard as wood).

working girl *n.* a euphemism for "prostitute."

-X-

X-rated (to be) *adj.* (mild) to be pornographic.
♦ NOTE: Movies which contain graphic sexuality are rated X and are restricted to anyone under the age of 18 years old. This expression may also be used to indicate anything which is sexy • *This party is turning X- rated!*; This party is becoming indecent!

-Y-

yacker (to be a) *n.* (mild) to be a talkative person.
♦ NOTE: to yack *v.* to talk excessively.

yank the yak (to) *exp.* (humorous) to masturbate • *He's yanking the yak;* He's masturbating.
♦ NOTE: In this expression, the term *"yak,"* literally a long-haired ox, is used to mean "penis."

yellow (to be) *adj.* coward
♦ VARIATION: **to be yellow-bellied** *adj.*

yellow *n.* lysergic acid diethylamide (L.S.D.)

yellow sunshine *n.* lysergic acid diethylamide (L.S.D.)

ying yang *n.* (mild) buttocks.
♦ NOTE: This term is commonly used in the expression *"up the ying yang"* meaning "in great quantity": *I don't need another dress. I've got dresses up the ying yang;* I don't need another dress. I've got lots of dresses.

york (to) *v.* (humorous) to vomit.
♦ NOTE: This verb describes the sound one makes when vomiting.

you-know-what *exp.* a euphemistic expression which is used to replace any vulgar word • *She's always so nasty! I think she's a real you-know-what!*
♦ NOTE: In this expression, it's up to the listener to guess which obscenity the speaker is replacing. Although the listener may not deduce the exact word, the sentiment is still the same.

-Z-

zone out (to) *v.* to drug overdose.

zonked out (to be) *adj.* to be drugged or tired.